Ovid's *Amores*, Book One

Oklahoma Series in Classical Culture

Oklahoma Series in Classical Culture

Series Editor

Ellen Greene, *University of Oklahoma*

Advisory Board

Susan Guettel Cole, *State University of New York, Buffalo*
Carolyn J. Dewald, *Bard College*
Thomas M. Falkner, *The College of Wooster*
Elaine Fantham, *Princeton University*
Nancy Felson, *University of Georgia*
Helene P. Foley, *Barnard College*
Sara Mack, *University of North Carolina, Chapel Hill*
Thomas R. Martin, *College of the Holy Cross*
John F. Miller, *University of Virginia*
Jon Solomon, *University of Arizona*
Richard F. Thomas, *Harvard University*

Ovid's Amores, Book One
A Commentary

Maureen B. Ryan and Caroline A. Perkins

University of Oklahoma Press : Norman

Library of Congress Cataloging-in-Publication Data

Ryan, Maureen B., 1951–
  Ovid's Amores, Book one : a commentary / Maureen B. Ryan and Caroline A. Perkins.
       p. cm.—(Oklahoma series in classical culture ; v. 41)
  Commentary in English, text in Latin.
  Includes bibliographical references and index.
  ISBN 978-0-8061-4144-2 (pbk. : alk. paper) 1. Ovid, 43 B.C.–17 or 18 A.D. Amores. Book 1. 2. Elegiac poetry, Latin—History and criticism. 3. Love poetry, Latin—History and criticism. I. Perkins, Caroline A., 1952– II. Ovid, 43 B.C.-17 or 18 A.D. Amores. Book 1. III. Title.
  PA6519.A73R93 2011
  871'.01—dc22
                                                    2010008802

Ovid's Amores, *Book One: A Commentary* is Volume 41 in the Oklahoma Series in Classical Culture.

The paper in this book meets the guidelines for permanence and durability of the Committee on Production Guidelines for Book Longevity of the Council on Library Resources, Inc. ∞

Copyright © 2011 by the University of Oklahoma Press, Norman, Publishing Division of the University. Manufactured in the U.S.A.

All rights reserved. No part of this publication may be reproduced, stored in a retrieval system, or transmitted, in any form or by any means, electronic, mechanical, photocopying, recording, or otherwise—except as permitted under Section 107 or 108 of the United States Copyright Act—without the prior written permission of the University of Oklahoma Press.

1 2 3 4 5 6 7 8 9 10

optimis parentibus

Contents

Preface	ix
Introduction	3
Glossary of Terms	19
P. Ovidi Nasonis Amorum: Liber Primus	25
Amores 1.1	27
Amores 1.2	35
Amores 1.3	43
Amores 1.4	50
Amores 1.5	59
Amores 1.6	65
Amores 1.7	74
Amores 1.8	83
Amores 1.9	95
Amores 1.10	102
Amores 1.11	111
Amores 1.12	117
Amores 1.13	122
Amores 1.14	129
Amores 1.15	136
Vocabulary	145
Bibliography	177
Index	181

Preface

The genesis of this book was a perceived need for a teaching text of the *Amores* geared to the intermediate Latin student. Current texts and commentaries either include English translations of the poems or provide extensive literary and textual information without the translation aids required by students at this level. Recently published Ovid readers have been keyed to the secondary school advanced placement test, and they include selections from both the *Amores* and the *Metamorphoses*. With this in mind, we have designed a complete reading text of *Amores* 1 for students who have completed the study of Latin grammar at the elementary level and have had some experience reading extended passages of Latin poetry.

The introduction provides an overview of the elegiac genre and Ovid's career as a poet and a basic discussion of elegiac meter and style. The text of the poems is our own, differing (though not substantially) from other established manuscripts of the *Amores*, and with very little textual commentary. We include short introductions to acquaint the student with each poem's subject matter and themes, and, to assist the student further, we offer a comprehensive vocabulary at the back.

We are well aware that in today's classrooms Latin students of varying abilities and experience may be enrolled in the same course, and we have tried to address their individual needs. The notes are designed to help students of different levels approach both the language and the poetry of Ovid with greater understanding. They offer the grammatical and syntactical assistance that a less experienced Latin student would depend on as well as basic background information. They also provide stylistic commentary and information of a literary and interpretative nature that a more experienced Latin student would welcome. As an additional aid, the notes for each poem are divided by subheadings so that the student will know the topic of each section in advance.

For those students interested in pursuing secondary sources on Ovid, elegy, and the Augustan age, we suggest readings (from one to three) following the notes on each poem. Multiple readings appear in their order of relevance rather than in alphabetical sequence. We also provide a more general bibliography at the back of the book.

We hope that students and teachers alike will use this text to kindle or rekindle an interest in this most clever and profound of the Roman elegiac poets.

FOR THE STUDENT

We recommend that a reader of this text have some experience with extended passages of Latin literature, especially poetry. Our assumption is that such a student has a basic familiarity with scansion and has had the pleasure of reading Latin aloud. The notes are intended, in large part, to assist with explanations of grammatical constructions, word order, ellipsis, and other complexities of the Latin language and literature that often challenge even the more experienced student. Repetition is the key to learning, and so we provide extensive and repeated help in the beginning, tapering off as the student's skill increases. A student, therefore, should expect help at the first few occurrences of a difficult or unfamiliar construction, after which time we expect the unfamiliar to become familiar and take root.

ACKNOWLEDGMENTS

This text would not have been possible without the support of many fine people. Our thanks go first to Judith Hallett for her many helpful suggestions and invaluable comments and criticisms and to Teresa Ramsby for her generous gifts of time and assistance throughout the writing process. We also wish to express our gratitude to the students of Latin 311, fall 2006 (Marshall University) and Barbara Blumenthal (Smith College), who field-tested versions of the text and provided valuable feedback. To Bill Regier go special thanks for his editorial advice, to Justina Gregory for her guidance and encouragement along the way, and to Brian Breed for his suggestions at the initial stages of the project.

We owe a large debt of thanks to our anonymous reviewers; our editor, Alice Stanton; copy editor Norma McLemore; and John Drayton, director of the University of Oklahoma Press, and his assistant, Astrud Reed.

Finally, a personal thank-you to Ron and Judie Hise, without whose generosity and moral support none of this would have ever transpired.

Ovid's *Amores*, Book One

Introduction

When he was a young man, Ovid fell headlong in love—with poetry. His family sought to prevent such an unseemly relationship, and almost succeeded.

> Often my father said, "Why do you pursue such a useless task? Homer himself died without a penny to leave behind!" I was moved by his words and completely abandoned poetry; I tried to write prose—in words free from rhythmic patterns. Yet on its own a poem would develop, in an appropriate meter, and whatever I tried to write became verse.
> (*Tristia* 4.10.21–26)

Ovid felt that through love he could bring something new to life in poetry, and that in turn poetry would awaken something new in him. His intense longing sought a lasting union, and to share his passion and his quest for a perfect union with poetry, Ovid wrote the *Amores*.

LIFE AND WORKS

Ovid himself gives a vivid account of his life in *Tristia* 4.10, an autobiographical poem composed in exile in the last years of his life. There we learn that he was born Publius Ovidius Naso on March 20, 43 BCE, in Sulmo, a town about ninety miles east of Rome. He tells us he came from a middle-class equestrian family, and in his teens he was sent to Rome and then abroad to complete his education. The goal his father had established for him was to undertake a military and political career typical of a young Roman

man of his class. Even though writing poetry had been his passion from an early age, Ovid tried to live up to his family's expectations. In his twenties, however, he abandoned plans for a senatorial career and threw himself into the life of a poet by publishing the five books that constituted the first edition of the *Amores*.

Ovid's choices came at a beneficial time for Rome and for himself. His birth in 43 BCE coincided with the penultimate conflict for supremacy in Rome, the one pitting Octavian, Julius Caesar's adoptive son and designated heir, and Mark Antony against the assassins of Caesar. In 31 BCE Octavian defeated Antony at Actium, and during Ovid's early years in Rome he was consolidating a power that would last beyond his own death in 14 CE. Ovid reached adulthood just as Rome had emerged from more than a century of civil war. External wars against the Germans and the Parthians would continue, but war on Italian soil effectively ceased until 69 CE after the fall of Nero.

Octavian's predecessor, Julius Caesar, had a mere five years to effect changes desperately needed in Rome. Octavian, who assumed the name Augustus in 27 BCE, had the luxury of decades both to resettle and reestablish Rome's political, military, and social systems. In support of the latter, Augustus worked to rebuild every aspect of the city, both physically (in terms of buildings, temples, and forums) and intellectually (in terms of literature and the arts). Through his advisor and close friend Maecenas, Augustus fostered the poetry of Horace, Vergil, and Propertius; Messalla, an orator, statesman, and soldier, emerged as the patron of Tibullus and Ovid himself. Poetry had a long history in Rome, but during the 40s, 30s, and 20s BCE there seemed to be a leisure that allowed Romans to engage in arts gentler than those of war and survival.

Ovid began his poetic career writing in the tradition of his older contemporaries, the great elegists Propertius and Tibullus. He published two editions of love poems in elegiac meter, aptly titled the *Amores*, or "Loves." Between these editions, he wrote the *Heroides*, a series of letters, also in elegiac meter, most of which were written in the voices of mythical and historical women to lovers who have abandoned them. At the same time that Ovid was composing the *Heroides* and revising the first edition of the *Amores* he was embarking on a lengthy mock-didactic poem, also in elegiac meter, called the *Ars Amatoria* (*Art of Love*). In this poem, Ovid created a narrator, a self-styled *praeceptor amoris* or "instructor of love," whose self-appointed task was to instruct the youth of Rome in the art of seduction. Two books of the *Ars* are directed to men, a third to women. Later, Ovid says, he felt compelled to write a sequel, the *Remedia Amoris,* which gave instruction on how to end a relationship. These works champion instant sexual gratification with as little conversation and commitment as possible, and breakups that involve very little mess. In both, the *praeceptor's* frivolous and flippant take on relationships countered the mutual marital devotion that Augustus was promoting for elite Romans.

From these amatory works Ovid advanced to writing poetry with larger themes and scope. He wrote a tragedy, a *Medea*, which has not survived, and then authored two longer works, the *Metamorphoses* and the *Fasti*. In the *Metamorphoses,* Ovid transforms 250 or so (mostly) mythological stories into a unified poem. These fifteen books begin with the creation of the universe, end with Rome's rise to power, and in between contain a vast array of tales of varying length that display the complete range of human and divine character. Befitting its genre, the *Metamorphoses* is written in dactylic hexameter and is the only work of all Ovid's extant poetry not in elegiac meter. The *Fasti* is a detailed examination of the Roman calendar of religious festivals with their attendant myths. Only six books of the intended twelve were completed. Taken together, both works have given us a rich store of Greek and Roman historical, mythological, and religious traditions and tales, much of which would be lost to us without Ovid.

In 8 CE Ovid, then at the height of his career and power as poet, was banished by Augustus for reasons that we can only guess. He cryptically attributes his exile to *carmen et error,* "a poem and a mistake" (*Tristia* 2.207). From urban Rome, Ovid, the most cosmopolitan of the Roman poets, was sent to Tomis, a wretched outpost on the Black Sea. There, he spent the remaining years of his life writing poetry, the *Tristia* and the *Epistulae ex Ponto,* which describe his exile, his life in Tomis, and his desire for restoration to Rome. But Ovid never returned to Rome. His hopes were raised by the death of Augustus in 14 CE, but Augustus's successor, Tiberius, did not rescind the orders of his predecessor, and three years later, in 17 CE, Ovid's life came to an end on the shores of the Black Sea.

ROMAN ELEGY

For his first published literary effort Ovid worked within a genre whose antecedents extended back to the poetry of Greece, but whose roots were firmly established by Roman poets of the first century BCE. In form, elegy came into being during the Archaic Age (c. 800–500 BCE), and, although its name in Greek, ἔλεγος, seems to indicate that it should be the poetry of lament, it was used, *inter alia*, for sympotic or drinking songs, love poems, battle exhortations, and funerary epitaphs. In topic and theme, Roman elegy of the first century BCE drew from Greek New Comedy, which itself inspired Roman comedy, the mimes of the great Hellenistic poets Callimachus, Theocritus, and Herodas (third century BCE), and the love poems of the Greek Anthology. In the larger context of poetics, elegy inherited from its Hellenistic predecessors a dispute about what constituted "better" poetry. In the prologue of the *Aetia,* Callimachus, poet and scholar at the Library in Alexandria, criticized certain of his contemporaries for their lengthy poems written in a grand style he considered more suited to epic; he favored shorter, more compact and refined poems with a personal style. Callimachus's viewpoint prevailed. His poetry, characterized by delicacy and brevity, complexity and wit, greatly influenced certain Roman poets, who followed him in promoting forms of poetry that were emphatically not epic, a genre they considered both outdated and too invested in political propaganda.

Earlier Roman poets had written short elegiac poems. Aulus Gellius, a late-second-century BCE writer, preserved four such examples in his *Noctes Atticae,* declaring, "I think that nothing more elegant, more charming, more polished, or more refined can be found in Greek or Latin than these" (*noct. Att.* XIX.9.10). The genre, however, found its true beginnings in the first century BCE in the poetry of Catullus, who experimented with various forms and genres. His poetic works range from lyric poetry, to wedding songs (*epithalamia*), to small epics called *epyllions*, to poems written in elegiac meter. Although he appears as a disinterested narrator in some of his longer poems, what characterizes his shorter lyric and elegiac poetry is the emphasis on the personal. Catullus establishes a poetic "I," a character (*persona*) that plays the role of narrator in his poems about love, ridicule of others, and the writing of poetry. His love poems in particular revolve around this narrator character, a poet in love whom he calls by his own name "Catullus," and the *puella,* or mistress, with whom he has an intense and dysfunctional relationship. He names his *puella* Lesbia in homage to the sixth-century BCE Greek female lyric poet Sappho of Lesbos. We witness the ups and downs in their complex relationship, the fire of their mutual passion, but also the jealousy and contempt he feels when his *puella* becomes emotionally and physically unavailable to him, and involved with other men. Catullus the narrator explores his feelings of love and despair toward his mistress in a manner that captures readers emotionally even today. The most powerful record of his torment is a short poem that attempts to analyze his very mixed feelings toward her and in so doing acknowledges the hopelessness of his situation (*carmen* 85).

> Odi et amo. Quare id faciam fortasse requiris.
> Nescio, sed fieri sentio, et excrucior.

> "I hate and I love. Perhaps you ask why I am doing this.
> I don't know. But I feel it happening, and I am crucified."

While Catullus did not establish the genre of elegy per se, his poetic situation of love and jealousy, and his use of such themes as subservience to his mistress, colored and perhaps inspired the poetry of later elegists.

Between Catullus and the two extant elegists from the first century BCE, Propertius and Tibullus, there lived the politician and poet Cornelius Gallus, who later scholars feel concretized the beginnings of elegy into an established genre. Regrettably, with the exceptions of a few papyri fragments found in Egypt, a pentameter quoted by a later authority, Vibius Sequester, and possibly some lines of Vergil's Tenth *Eclogue* (52–61) that many believe contain quotes from Gallus's poetry, all four books of his love elegies have been lost. Following Catullus's example, he calls the narrator of his poems by his own name, and he gives his *puella* the name Lycoris. As procurator of Egypt, Gallus made the unfortunate decision to challenge Augustus's authority. He lost and was forced to commit suicide, and then his name was literally erased from all written historical records (*damnatio memoriae*). Gallus is mentioned in poems by authors such as Vergil (*Ecl.* 10), Propertius (2.34.91–92), Ovid (*Am.* 1.15.29–30 and 3.9.63–64) and Quintilian (*Inst.* 10.1.93), and the latter three affirm his importance as an elegiac poet. Nevertheless, we are left with a memory that is vague and intriguing at best, and we can only guess at Gallus's contribution to the genre by looking at the poetry of his younger contemporaries.

These contemporaries were Propertius and Tibullus, each of whom left a unique stamp on the genre of love poetry while acknowledging and preserving what seem to be its salient features. Again, these features typically include a poet as narrator, a *puella*, or mistress, and a love relationship that is at times difficult and volatile. Their topics include the poet's jealousy and fear of rivals, his exclusion from and by his mistress, his critical assessment of his mistress's behavior and appearance, his desire to spend leisure time with his mistress, and his concomitant rejection of the political and military life required of elite Roman males. He claims an allegiance to *militia amoris*, the "soldiering of love," and by doing so asserts the superiority of his idle life (*otium*) of love and love poetry over the active public duty (*negotium*) of a real soldier. Other themes include an interest in magic, sex for sale, and the role of poetry as an enchantress, persuader, and immortalizer. The two poets also treat subjects outside the love relationship. Like Catullus before them, Propertius and Tibullus were politically and culturally engaged, and they offer their own views on important issues of the day. They also, through their poetry, define and defend themselves as poets.

Propertius memorably portrays the protagonist of his elegies, named "Propertius," as a masochist who views love as a burden and the love relationship as extremely harmful to the health and well-being of the lover. Unlike Catullus, who celebrates his new love for Lesbia with the exuberant *uiuamus atque amemus* ("Let us live and love!" *carmen* 5.1), Propertius describes how his mistress Cynthia took control of him and how, consequently, Love stepped on his head (*et caput impositis pressit Amor pedibus,* 1.1.1–4). His relationship with Cynthia is turbulent, and he weeps more tears of disillusion and distress than do the heroines of modern romance novels. He also subscribes enthusiastically to the concept of *seruitium amoris* ("enslavement to love"), whereby he casts himself as a slave to the woman he loves. As a *seruus amoris* Propertius is passive, while the *puella* asserts her domination and control as if she were his master (*domina*) and he were her slave. He, however, never loses his identity as a Roman male.

Tibullus is calm and reflective in contrast, and the poems of his first book celebrate the joys of a rustic life in the country with his mistress Delia: *quam iuuat immites uentos audire cubantem / et dominam tenero continuisse sinu (*"how pleasurable, lying in bed, to have pressed my mistress close in tender embrace, while listening to the roar of the winds," Tibullus 1.1.45–46). He also writes about his love for a boy named Marathus. Tibullus, like Propertius, expresses reluctance to participate in war and military campaigns, activities deemed important for elite young men of his day, but which he views as motivated by power and greed. There is a dark side to his poetry that even in happier moments leaks out through descriptions of witchcraft, dire omens, and predictions of future mishaps. It is no surprise that his second interest is a woman whom he calls Nemesis, or "Retribution," a greed-driven *puella* who goes off to the country with a wealthy ex-soldier (Tibullus 2.3.33–42).

To hear the voice of the only female poet whose elegies have survived, we must turn to Sulpicia, whose poems, along with those composed by members of Messalla's literary circle, are now found in book 3 of Tibullus. Sulpicia presents her narrator as a young aristocratic girl—proud, openly passionate, and fearless in the face of social convention. Her love interest is Cerinthus, and she declares outright her sexual success with him: *exorata meis illum Cytherea Camenis / attulit in nostrum deposuitque sinum* ("Won over by the entreaties of my Muses, Venus brought him to me and placed him in the folds of my lap," Tibullus 3.13.3–4). Conversely, the author of six elegies in this collection who calls his narrator "Lygdamus" gives lost love primacy in his poetry. When speaking of his beloved, Neaera, he writes with profound and persistent longing. His language is sometimes strikingly similar to Ovid's (cf. Tibullus 3.5.15–20 and Ovid, *Amores* 2.14.23f.), leading some to speculate that he may actually be the young Ovid.

OVID'S CONTRIBUTION

This, then, was the literary atmosphere into which Ovid inserted his own contribution. But Ovid did not merely repeat what had been accomplished previously. He retained the characters of elegy, the poet as narrator and the *puella*, but shaped them to suit his own literary purposes. He does not announce, for instance, in the opening poem of his *Amores* that a *puella* has captured his heart; nor does he name his mistress. Instead he happily makes himself and his poetry the center of attention. This focus continues throughout book 1, and it seems that the elegiac themes and situations that Ovid adapts are subordinated to this primary purpose.

In similar fashion, Ovid takes elegiac situations and reshapes them. In *Amores* 1.4, the *puella* is amenable to an affair with the poet, yet she makes his life difficult by appearing at a dinner party with another man. In *Amores* 1.6 and 1.12, she refuses to allow the poet to visit. In *Amores* 1.10, she asks for gifts. And in *Amores* 1.14, she becomes overly concerned with her appearance. All of these situations are typical of elegy, but Ovid stamps them with humor, seriousness, or both, so that his poems seem to operate on a multitude of levels simultaneously. *Amores* 1.6, for instance, is a *paraclausithyron*, a song sung by a lover "beside a closed door," which is found in comic playwrights and elegiac poetry. Typically the poet, on his way home from a party, drunk and wearing a garland, addresses his mistress's locked door in tears. He has become the *exclusus amator*, "the shut-out lover," and he complains that his mistress is sleeping unmindful of him or, worse, sleeping with someone else. He accuses the door of heartlessness and obstinacy, he becomes violent, and when he has lamented all night long without success (and he is never successful), he leaves a token of his love affixed to the door or lying on the steps. Ovid embraces the scenario, but changes it so that it is not the door that the poet is addressing, or the *puella* within, but the *ianitor*, the doorkeeper. This change allows the poet to indulge in a wonderful opening joke, to identify to a degree with the servile status of the *ianitor*, and to avoid turning his mistress into the stereotypical hard-hearted woman of elegy who denies him admittance.

Important themes of elegy undergo the same scrutiny and renovation in Ovid's elegies. Found first in the poetry of Catullus (e.g., *c.* 68.68) and developed further in Propertius's elegies is the idea of *seruitium amoris*. Although Ovid acknowledges this idea, he does not entirely convince us that his *seruitium* is in service of his *puella*. *Amores* 1.3, for example, begins with expressions of servile devotion but ends with emphasis on the poet's own triumph as immortalizer. Indeed, it is to the service of elegy and to the process of writing that Ovid devotes the *Amores*. His opening poem is about poetics and the writing of poetry. It is couched as a *recusatio*, a set poem in which a poet begs to be excused from writing of weightier themes in order to pursue love and the writing thereof, but the poem is not so much about love and love poetry as it is about meter. Throughout book 1 of the *Amores*, when we see the adjectives *tenuis* and *leuis* and their opposites, *fortis* and *durus*, we are to be reminded that the former pair are key poetic terms for the writing of elegy, whereas the latter are characteristic of epic and tragedy. With his discussion of poetics, Ovid reveals himself as a serious poet very much in control of his genre.

Ovid has taken love elegy, an established genre, and made it his own, and he imbues the whole with a wit that does not hide the seriousness of his intention. He has been called the most modern of poets, but his modernity extends beyond the alleged impetus for elegy, the love relationship, to encompass the very act of writing poetry. As you read the poems of this collection, be alert to the various ways that Ovid subverts the experiences of love, and listen for the contrived and self-aware voice of Ovid as narrator.

METER

Every genre of Latin poetry had a specific meter attached to it. Because the *Amores* falls into the genre called elegiac love poetry, Ovid wrote in a specific rhythm or meter called the **elegiac couplet**. The elegiac couplet is based on two alternating lines of poetry. The first is a **dactylic hexameter** ("a finger-shaped six measure"), which consists of six metrical feet. The second, a **pentameter** ("a five measure"), contains five: two and a half + two and a half metrical feet.

In the **hexameter** line, each foot is made up of either a dactyl (-⏑⏑) or a spondee (--). The **final** (or sixth) **foot** is always two syllables, either a spondee (--) or a trochee (-⏑). The **second-to-last** (or fifth) **foot** is generally a dactyl (-⏑⏑). Although a spondee (--) is possible in the fifth foot, it is much less common in elegy than in epic poetry.

— ⏑̆ — ⏑̆ — ⏑̆ — ⏑̆ — ⏑̆ — ⏑̆

cĭn-gĕ-rĕ | lī-tŏ-rĕ- | ā flā- | uĕn-tĭ-ă | tēm-pŏ-ră | mȳr-tŏ |
"Bind your golden temples with myrtle from the shore"

The **pentameter** line consists of two halves, called **hemistichs**. The first half, or hemistich, contains two and a half feet; each full foot consists of either a dactyl (-⏑⏑) or a spondee (--), and the half foot is a long syllable (-). In the second hemistich, *no* substitution is permitted. It may consist only of two dactyls (-⏑⏑) followed by an *anceps* syllable (- or ⏑).

    — ⏑⏑ — ⏑⏑ — ‖ — ⏑⏑ — ⏑⏑ ⏓

Mū-să pĕr | ūn-dĕ- | nōs ‖ ē-mŏ-dŭ- | lān-dă pĕ- | dēs |
"O Muse, about to be set to the rhythms of eleven feet"

In reading poetry, pauses generally occur within the line as well as at its end. A pause is determined, to some degree, by the sense of the passage. There are two types of pauses in a line of poetry: (1) the **caesura**, and (2) the **diaeresis**.

(1) A **caesura** is a pause between two words in the *middle* of a foot. In the hexameter line, the **principal caesura** is frequently found in the third foot, splitting the line into two parts.

    Amores 1.1.1
Arma graui numero uiolentaque bella parabam
"I was preparing weapons in a weighty meter and violent wars . . ."

Ar-ma gra- | ui nu-me- | ro ‖ ui-o- | len-ta-que | bel-la pa- | ra-bam |

However, the **principal caesura** may also occur in the fourth foot, in which case there may be another caesura in the second foot (or vice versa). Thus the line is divided into three parts.

    Amores 1.3.11
at Phoebus comitesque nouem uitisque repertor
"but Apollo and his nine companions and the discoverer of the vine . . ."

at Phoe- | bus ‖ co-mi- | tes-que no- | uem ‖ ui- | tis-que re- | per-tor |

(2) A **diaeresis** is a pause between two words at the *end* of a foot. In the pentameter line, there must be a **diaeresis** between the two hemistichs.

Amores 1.1.27–28
sex mihi surgat opus numeris, in quinque residat;
   ferrea cum uestris bella ualete modis.
"my work rises in six meters and subsides in five;
   iron wars with your meters, farewell."

fer-re-a | cum ues- | tris ǁ bel-la ua- | e-te mod- | is |

In either the hexameter or pentameter line, there may be a **diaeresis** after the first foot for emphasis, especially if a word or phrase is carried over from one line to the beginning of the next (enjambment).

Amores 1.6.37–38
ergo Amor et modicum circa mea tempora uinum
   mecum est et madidis lapsa corona comis.
"therefore Love and a little wine around my temples
   is with me and a lopsided garland on my damp hair."

me-cumst ǁ et ma-di- | dis ǁ lap-sa co- | ro-na co- | mis |

OVID'S METRICAL AND STYLISTIC PRACTICES

Poets of the epic dactylic hexameter tended to avoid bringing a sentence or clause to a close at the end of the line. Ovid, however, was just the opposite. He followed the practice of **end-stopping** used by the other love poets, who completed a sense-unit at the end of the pentameter. As a result of end-stopping, Ovid has very few lengthy periodic sentences that continue for many couplets.

   In addition, the completion of thought achieved by end-stopping is reinforced by the rhythm of the pentameter's second hemistich. Remember that only two dactyls can be used in the second half of the pentameter. The repetitive pattern of those long and short syllables (-ᵕᵕ -ᵕᵕ ᵕ̱) creates a **rhythmical refrain** that the audience comes to expect, which in turn helps to bring a sense of closure to every couplet. (It is worth noting that by Ovid's time the elegiac couplet was generally brought to a close by a two-syllable, or disyllabic, word to preserve and emphasize the dactylic rhythm. For example, *nudaque simplicitas purpureusque pudor* [1.3.14].)

Internal rhyme occurs often in both the hexameter and the pentameter line. In the hexameter, an adjective and a noun with identical case and declension endings frequently stand one at the caesura, the other at the end of the line; in the pentameter, they may stand at the end of the first hemistich and the second. For example, *ut stetit ante* **oculos** */ posito uelamine* **nostros** (1.5.17). Internal rhyme gives the line a greater cohesiveness through balance and sound.

In his elegiac verses, Ovid employs dactyls much more frequently than do the other love poets. (He is closer to the original Greek elegists in this practice.) The lightness of the **dactylic rhythm** (versus the more weighty spondee) seems most appropriate to Ovid, who appears to take a more detached and light-hearted approach to love and the poet-lover. Dactylic rhythm also keeps Ovid's verses moving quickly. Short clauses and clauses split into two parts add a sense of **brevity**, while also contributing to the impression of **speed**. Moreover, since his meter is predominantly dactylic, when Ovid uses the slower and more ponderous spondaic rhythm, its effect can be striking.

The Greek poets of the Archaic Age used elegiac couplets to express a variety of moods and for many different subjects (see the section above titled "Roman Elegy"). For them, the metrical form was not intended to impose any specific mood or subject matter on the poet. The Roman elegiac poets, and especially Ovid, embraced this **adaptability of the elegiac couplet** to obtain a greater freedom in giving expression to their inventiveness.

Because their poetry was written to be delivered orally (as well as to be read in private), poets applied the **techniques of rhetorical training** that as students they had learned and practiced in their *declamationes*, or practice speeches. Ovid was no exception. Just like an orator, he is aware of his audience and how he can manipulate their emotions and feelings. His elegies are, thus, distinctly **dramatic**: his scenes are clearly set and lively, and his characters (of which the poet as narrator is one) speak out directly and may address a person or thing in the poem or make side comments. Short, concise observations on life, or *sententiae*, are especially well suited to the end-stopped elegiac couplet, and they are sprinkled throughout Ovid's poems. Like the exercises in schools of rhetoric, many of his elegies deal with **a single topic**, which is made clear at the outset. One type of rhetorical exercise, in particular, appears frequently in the *Amores*: the *suasoria*, a speech designed to persuade someone to adopt a certain course of action (see, for example, *Amores* 1.13).

Orator and poet alike were also careful to infuse their works with the proper adornments of rhetorical style, and Ovid has his own favorite devices with which to impress and charm an audience. He is particularly fond of **balanced structure**, both within the couplet itself and within each line of a couplet. One way he creates balance within individual lines is through **internal rhyme**; another is the **symmetrical arrangement** of words. The **golden line** is the perfect example of the latter type of artful symmetry, in which a five-word line is arranged with two adjectives first, a verb in the center, and two nouns at the end, an ABverbAB order. **Chiasmus** affords another of Ovid's favored arrangements, wherein adjectives and their nouns are placed in an inverse ABBA order. He also favors **antithesis**, which he frequently couples with chiasmus for the sake of contrast. Balance within the couplet or successive couplets is achieved through parallel phrases or clauses: the **tricolon** ("three clauses"), often with anaphora, is especially frequent in the *Amores*. Ovid, however, prevents the monotony that his tendency toward balance might engender by employing a rhetorician's *uariatio* ("variation"). He skillfully rearranges the order of words and varies the placement of phrases to avoid complete symmetry; he precedes main clauses with their relative clauses and inserts one clause inside another; he changes moods (for example, a jussive subjunctive may parallel a direct command) and parts of speech.

This section has focused primarily on the "greatest hits" in Ovid's repertory of style, and the next section elaborates on these particular practices with an alphabetical list of grammatical terms, rhetorical figures of speech, and metrical expressions, each accompanied by a specific example from the text. Additional information and greater detail on style are given in the notes of the individual poems—all designed to enhance the understanding of Ovid's craftsmanship as a poet and of poetry in general.

Glossary of Terms

alliteration: the repetition of the same consonant sound, usually at the beginning of successive words or syllables, as the sound of -t- in *tumidi ritu torrentis*, or the s- in "**s**imilar to a **s**wollen **s**tream," 1.7.43.

anaphora: the repetition of a word in the same or similar form at the beginning of successive clauses or phrases, as in *scit bene **quid** gramen, **quid** torto concita rhombo / licia, **quid** ualeat uirus amantis equae,* "She knows well **what power** herbs have, **what power** the cords that set the whirling wheel in motion have, **what power** the secretions of a mare in heat have," 1.8.7–8.

anastrophe: the reversal of the usual order of words, in particular the preposition and its object, as in *ancillas inter,* "among maidservants," 1.11.2.

antithesis: the balancing of opposing words or ideas against each other, for contrast, as in *cur mihi sit **damno**, tibi sit **lucrosa** uoluptas?* "Why should pleasure be **a loss** for me, **full of profit** for you?" 1.10.35.

apostrophe: an address in the second person to some person or object, absent or present, often used for emotional effect, as in *dum licet, Argeas frangite, **Troes**, opes,* "While you may, **Trojans**, break the might of the Argives," 1.9.34.

assonance: the repetition of the same or similar vowel sounds in successive words or syllables, as the sound of -a- in *qualiter abiecta de niue manat aqua,* "just as water drips from snow tossed aside," 1.7.58.

asyndeton: the omission of conjunctions, like *et* and *-que,* in a series of words or phrases, as in *scindentur uestes, gemmae frangentur et aurum; / carmina quam tribuent, fama perennis erit,* "Clothes will be torn, (and) jewels and gold will splinter, / (but) the fame that poetry gives will be everlasting," 1.10.61–62.

bracketing: the placement of two grammatically related words, one at the beginning of a line, the other at the end; also called "framing," as in *uirginea tenuit cornua uara **manu***, "She held the curved horns **in her maiden hand**," 1.3.24.

caesura: a pause in the middle of a metrical foot that corresponds with the end of a word. In the hexameter line, the caesura most commonly occurs within the third foot, or in both the second and fourth feet. (See the earlier section titled "Meter.")

chiasmus: two parallel phrases or clauses, the second of which is reversed in order (ABBA), as in *Mars dubius, nec certa Venus,* "Mars is unreliable, and not dependable is Venus," 1.9.29.

diaeresis: a pause at the end of a metrical foot that corresponds with the end of a word. In the hexameter line, a diaeresis after the first foot is not uncommon. In the pentameter, the diaeresis stands at midpoint. (See the earlier section titled "Meter.")

diastole: the lengthening of a vowel that is usually short by nature, for metrical convenience, as in *quae tu reddide**ris** ego primus pocula sumam,* "I will be the first to take the cups that you give back," 1.4.31.

diminutive: nouns or adjectives with suffixes such as *-ellus, -olus,* and *-ullus* that indicate smallness in size, often used to express affection, pity, or contempt, as in *cum bene deiectis gremium spectabis **ocellis**,* "when you will look at your lap, your **sweet little eyes** suitably cast down," 1.8.37.

ellipsis: the omission of one or more words that can be understood from context (often a form of *esse*) but that must be supplied in order for the sentence to be grammatically complete, as in *an, quod ubique, tuum est? = an **(id)**, quod ubique **(est)**, tuum est?* "Or is **that**, which **is** everywhere, yours?" 1.1.15.

enjambment: the opposite of end-stopping, where the final word or phrase of a sentence is carried over from one line to the beginning of the next, as in *aspice quot somnos iuueni donarit amato / **Luna**,* "consider how many nights of sleep to a beloved youth gave / **Luna**," 1.13.43–44. Enjambment is much more extensively used by the poets of epic than by the elegiac poets.

genre: a category of literature, e.g., epic, tragedy, pastoral, lyric, elegy, comedy.

gnomic perfect: the perfect when used to express a general truth, or gnome, especially in negative statements, to indicate that what has been true in the past is still true and will always be true, as in *nec **nocuit** simulatus amor*, "Nor **does** a feigned passion **do harm**," 1.8.71.

golden line: the "ideal" hexameter line, in which five words are arranged symmetrically as follows: adjective A, adjective B, verb form, noun A, noun B, as in *roscida purpurea supprime lora manu,* "Check the dewy reins with your rose-colored hand," 1.8.10.

hendiadys: the use of two nouns connected by a conjunction, in place of one noun modified by an adjective (the effect is to give equal prominence to the images, one of which would otherwise be subordinate to the other), as in *facta **manu** culpaque tua,* "done **by** your **guilty hand**," 1.14.43.

hiatus: a separation of two words that should elide but do not. This exception to metrical rules is a rare occurrence in Ovid's elegiac poetry.

hyperbaton: the violation of the usual order of words, as in *pugnabat tunica **sed tamen** illa tegi,* "**but nevertheless** she was fighting to be covered by her tunic," 1.5.14. Hyperbaton is a distinctive feature of poetry, which allows the artful arrangement of words and sounds.

hyperbole: an extreme exaggeration or overstatement, for rhetorical effect, as in *nigri non illa parentem / Memnonis in roseis **sobria** uidit equis,* "that one **except when drunk** has not seen black Memnon's mother on her rosy steeds," 1.8.3–4.

iambic shortening: the shortening of a long syllable preceded by a short syllable when the word accent falls on that preceding short syllable, as *puto* in *nam, puto, sentirem,* "For, I think, I would feel," 1.2.5.

interlocked word order: the symmetrical arrangement of two pairs of related words so that one word of each pair stands between each word of the other pair (ABAB); also called **synchesis**, as in

22 Glossary of Terms

aspice **cognati felicia Caesaris arma**, "Consider the successful wars of your kinsman Caesar," 1.2.51.

invective: a form of literature whose intent was to denigrate an individual publicly by attacking him or her on the grounds of birth, upbringing, moral defects, physical defects, and so on.

litotes: the expression of an affirmative quality by negating its opposite, as in ***nil non*** *laudabile uidi*, "I saw **nothing not** worthy **of praise**" (i.e., "Everything I saw [was] worthy of praise"), 1.5.23.

metonymy: the substitution of one word, usually a noun, for another with which it is closely associated, as in *dum cadet incurua falce resecta* ***Ceres***, "As long as **the grain** falls, cut with a curved sickle," 1.15.12.

patronymic: a designation derived from the name of one's father or paternal ancestor, as in *summa ducum,* ***Atrides***, *visa* ***Priameide***, *fertur . . .* , "Highest of leaders, **the son of Atreus** (= Agamemnon), when **the daughter of Priam** (= Cassandra) had been seen, is said to . . . ," 1.9.37.

periphrasis: a roundabout and extended way of expressing something that could be expressed in a shorter, more direct manner, as in *uitis repertor,* "discoverer of the vine" (= Bacchus), 1.3.11.

personification: the attribution of human characteristics to plants, animals, inanimate objects, and abstract concepts, as in *Mens Bona ducetur manibus post terga retortis / et Pudor*, "Good Sense will be led with her hands twisted behind her back, and Sense of Honor too," 1.2.30–31.

polysyndeton: the excessive use of conjunctions in a series of words or phrases, as in *di tibi dent nullos****que*** *lares inopem****que*** *senectam /* ***et*** *longas hiemes perpetuam****que*** *sitim*, "May the gods give you no home **and** an old age of poverty **and** long winters **and** unending thirst," 1.8.114.

prolepsis: the attribution of a characteristic to a person or a thing that anticipates what will happen at a later time; also called "anticipation," as in *hos (animos) petit in* ***socio*** *bella puella*

Glossary of Terms 23

viro, "A beautiful girl looks for this (type of character) in a man who **will be her partner,**" 1.9.6.

rhetorical question: a question asked not to gain information but to create an effect, as in *Quid mihi, Liuor edax, ignauos obicis annos . . . ?* "Why, biting Envy, do you condemn me for my inactive years . . .?" 1.15.1.

ring composition: the echoing of words from the opening lines of a poem in its final lines, as in *mediamque **dies** exegerat horam,* "The **day** had passed **the middle** hour" (1.5.1), echoed in *proueniant **medii** sic mihi saepe **dies**,* "May **the middle of days** often arise for me in this way," 1.5.26.

sententia: a short, concise, and pointed opinion or observation, as in *leue fit, quod bene fertur, onus,* "A heavy burden that is borne with a good attitude becomes light," 1.2.9.

syncope: the loss of a letter or syllable within a word, usually a verb, for metrical convenience, as in *audierit* (= *audi**u**erit*), I.3.4, and *norit* (= *nou**e**rit*), 1.3.6.

synecdoche: the use of a part of something to express its whole, as in *optaui quotiens . . . uentus frangeret **axem**,* "How many times have I longed for the wind to break your **chariot**," 1.13.29.

synizesis: the merging of two vowels into one sound for metrical convenience, as in *ipse deus uatum palla spectabilis **aurea**,* "the very god of poets, noteworthy in his golden cloak," 1.8.59; *au-rea* scans as two syllables.

systole: the shortening of a vowel that is usually long by nature, for metrical convenience, as in *ludunt formosae: casta est quam nemo rogauit,* "Beauties play around: the woman whom no one has propositioned is chaste," 1.8.43.

tmesis: the division of a compound word into its two parts, with one or more words inserted between them, as in ***ante** ueni quam uir,* "Come **before** your man does," 1.4.13.

transferred epithet: an adjective that agrees with one noun grammatically but logically belongs with another noun, as in *inque ministeriis **furtiuae** cognita noctis / utilis,* "and (you,) recognized as useful in **secret** services of the night," 1.11.3.

tricolon: a series of three related clauses; often each subsequent clause becomes progressively longer than the preceding one (called **tricolon crescens**), as in *quos umeros, quales uidi tetigique lacertos / forma papillarum quam fuit apta premi*, "What shoulders, what arms I saw and touched! How suitable for squeezing were the shape of her breasts!" 1.5.19–20.

word picture: the careful placement of the words of a phrase so that their arrangement visually reflects the image being described in the verse, just as when the narrator and his girl are in the midst of "that crowd" in ***agmine** me inuenies aut inuenieris in **illo***, "In that crowd you will find me or you will be found," 1.4.57.

zeugma: the use of a single word (esp. a verb) to apply to two (or more) nouns, when it has one meaning with one noun and another meaning with the other, as in ***collige** cum uultu mentem*, "**Get** your emotions **under control** and **compose** your face," 1.14.55.

P. Ovidi Nasonis Amorum
Liber Primus

Epigramma Ipsius

Qui modo Nasonis fueramus quinque libelli,
   tres sumus: hoc illi praetulit auctor opus.
ut iam nulla tibi nos sit legisse uoluptas,
   at leuior demptis poena duobus erit.

"We who had recently been Naso's five little books
   are now three: the author preferred this opus to that.
Although now to read us may be no pleasure to you,
   yet the punishment will be lighter, with two removed."

Amores 1.1

Ovid opens the *Amores* with a humorous encounter between himself as narrator and Cupid, the mischievous god of love. The narrator chastises the youthful deity for interfering with his intention to write epic and haughtily advises him to keep to his traditional role as a god who inspires love, not poetry. Not surprisingly, the aspiring epic poet fails to persuade the powerful god of love. Cupid answers his complaints with an arrow; the narrator burns with desire and has no choice but to embrace the writing of love poetry.

With his first word, *arma*, the first word of the *Aeneid*, Vergil's great epic poem, Ovid reveals his intention of writing a type of elegy different from that of his predecessors. Although he is working within the elegiac tradition by introducing his narrator and by establishing the circumstances under which he will write love poetry, these circumstances are unique. Propertius begins his first poem with the words *Cynthia prima*, which establishes his *puella* as first in his heart and his poetry; Tibullus, in his introductory poem, chooses the quiet country life with *Delia* over any other occupation. Ovid, however, begins *arma . . . parabam edere* ("I was preparing to write of weapons"), thereby informing his audience that his focus is on the poet and the process of writing. Even after Cupid strikes and the narrator responds with the wretched cry of a young man in love (*me miserum!*), there is no expression of passion for a girlfriend. Instead Ovid composes an elegiac couplet about an elegiac couplet (27–28) in language that is distinctly sexual. In this first poem, Ovid reveals himself to be an innovative writer of elegy. Wittily, he makes it clear that he is concerned more with the form of elegy than with its standard content.

Amores 1.1

Arma graui numero uiolentaque bella parabam
  edere, materia conueniente modis.
par erat inferior uersus; risisse Cupido
  dicitur atque unum surripuisse pedem.
'quis tibi, saeue puer, dedit hoc in carmina iuris?   5
  Pieridum uates, non tua turba, sumus.
quid, si praeripiat flauae Venus arma Mineruae,
  uentilet accensas flaua Minerua faces?
quis probet in siluis Cererem regnare iugosis,
  lege pharetratae uirginis arua coli?   10
crinibus insignem quis acuta cuspide Phoebum
  instruat, Aoniam Marte mouente lyram?
sunt tibi magna, puer, nimiumque potentia regna:
  cur opus affectas, ambitiose, nouum?
an, quod ubique, tuum est? tua sunt Heliconia tempe?   15
  uix etiam Phoebo iam lyra tuta sua est?
cum bene surrexit uersu noua pagina primo,
  attenuat neruos proximus ille meos;
nec mihi materia est numeris leuioribus apta,
  aut puer aut longas compta puella comas.'   20
questus eram, pharetra cum protinus ille soluta
  legit in exitium spicula facta meum
lunauitque genu sinuosum fortiter arcum
  'quod'que 'canas, uates, accipe' dixit 'opus.'
me miserum! certas habuit puer ille sagittas: 25
  uror, et in uacuo pectore regnat Amor.
sex mihi surgat opus numeris, in quinque residat;
  ferrea cum uestris bella ualete modis.
cingere litorea flauentia tempora myrto,
  Musa per undenos emodulanda pedes.   30

Notes

1–4 *I was planning to write an epic poem, but Cupid, as a joke, stole a foot from my second verse.*

1 **Arma . . . uiolentaque bella**: By calling to mind the opening words of Vergil's famous Roman epic, the *Aeneid* (*Arma uirumque cano* . . .), the narrator creates the impression that he is writing an epic poem. The meter of elegiac poetry supports this ruse, since the first verse of the elegiac couplet is always dactylic hexameter, the meter used for epic poetry.

parabam: In accordance with the conventions of love elegy, the "I" of "I was preparing" is a *persona*, or character, named "Ovid" who plays the role of poet and lover in the *Amores* (see the introduction). To distinguish him from Ovid, the real author of the *Amores,* we will refer to this character as "narrator."

graui numero: i.e., dactylic hexameter. A "weighty meter" is suitable for the very serious world of war and epic poetry, in which the heroic qualities of manly military men are displayed.

2 **materia conueniente**: Experiment with different ways to translate the ablative absolute—avoid being literal.

modis: "rhythms"; dative object of *conueniente*.

par erat inferior uersus: In epic poetry, every line is dactylic hexameter and therefore every line is made up of six feet (hex < Greek ἕξ = "six"). In the elegiac couplet, however, the first verse is dactylic hexameter, but the second, or "lower," verse is a pentameter (penta < Greek πέντα = "five").

risisse . . . surripuisse (4): The hissing repetition of *-isse* emphasizes the impertinence of Cupid's behavior.

4 **dicitur**: By whom? The passive verb form creates a distancing effect, casting doubt on the "reality" of Cupid's appearance.

unum . . . pedem: Note the separation of the adjective and noun, with *unum* placed at the pause in the line (here, the diaeresis) and *pedem* at the line's end. Ovid often connects an adjective and a noun by using this type of word placement. Look for other examples.

5–16 *I warned him that poetry was not under his sphere of influence and that it would not be right for gods to trespass in each other's domains.*

5 **quis . . . quid** (7) **. . . quis** (9) **. . . quis** (11): The repetition of interrogative pronouns, the first three at the beginning of successive couplets, is an example of *anaphora* (see the glossary) and is meant to emphasize the narrator's outrage at Cupid's interference.

quis tibi: This beginning may recall Propertius's *recusatio* (excuse for <u>not</u> writing epics): *quid tibi cum tali, demens, est flumine? quis te / carminis heroi tangere iussit opus?* "What are you doing, madman, with such a mighty stream? Who bid you to set your hand to the task of epic poetry?" (3.3.15ff.) Apollo, the god of poetry, is addressing the poet Propertius and castigating him for attempting to take on something beyond his scope. In Ovid's poem, the situation is reversed: the narrator claims he is quite capable of writing epic, and *he* castigates the god for trying to stop him.

hoc: The vowel is metrically long, the result of the original spelling *hocc < hocce*.

iuris: partitive genitive, with *hoc*.

6 **Pieridum**: Greek genitive plural of *Pieris, Pieridos*, feminine, "a daughter of Pierus (a Macedonian king)," i.e., a Muse. The suffixed form of a father's name used to identify his offspring is called a patronymic (see the glossary). The Muses were female divinities who, with Apollo, presided over literature and the arts. The Pierides were first identified with the Muses in extant Latin by Lucretius (*de rerum natura*, 1.926), and later by Vergil in his pastoral poems, the *Eclogues*. The lofty term, as McKeown suggests, is used here to add a touch of the grandiose.

uates: predicate nominative. The narrator is being pompous. He calls himself a *uates* and insults Cupid by calling him *saeue puer* (5). *Vatis* is a solemn and archaic term originally applied to prophets who delivered their predictions of the future in verse form (cf. Varro, *de lingua latina* 7.36). The poets of the Augustan Age adopted *uatis*, "inspired prophet or bard," to describe a poet in his inspired state (cf. Horace, *carmen* 1.1.35).

7–12 The narrator argues his point by using mythological *exempla* to demonstrate that each individual god has his or her own sphere of influence. These examples are supposed to represent impossibilities, namely that it is unacceptable for certain deities to operate outside their traditional roles, and therefore Cupid should not interfere in Apollo's realm of poetry. The rhetorical questions add emphasis (see the glossary).

7 **quid**: "what would happen . . . ," the understood apodosis to the following *si*-clauses (protases). Ovid uses a future less vivid condition to emphasize the potentially dire and chaotic consequences that could be unleashed in the divine world if Cupid usurps Apollo's role. The repetition of the *-ae-* vowel sound in *praeripiat . . . flauae . . . Mineruae*, known rhetorically as assonance (see the glossary), helps represent the ominous nature of such behavior.

7–8 The word order of this couplet aptly represents the role reversals as the narrator imagines them. In the first verse, *Venus* and *arma* are juxtaposed and encircled by Minerva, the victim of Venus's attack (*flauae . . . Mineruae*): adjective B, deity A, emblem B, deity B. In the second verse, in an almost parallel arrangement, *flaua Minerua* is hemmed in by the emblem of her victim Venus (*accensas . . . faces*): adjective A, adjective B, deity B, emblem A. The goddesses and their emblems change positions in the line in the same way the goddesses themselves exchange emblems.

8 **uentilet**: *si* is to be repeated.
accensas . . . faces: literally "torches set ablaze," but figuratively the fiery passions of love caused by Venus. For the adjective/noun placement, cf. *unum . . . pedem* (4).

10 **pharetratae uirginis**: Diana, virgin goddess of hunting, is introduced in an indirect rather than direct way, a rhetorical device known as periphrasis (see the glossary).
arua coli: an accusative-infinitive construction introduced by *quis probet* and parallel to *Cererem regnare* (9). The language could be sexual: "plowing fields" is a sexual metaphor that extends at least as far back as Sophocles's *Antigone*; see Adams 1982: 154.

11 **crinibus**: ablative of respect, with *insignem*.

12 **Aoniam**: "of Aonia." Aonia was that region in Boeotia where Mt. Helicon, the home of the Muses, was located.
Marte mouente: For translating the ablative absolute, see *materia conueniente* above (2).

15 **an, quod ubique, tuum est**: = *an (id), quod ubique (est), tuum est*, "or is that, which is everywhere, yours," i.e., "or is everything everywhere under your power." Ellipsis, the omission of words that can be supplied from context, is a common feature of Latin poetry (see the glossary).
tempe: "valley," indeclinable Greek neuter plural. Originally, *Tempe* was the name of a mountain valley in Thessaly near Mt. Olympus. The Helicon valley was the stamping grounds of the Muses.

16 **sua**: reflexive adjective, referring back to the logical subject "Phoebus."

17–20 *I protested that Cupid had reduced my epic poetry to love poetry, which I could not write: I was not in love.*

17 **cum . . . surrexit**: frequentative indicative (*cum*-temporal), "every time that . . ."

18 **neruos**: "vigor / power," with a reference to both literary work and the male sexual organ. Through sexual innuendo, Ovid suggests that the rising

32 Amores 1.1

(*surrexit*) first verse of the elegiac couplet, i.e., the epic and therefore masculine verse, becomes enervated in the falling (*attenuat*) second verse. For *neruus* as the male sexual organ, see Adams 1982: 38. *Attenuat* also makes an important poetic point: *tenuitas* was a Callimachean poetic ideal, indicating the "slender style" that the Roman love poets preferred to the elevated and inflated style of epic poetry (cf. Callimachus, *Aitia*, frag. 1.11: κατὰ λεπτόν and 1.24: Μοῦσαν λεπταλέην).
proximus ille: i.e., the *inferior uersus* mentioned in 3.

19 **numeris leuioribus**: *Leuis* is the opposite of '"weighty" and "serious" (*grauis*) and is therefore a suitable description for the frivolous and unmanly quality of love and love poetry; cf. *graui numero* above (1).

20 **aut puer aut ... puella**: Either sex will provide a suitable object for the narrator's love. Poems to young males were part of Archaic and Hellenistic poetry, and Roman poets followed this trend: Catullus wrote of Iuuentius, and Tibullus of Marathus.
compta ... comas: "having done up *her own* hair"; a perfect passive participle with an accusative of respect. In this construction, the passive voice often takes on a reflexive meaning, an essentially poetic usage that corresponds closely to the Greek middle voice.

21–26 *Cupid's answer was to shoot me with an arrow and thus inflame me with the appropriate topic for my poetry.*

21 **questus eram** < *queror, queri*.
pharetra cum: = *cum pharetra*; *cum* is a conjunction here, not a preposition. Postponement of conjunctions, like *cum*, is not unusual in poetry. The postponement gives emphasis to *pharetra*.
pharetra ... soluta: See 2 above.
ille: = *Cupido*.

22 **in exitium ... meum**: accusative of purpose, "for my destruction."
spicula: plural for singular.

23 **-que ... -que** (24): The swiftness of Cupid's response is emphasized by polysyndeton, the use of more conjunctions than necessary (see the glossary).
fortiter: of stringing the bow, referring to his physical strength.

24 **quod**: a relative pronoun whose antecedent is *opus*. Like other poets, Ovid is fond of placing the relative clause <u>before</u> its antecedent. The relative clause expresses purpose; therefore, translate as a purpose clause.
accipe ... opus: Cupid "inspires" the narrator to write elegy. Deities are supposed to inspire poets, as Hesiod shows in *Theogony* 1.29–32

when he writes, "[The eloquent daughters of great Zeus] plucked and gave me a rod, a branch of everlasting laurel . . . and breathed into me their divine voice so that I might celebrate things future and things past." Yet Cupid's "inspiration," though appropriate to his traditional depiction, is markedly hostile—and sexual. For *opus* as the male sex organ, see Adams 1982: 57. (The bow stretched taut also has a related sexual connotation, as do references to *arma* in general; see Adams 1982: 21).

uates: Cupid mocks the narrator by using his own self-designation (see *Pieridum uates*, 6) against him.

25 **me miserum**: an accusative of exclamation, which marks the narrator's transformation into a love poet. Propertius, and Ovid in particular, adopted this phrase of lament from the young men in love (*adulescentes amantes*) depicted in Roman comedy who were continually blocked from getting the girls they desired. Ovid may also be recalling the first line of Propertius's first poem, *Cynthia prima suis miserum me cepit ocellis:* "Cynthia first captured wretched me with her eyes."

26 **uror**: part of the vocabulary of love. The image of fire and burning to represent the passion of love is conventional in love poetry; cf. *accensas . . . faces* above (8).

uacuo: in the sense that the narrator does not yet have anyone he is in love with.

pectore: *pectus* as the seat of love.

27–30 *Now that the subject matter and the meter of my poetry match, I am no longer an epic poet but a love poet.*

27 **sex . . . quinque**: Both modify the ablative *numeris*.

surgat . . . residat: The sexual imagery of *surrexit . . . attenuat* (17–18 above) is echoed. The omission of a conjunction between the two verbs, known as asyndeton (see the glossary), emphasizes the swift result of Cupid's onslaught.

29 Poets considered a hexameter line constructed of only five words particularly elegant. It seems a most appropriate way to address the Muse of love poetry and to bring the poem to a close. To enhance the elegance, Ovid uses his favorite adjective/noun arrangement. The adjectives are placed first, and their nouns second. The first and last words go together (*litorea . . . myrto*), and the second and third words (*flauentia tempora*). This creates a crisscross pattern, ABBA, known as chiasmus. It also creates a word picture in which the goddess's brow is encircled by the garland (*litorea . . . myrto*). See "chiasmus" and "word picture" in the glossary.

cingere ... tempora: "wreathe *your own* ... brow"; an imperative singular in the passive voice with an accusative of respect; cf. *compta ... comas* above (20).
myrto: Names of plants and trees are typically feminine in Latin. The myrtle was sacred to Venus and can therefore be a symbol for love poetry.

30 **Musa**: vocative singular.
emodulanda: a gerundive used as a simple participle (future passive), "about/worthy to be ... " This word is Ovid's creation and does not appear elsewhere in Latin literature.

For Further Reading

Keith, A. M. 1992. "*Amores* 1.1 and the Propertian Programme." *Studies in Latin Literature* 6 (Collection Latomus): 327–44.

Cahoon, L. 1985. "A Program for Betrayal: Ovidian *Nequitia* in *Amores* 1.1, 2.1, 3.1." *Helios* 12: 29–39.

Amores 1.2

In this poem Ovid brings together three standard themes of elegiac poetry but spins them in his own unique way. His first theme, that the narrator is experiencing a classic symptom of love—sleeplessness, is wittily undercut when the narrator does not recognize his insomnia as a symptom of love. He seems unaware that Cupid's arrow had inflamed him at the end of 1.1. He gradually begins to understand the truth, and after some debate accepts his fate. Thus Ovid introduces his second theme, the narrator's surrender to love, expressed in the standard language of *seruitium amoris* (see the introduction). The word *seruitium* is actually used (its only appearance in the *Amores*), and the narrator further defines himself as Cupid's spoils of war (*praeda*) and victim. Though earlier love poets also subjugated themselves to a superior power, their slavery was to their mistresses. In this poem, however, Cupid, not a *puella*, enslaves the narrator.

   Finally, Ovid engages the triumph theme to demonstrate Cupid's control over the narrator in an extended metaphor of twenty-eight lines. This theme has also appeared often in elegiac poetry, but never with Cupid as triumphator in such a prominent position. The triumph as Ovid depicts it becomes deliciously humorous because at every turn he substitutes attributes and associates of Cupid and love for those more typical of a victorious Roman general. He caps the whole scenario by associating Cupid with the emperor Augustus himself, a familial connection that is technically accurate but that in these circumstances must shock and amuse his audience. The result is the blending of love and war that was introduced in *Amores* 1, and this has the effect of making love as important as war. The focus remains on the narrator and his relationship not with his girlfriend, but with Cupid. It may be elegy and the narrator may at last be in love, but we have yet to meet the other important component of a love relationship.

Esse quid hoc dicam, quod tam mihi dura uidentur
   strata, neque in lecto pallia nostra sedent,
et uacuus somno noctem, quam longa, peregi,
   lassaque uersati corporis ossa dolent?
nam, puto, sentirem, si quo temptarer amore— 5
   an subit et tecta callidus arte nocet?
sic erit: haeserunt tenues in corde sagittae,
   et possessa ferus pectora uersat Amor.
cedimus, an subitum luctando accendimus ignem?
   cedamus! leue fit, quod bene fertur, onus. 10
uidi ego iactatas mota face crescere flammas
   et uidi nullo concutiente mori.
uerbera plura ferunt quam quos iuuat usus aratri,
   detractant prensi dum iuga prima, boues;
asper equus duris contunditur ora lupatis: 15
   frena minus sentit, quisquis ad arma facit.
acrius inuitos multoque ferocius urget,
   quam qui seruitium ferre fatentur, Amor.
en ego, confiteor, tua sum noua praeda, Cupido;
   porrigimus uictas ad tua iura manus. 20
nil opus est bello: ueniam pacemque rogamus;
   nec tibi laus armis uictus inermis ero.
necte comam myrto, maternas iunge columbas;
   qui deceat, currum uitricus ipse dabit
inque dato curru, populo clamante triumphum, 25
   stabis et adiunctas arte mouebis aues.
ducentur capti iuuenes captaeque puellae:
   haec tibi magnificus pompa triumphus erit.
ipse ego, praeda recens, factum modo uulnus habebo
   et noua captiua uincula mente feram. 30
Mens Bona ducetur manibus post terga retortis
   et Pudor et castris quidquid Amoris obest.

omnia te metuent; ad te sua bracchia tendens
    uulgus 'io' magna uoce 'triumphe' canet.
Blanditiae comites tibi erunt Errorque Furorque,   35
    assidue partes turba secuta tuas.
his tu militibus superas hominesque deosque;
    haec tibi si demas commoda, nudus eris.
laeta triumphanti de summo mater Olympo
    plaudet et appositas sparget in ora rosas.   40
tu pinnas gemma, gemma uariante capillos,
    ibis in auratis aureus ipse rotis.
tunc quoque non paucos, si te bene nouimus, ures;
    tunc quoque praeteriens uulnera multa dabis.
non possunt, licet ipse uelis, cessare sagittae;   45
    feruida uicino flamma uapore nocet.
talis erat domita Bacchus Gangetide terra:
    tu grauis alitibus, tigribus ille fuit.
ergo cum possim sacri pars esse triumphi,
    parce tuas in me perdere uictor opes.   50
aspice cognati felicia Caesaris arma:
    qua uicit, uictos protegit ille manu.

Notes

1–8   *Why do I toss and turn, unable to sleep? Could it be love? It must be.*

  1   **quid ... dicam**: a deliberative subjunctive introducing a four-part question. The repetition of harsh *k*, *d*, *t* and *s* sounds reflects the restless agitation the narrator is experiencing.
      hoc ... quod: "the reason ... that ... "
  2   **nostra**: = *mea* (plural for singular).
  3   **somno**: ablative of separation, with *uacuus*.
      quam longa: = *quam longa fuit nox!* (LaFleur); ellipsis.
  4   **uersati**: The vivid image of the narrator's torment may recall Catullus *carmen* 50.10–11: *sed toto indomitus furore lecto / uersarer*, "but wild with passion I tossed and turned over the whole bed." In *c.* 50, Catullus is completely aware that his sleeplessness results from the passion he feels for the charming verses of his fellow poet Licinius,

38 Amores 1.2

and he links this passion with the creation of his poem. Our narrator, however, does not recognize why he cannot sleep. His obtuseness emphasizes that the creation of love poetry itself is far more important than any "Licinius" (or "Licinia") who might inspire it.
Ovid uses his favorite adjective/noun arrangement in line 4; cf. the chiastic (ABBA) pattern of 1.29. The adjectives are placed first (*lassaque uersati*), the nouns second and in reversed order (*corporis ossa*).

5 **puto**: an ironic aside that distances the narrator from his conclusion. The final *-o* is shortened (see "iambic shortening" in the glossary), as it often is in colloquial speech.

quo: = *aliquo*. After *si, nisi, num* and *ne*, the indefinite adjective means "some" or "any."

6 **subit et . . . nocet**: The subject *Amor* is supplied from *amore* in the preceding line (ellipsis); *amore* (5) has become personified. For Love's sneakiness, cf. 1.3–4.

7 **sic erit**: "that must be it" (McKeown).

tenues . . . sagittae: The language in these lines recalls Cupid's successful attack in *Amores* 1.25–26. The narrator calls the arrows of Amor *tenues* to continue to draw attention to the insidiousness of love, but *tenues* also has a poetic connotation. The idea of "slender style" was an important way that Roman love poetry distinguished itself from the grandiloquence of epic poetry; cf. *attenuat* (1.18). There is some irony in having *ferus Amor* (8) inflict wounds with such arrows. His warlike description and actions are typical of soldiers in battle, yet his arrows are elegiac.

8 **possessa . . . uersat**: In English we would use two finite verbs to express the Latin perfect passive participle and present indicative verb, "seizes and assails." *Amor*'s attack, *uersat*, picks up and plays on *uersati* (4).

ferus . . . Amor: cf. *saeue puer* (1.5).

9–18 *I will not fight it. The more you struggle against love, the greater your suffering will be.*

9 **cedimus . . . accendimus . . . / . . . cedamus** (10): plurals for singulars. Note the wordplay in spelling and sound. The transformation of the quick dactylic *cedimus* to the slow spondaic *cedamus* underscores the narrator's resolution.

leue fit, quod bene fertur, onus: a short, clever saying, known rhetorically as a *sententia* (see the glossary). For the poetic connotations of *leuis*, see 1.19.

11 **mota face**: cf. 1.2.

flammas: accusative subject of both *crescere* and *mori* (12).

13 **ferunt**: *Boues*, the subject, is at the end of the next line (14). Translate in this order: *boues prensi, dum iuga prima detractant, plura uerbera ferunt quam (boues) quos usus aratri iuuat.* Such inversion of the usual order of words is called hyperbaton (see the glossary). The narrator as a tamed animal plays into the traditional elegiac pose of *seruitium amoris*. The notion that some oxen actually enjoy being subjected to the plow anticipates the narrator's capitulation to *Amor* (19–22).
usus aratri: "experience with the plow." The sexual innuendo (cf. 1.10) ties these *boues* even more closely to the narrator.

14 **detractant prensi**: Slow, heavy spondees in initial position are much less common than dactyls in the *Amores* and befit the oxen's resistance to coercion.

15 **ora**: accusative of respect, with *contunditur*. Though similar in form to the accusative of respect with a passive verb (cf. 1.20 and 1.29), there is no reflexive idea here. The horse does not make his own mouth sore; rather, the mouth is made sore by some action done to it.

16 **ad arma facit**: "adapts to the harness" (literally, "acts in accordance with his equipment"). The metrical balance (- ˘ ˘ -) of the two hemistiches and unusual rhyme (*sentit . . . facit*) gives the pentameter a singsong quality, the effect of which is to undercut the seriousness of the narrator's observations.

17 **multo**: ablative of degree of difference, with *acrius* and *ferocius*.

18 **qui**: Understand *eos* as the antecedent. It is common practice for the pronoun forms of *is, ea, id* to be omitted in poetry when they can be understood from context (ellipsis).

19–28 *You have conquered me, Love. Now, for this victory of yours, you deserve a triumphal parade.*

20 **ad tua iura**: "to the terms you impose."

21 **nil**: adverbial, "not at all."
ueniam pacem rogamus: The soothing sound of *m* here and in the following lines suggests the comfort, rather than torment, that submission to Cupid's power brings the narrator.

22 **laus**: "a source of glory"; predicate nominative.
uictus: used as an adjective modifying the subject "I" in *ero*, not as part of a future perfect passive.

23 **myrto**: a plant sacred to Venus; cf. 1.29.
maternas . . . columbas: Doves were sacred to Venus, Cupid's mother, and have often been shown drawing her chariot across the sky.

24 **qui deceat**: relative clause of purpose (cf. 1.24), with *currum* as its antecedent; understand *te* as the direct object. It is common practice

for the forms of the pronouns *ego* and *tu* to be omitted in poetry when they can be understood from context; cf. 18 above.

uitricus: i.e., Vulcan, Venus's husband, god of the forge. Typically, Cupid's father is Mars.

25 **triumphum**: The triumph was the procession of honor awarded to a Roman general for a major military victory over Rome's enemies. The general, wearing a crown of laurel leaves, rode in a chariot through the city up to the temple of Jupiter Optimus Maximus at the top of the Capitoline Hill. His army accompanied him, and behind him he displayed his most important prisoners of war, the spoils he had acquired, and animals to be sacrificed. As he passed by, the crowds of spectators shouted out the ritual cry "*io triumphe!*"

For Propertius (2.10), the triumph stood for the "official" poetry that he chose not to write (Galinsky 1969: 84). Ovid, in celebrating the conquests of Cupid, is able to conflate "official" poetry and love poetry.

26 **arte mouebis**: "You will skillfully guide."

27 **ducentur capti**: Cf. *detractant prensi* (14). The use of similar verb forms in the same spondaic meter and the same metrical position recalls the plight of the *boues*. Though *prensi* and *capti* are nearly synonymous and indicate the forceful seizure of both groups, the struggle of the oxen (*detractant*) has been replaced by a stately procession of submissive young lovers.

29–34 *I, recently wounded, will be paraded as a captive before the cheering crowds, along with your great enemies.*

31 **Mens Bona . . . / et Pudor** (32): The narrator gives human characteristics to these two natural enemies of Love (see "personification" in the glossary), making them deities who have been taken prisoner by him. Ovid may be alluding to Vergil's *Aeneid* 1.291–96 and the scene of Jupiter's prophecy of Rome's greatness under the Julians *gens*, in which *Fides* and *Vesta* (to whom Ovid's *Mens Bona* and *Pudor* are analogous) are free and victorious, but *Furor* is a prisoner, hands chained behind his back (*post tergum*).

33 **te . . . te . . . tibi** (35) **. . . tu** (37) **. . . tibi** (38): The anaphoric repetition of the second-person pronoun, a characteristic of a prayer addressed to a deity, continues all the way to the end of the poem.

35–42 *You will be accompanied by your faithful comrades-in-arms, and from on high your mother will acclaim you sparkling in your jewels and gold.*

35 **Blanditiae . . . Errorque Furorque**: These personifications are suitable companions for Love, just as *Mens Bona* and *Pudor* are appropriate

enemies. *Furor* is personified in Roman poetry for the first time here and in Vergil's *Aeneid* 1.294, discussed above (31).

36 **partes . . . secuta tuas**: "having faithfully supported your (political) program."

37 **hominesque deosque**: *-que . . . -que* is an epic convention (see *Errorque Furorque* above, 35). Here, the polysyndeton emphasizes Cupid's omnipotence both in heaven and on earth.

38 **tibi**: a double-duty pronoun: dative of disadvantage, with *demas*, and dative of advantage, with *commoda*. Both uses fall under the heading "dative of reference."

demas: the generalizing second-person singular subject ("someone").

nudus: a play on both the military meaning "unarmed/defenseless" and on Cupid's traditional nakedness (along with that of those engaged in love's tussles).

39 **triumphanti**: Understand *tibi;* for the omission of pronouns, see 18 above.

41 **pinnas gemma, gemma . . . capillos**: Both *pinnas* and *capillos* are objects of *uariante*. The chiasmus, repetition, and asyndeton emphasize Cupid's resplendence.

42 **rotis**: a part of a chariot (*currum*) used to represent the chariot as a whole (see "synecdoche" in the glossary).

43–48 *As you pass by, your mere presence will cause the crowds to be afflicted with Love. Bacchus has a similar effect.*

43–46 **non paucos . . . ures / . . . uulnera multa dabis** (44) / . . . **sagittae** (45) / . . . **flamma** (46): the extended chiasmus (action A, action B, weapon B, weapon A) vividly encapsulates Cupid's belligerent amatory power, which was introduced in the first poem (1.25–26) and recalled earlier in this poem (7–9, 29, and 37).

43 **non paucos**: = *multos*. This is an example of litotes, or understatement, whereby a positive idea is formed by the negation of its opposite (see the glossary); the effect is to intensify the idea.

44 **praeteriens**: "as you pass by (in your chariot)."

45 **licet**: as a conjunction introducing a concessive clause, "although/even though."

46 **flamma**: i.e., Cupid's torch.

47 **Bacchus Gangetide terra**: The Ganges River was in India, and it marked the eastern boundary of the area where Bacchus, another god of passion, overcame opposition and established his religious cult. In his victorious return from the East to Greece, Bacchus rode in a chariot drawn by panthers.

48 **grauis alitibus**: an oxymoron; the *grauitas* of the conquering Roman general is juxtaposed to its opposite, the *leuitas* of the frivolous god

42   *Amores* 1.2

of love. For the poetic connotations of *grauis* and *leuis*, see 1.1 and 19. The chiasmus *tu . . . alitibus tigribus ille* and asyndeton emphasize the contrast between Amor and Bacchus; cf. 41 above.

49–52   **Be merciful to me, your captive, just as Caesar was merciful to those he conquered.**

50   **parce . . . perdere**: *Parce* + the infinitive *perdere* function similarly to *noli* + the infinitive, i.e., to express a negative command, but with a slightly different nuance: "refrain from . . ."

51   **cognati . . . Caesaris**: Based on the claims of the Julian *gens*, Augustus could trace his family line back to Iulus, son of Aeneas and grandson of Venus, Aeneas's mother. Cupid, as the son of Venus, was stepbrother to Aeneas and therefore a kinsman of Augustus.

52   **qua**: *Manu* is its antecedent; for the placement of the relative clause before its antecedent, see *quod* (1.24).

For Further Reading

Miller, J. F. 1995. "Reading Cupid's Triumph." *Classical Journal* 90: 287–94.
Moles, J. 1991. "The Dramatic Coherence of Ovid, *Amores* 1.1 and 1.2." *Classical Quarterly* 41: 551–54.

Amores 1.3

Having submitted unwillingly (1.1) and then willingly (1.2) to Cupid and the demands of love poetry, Ovid now introduces the *puella*, the mistress or "girl," although not by name. We might expect expressions of joy and rapture, but instead the narrator seems concerned that his love will not be returned. Initially he portrays the *puella* as a conqueror (*praedata est*) like Cupid in 1.2, which makes the narrator *her* spoils of war, and he uses the language of *seruitium amoris* to describe his subservient relationship to her. Yet he clearly wants her surrender in return, and to that end he offers as qualifications his poetic genius, his fidelity, his desire to die with his girl at his side, and the promise of poetic immortality. All of these assertions are typical of other love poets, but here they seem suspect, especially his declaration of fidelity.

The narrator loses credibility when he exemplifies his final argument, the immortalizing power of poetry, with three mythological maidens, Io, Leda, and Europa. These *exempla,* while demonstrating the fame a *puella* can achieve, also allow him implicitly to compare himself to Jupiter, the seducer in each instance—and an unfaithful lover. More significant, the narrator has used the elegiac conventions to shift focus away from the potentially predatory *puella* and onto himself and his poetry. He reduces his girl to poetic subject matter (*materies*) in line 19, which also counters his earlier avowals of love. Thus a poem that begins with the *seruitium* of the narrator and ends with his power as immortalizer reveals again that Ovid's plan is to write poetry about poetry. Love, although necessary, may not be central to his plan.

Iusta precor: quae me nuper praedata puella est
   aut amet aut faciat cur ego semper amem.

44 Amores 1.3

a, nimium uolui! tantum patiatur amari;
  audierit nostras tot Cytherea preces.
accipe, per longos tibi qui deseruiat annos;   5
  accipe, qui pura norit amare fide.
si me non ueterum commendant magna parentum
  nomina, si nostri sanguinis auctor eques,
nec meus innumeris renouatur campus aratris,
  temperat et sumptus parcus uterque parens,   10
at Phoebus comitesque nouem uitisque repertor
  hac faciunt et me qui tibi donat Amor
et nulli cessura fides, sine crimine mores,
  nudaque simplicitas purpureusque pudor.
non mihi mille placent, non sum desultor amoris: 15
  tu mihi, si qua fides, cura perennis eris;
tecum, quos dederint annos mihi fila sororum,
  uiuere contingat teque dolente mori;
te mihi materiem felicem in carmina praebe:
  prouenient causa carmina digna sua.   20
carmine nomen habent exterrita cornibus Io
  et quam fluminea lusit adulter aue
quaeque super pontum simulato uecta iuuenco
  uirginea tenuit cornua uara manu.
nos quoque per totum pariter cantabimur orbem   25
  iunctaque semper erunt nomina nostra tuis.

Notes

1–4 *Allow me, I pray, to love and be loved by the girl who has captured my heart.*

> 1 **Iusta precor**: Although *precor* seems to indicate the subservient position of the narrator, the opening word *iusta* ("fairness") reveals his interest in seeking a balance of power between himself and the *puella*. Note how *precor* is picked up by *preces* in line 4, rounding off the opening section of the poem.
> **praedata puella est**: The metaphor of the mistress as "conqueror in war" may be based on Propertius 2.1.55, *una meos quoniam praedata est*

femina sensus, "since one woman has taken my senses as spoils." In *Amores* 1.2 the narrator called himself the spoils (*praeda*, 19) of Cupid; in the current poem Cupid's control over him seems to pass to the *puella*. The repetition of the *p* sound, an example of alliteration (see the glossary), suggests the narrator's indignation.

The use of the word *puella* ("girl") in elegiac poetry leaves the marital status or social position of the female ambiguous. This ambiguity allows the *puella* to operate outside the traditional domestic and marital structures (and strictures) in Roman society.

puella: the antecedent of *quae*; *puella* has been attracted into the relative clause, but functions syntactically as the subject of *amet* and *faciat* (2) (jussives). This arrangement is especially common when the relative clause precedes the main clause.

2 **amet . . . amem**: The balance of power between narrator and *puella* is made explicit by the active behavior of the girl (*amet*) at the beginning of the line and the active behavior of the narrator (*amem*) at the end. *Amem* is a deliberative subjunctive used in an indirect question.

faciat cur: "Let her give reasons why."

3 **patiatur amari**: *Puella* is the subject of *patiatur*; understand *se* as the accusative subject of *amari*. The narrator's willingness to love without being loved in return is a theme found in both Propertius (1.6.25) and Tibullus (1.1.57).

4 **audierit**: syncopated form of *audiuerit* (see "syncope" in the glossary). Most take it as future perfect indicative with an understood protasis, "If that happens, then Cytherea . . . " Cairns (1993: 105), however, treats it as perfect subjunctive, which is standard in prayers solemnly invoking deities.

nostras: plural for singular; cf. 2.2.

Cytherea: "the Cytherean," i.e., Venus, since the island of Cythera was sacred to her.

5-6 *I promise to be your faithful and devoted slave.*

5 The narrator begins a speech of persuasion (called a *suasoria* in rhetorical terms) that is carefully designed to prove the worthiness of his love and to persuade the girl to accept him as a lover. The *suasoria* continues through line 26.

accipe . . . accipe (6): Repetition highlights the narrator's urgency.

tibi qui: The centrally placed conjunction of the girl (*tibi*) and the narrator (*qui*) continues the emphasis on balance of power.

deseruiat: language of *seruitium amoris*.

6 **norit**: contracted from *nouerit* < *nosco, noscere*; cf. *audierit* above (4).

46 Amores 1.3

7–12 *My humble background and limited resources are balanced by the favor the gods of love elegy bestow on me.*

7   **me . . . meus** (9) **. . . me** (12) **. . . mihi non sum** (15): The balance between *puella* and narrator abates as the narrator focuses primarily on himself.

8   **nomina**: As the first word in line 8 and the final word of the clause begun in line 7, *nomina* puts strong emphasis on "fame," a key concept of this poem; cf. *nomen* (21) and *nomina* (26). The poetic term for one line carrying over to the next is "enjambment" (see the glossary). While enjambment within the couplet is not uncommon, it is extremely rare between couplets; Ovid preferred to complete a sentence or clause by the end of each couplet.

   auctor eques: *Eques* is predicate nominative; understand *est* by ellipsis. The poverty of the love poet was conventional in elegy, but Ovid himself was by no means poor.

9   The first golden line in the *Amores*. As "golden" implies, this hexameter line exemplifies the ultimate in artful arrangement: the adjectives precede, the verb stands in the center, and the nouns follow. The word order is in an interlocked ABverbAB pattern, known rhetorically as synchesis. (See "golden line" and "interlocked word order" in the glossary.)

10 **temperat et**: = **et temperat**; for the postponement of the conjunction, see *pharetra cum* (1.21).
    sumptus: accusative plural, "spending/expenses."

11 **-que . . . –que . . . / . . . et** (12) **. . . / et** (13) **. . . / -que . . . -que** (14): This is an excellent example of polysyndeton, used to impress the *puella* with the narrator's overwhelming number of positive attributes.
    uitis repertor: periphrasis for Bacchus, god of wine and here a god of poetry, in company with Apollo and the nine Muses. Ovid clearly draws on Propertius 3.2 for his claims of surpassing poetic ability: *miremur, nobis et Baccho et Apolline dextro / turba puellarum si mea uerba colit?* (9–10) . . . *at Musae comites* (15), "Should I wonder, with both Bacchus and Apollo at my side, that a crowd of girls cherishes my words? . . . The Muses are my companions."

12 **hac faciunt**: "are active in this cause," i.e., "are on my side."
    Amor: also subject of *hac faciunt*. The suspension of *Amor* to the couplet's end sets it in contrast with *Phoebus* (11) at the beginning and reminds us of Cupid's power over the narrator. In this same line, *donat* repeats the metaphor of enslavement found in *deseruiat* (5).

13–18 *My humble background and limited resources are balanced out as well by my faithfulness—by other qualities, yes, but especially my enduring faithfulness.*

13 **fides ... mores / ... simplicitas ... pudor** (14): These four very Roman virtues parallel the divinities of poetry mentioned above (11–12) and are also subjects of *hac faciunt* (12).
15 **mille**: Understand *puellae*.
desultor amoris: The *desultores* were performers at the Circus Maximus (the Roman race course) who leapt from one horse's back to another at full gallop. The vivid image brings to mind fickleness rather than fidelity.
The *-or-* sound leaps from line end to line end in 11–15 (*repertOR, amOR, mORes, pudOR, desultOR amORis*) just as the lover from bed to bed (Ferguson 1978: 123).
16 **tu ... / tecum ...** (17) / **teque** (18): The anaphora of the second-person singular pronoun, which imitates the style of a prayer to a deity (cf. 2.33), suggests that the girl is being addressed as a goddess. Note that although the focus is now on the *puella*, the narrator is equally present with her: *tu mihi* (16), *tecum ... mihi* (17), *teque* (18), *te mihi* (19). While this word placement can be called rhetorical—it is a favorite technique of Cicero, for instance, to "place" himself next to his client through conjoining pronouns, it gives this poem a meaning that transgresses the ostensible elegiac relationship of narrator as slave and *puella* as master.
mihi: dative indicating possession.
si qua fides: Understand *est* by ellipsis.
qua: = *aliqua*; for *qui qua quod* following *si*, see *quo* (2.5).
17–18 The narrator's wish that his mistress be at his side as he dies is most likely based on Tibullus 1.1.59–62: *te spectem, suprema mihi cum uenerit hora / et teneam moriens deficiente manu. / flebis et arsuro positum me, Delia, lecto / tristibus et lacrimis oscula mixta dabis*, "May I gaze upon you when my final hour is at hand and may I hold you in my weakened arms as I die. You will weep when I am placed on the funeral pyre, Delia, and your tears will intermingle with kisses."
17 **annos**: accusative of duration of time. *Annos*, the antecedent of *quos*, has been attracted into the relative clause, but functions with *uiuere* (18); cf. *puella* above (1).
sororum: i.e., the Parcae = the three Fates: Clotho, who spins out the thread of life; Lachesis, who measures the thread; and Atropos, who cuts it off and brings life to an end.
18 **contingat**: impersonal verb with *mihi* (17). Optative: literally, "May it happen to me to live ...," i.e., "May I be lucky enough to live ..." *Mihi* does double duty as indirect object with *dederint* (17) and reference with *contingat*.
mori < *morior, mori*; antithetical to *uiuere*. The opposition in meaning of *mori* and *uiuere* is physically represented by their extended separation—they bracket the line.

48   *Amores* 1.3

19–20   *Deign to be the inspiration of my poetry; then my poetry will be inspiring.*

19   **materiem felicem**: predicate accusative with *te*, "yourself (as) a . . . " The agricultural meanings of *felicem*, "fruitful" (referring to plants and trees), and of *prouenient* (20), "sprout/spring forth," create a vivid image of fertility, growth, and vitality.
in carmina: for the accusative of purpose, see *in exitium . . . meum* (1.22).

20   **causa . . . sua**: ablative singular, with *digna*; *causa*, here, "source of inspiration."

21–26   *The fame that the maidens loved by Jupiter have attained through poetry—that same fame will unite you and me for eternity.*

21   **carmine**: ablative of cause.
nomen: Cf. *nomina* above (8). The narrator's claim that poetry brings eternal fame (= immortality) draws again on Propertius 3.2: *fortunata, meo si qua est celebrata libello! / carmina erunt formae tot monumenta tuae* (17–18), "Fortunate the girl who is celebrated in my book of poetry! My poems will create a memorial to your beauty."
exterrita cornibus Io: After having his way with the maiden Io, Jupiter transformed her into a heifer to hide her, and his deed, from his (rightly) mistrustful wife, Juno.
Io: the first of the three subjects of *habent*.

22   **quam**: Understand *ea* (= Leda, unnamed) as the antecedent of *quam* (cf. 2.18) and as the second subject of *habent*. Jupiter disguised himself as a swan (*fluminea aue*) to seduce Leda.
adulter: i.e., Jupiter.

23   **quaeque**: Understand *ea* (= Europa, also unnamed) as the antecedent of *quae* and as the third subject of *habent*. The maiden Europa was tricked into climbing onto a playful young bull's back (Jupiter in disguise), so that he could carry her off across the sea to Crete.
uecta < *ueho, uehere*.

25   **nos . . . nostra tuis** (26): the bracketing (see the glossary) of the couplet underscores that the narrator will share the immortal fame he offers as enticement to the *puella*.
pariter: "to an equal degree," on the one hand, with Jupiter and his loves (Io, Leda, and Europa) and, on the other, with each other.

26   **nomina nostra**: plural for *nomen meum*, in view of the following *tuis*.
tuis: Understand *nominibus* by ellipsis.

For Further Reading

Curran, L. C. 1966. "*Desultores Amoris:* Ovid *Amores* 1.3." *Classical Philology* 61: 47–49.
Olstein, K. 1975. "*Amores* 1.3 and Duplicity as a Way of Love." *Transactions of the American Philological Association* 105: 241–57.
Davis, J. T. 1988. "*Desultores Amoris*, Publicity-Seeking and Ovid, *Amores* 1.3." *Augustan Age* 8: 22–26.

Amores 1.4

The scenario of 1.4 is a forthcoming dinner party at which the narrator, his mistress, and her husband or lover (*uir* can mean both) will be guests. Obstacles to the love relationship are standard in elegy. They can range from a locked door to an overzealous slave or, as here, to the presence of a rival. In this poem Ovid reverses the usual situation by casting the legitimate *uir* as the interloper and the narrator as the wronged party. The girl, still unnamed, is a passive party in the imagined sequence of events, and her subordinate status is brought into sharp focus when the narrator begins a series of directives designed to control her behavior. His initial instructions center on their shared intimacies and call for secret communications typical of lovers (and love poetry): writing messages on tables with wine or using a variety of winks, nods, and hand gestures.

    As the poem and party advance, however, the narrator turns to his real concern, that his mistress and her *uir* will engage in sexual play. Now his directives change from "don't let your lips touch the same food as his" to "don't let your lips (and other parts) touch him"! The more forceful and legalistic his language becomes, the more we can imagine that the *puella* and her *uir* are in fact engaging in the very behavior the narrator hopes to prevent and that he is becoming increasingly anxious. His obsession with sex actually arouses him, and, in an amusing aside and with irony so typical of Ovid, the narrator reveals that what motivates his deepest fears is the sexual activity he himself has often engaged in at dinner parties. As the poem and party end, the narrator continues to imagine the worst, and in a last-ditch effort to retain the pose of control—even as it becomes clear he has no control—he orders his *puella* to reject the act itself, or, if she cannot, to at least deny to him that it happened.

Vir tuus est epulas nobis aditurus easdem:
 ultima cena tuo sit precor illa uiro.
ergo ego dilectam tantum conuiua puellam
 aspiciam? tangi quem iuuet, alter erit,
alteriusque sinus apte subiecta fouebis?   5
 iniciet collo, cum uolet, ille manum?
desine mirari, posito quod candida uino
 Atracis ambiguos traxit in arma uiros;
nec mihi silua domus, nec equo mea membra cohaerent.
 uix a te uideor posse tenere manus.   10
quae tibi sint facienda tamen cognosce, nec Euris
 da mea nec tepidis uerba ferenda Notis.
ante ueni quam uir; nec quid, si ueneris ante,
 possit agi uideo, sed tamen ante ueni.
cum premet ille torum, uultu comes ipsa modesto 15
 ibis ut accumbas, clam mihi tange pedem;
me specta nutusque meos uultumque loquacem;
 excipe furtiuas et refer ipsa notas.
uerba superciliis sine uoce loquentia dicam;
 uerba leges digitis, uerba notata mero.   20
cum tibi succurret Veneris lasciuia nostrae,
 purpureas tenero pollice tange genas;
si quid erit, de me tacita quod mente queraris,
 pendeat extrema mollis ab aure manus;
cum tibi, quae faciam, mea lux, dicamue, placebunt, 25
 uersetur digitis anulus usque tuis;
tange manu mensam, tangunt quo more precantes,
 optabis merito cum mala multa uiro.
quod tibi miscuerit, sapias, bibat ipse iubeto;
 tu puerum leuiter posce quod ipsa uoles;   30
quae tu reddideris, ego primus pocula sumam,
 et, qua tu biberis, hac ego parte bibam.
si tibi forte dabit quod praegustauerit ipse,
 reice libatos illius ore cibos.
nec premat impositis sinito tua colla lacertis,   35
 mite nec in rigido pectore pone caput,

Amores 1.4

nec sinus admittat digitos habilesue papillae;
　oscula praecipue nulla dedisse uelis.
oscula si dederis, fiam manifestus amator
　et dicam 'mea sunt' iniciamque manum.　　　　　　40
haec tamen aspiciam, sed quae bene pallia celant,
　illa mihi caeci causa timoris erunt.
nec femori committe femur nec crure cohaere
　nec tenerum duro cum pede iunge pedem.
multa miser timeo, quia feci multa proterue,　　　　45
　exemplique metu torqueor ipse mei:
saepe mihi dominaeque meae properata uoluptas
　ueste sub iniecta dulce peregit opus.
hoc tu non facies; sed, ne fecisse puteris,
　conscia de tergo pallia deme tuo.　　　　　　　　　50
uir bibat usque roga (precibus tamen oscula desint),
　dumque bibit, furtim, si potes, adde merum.
si bene compositus somno uinoque iacebit,
　consilium nobis resque locusque dabunt.
cum surges abitura domum, surgemus et omnes,　　　55
　in medium turbae fac memor agmen eas:
agmine me inuenies aut inuenieris in illo;
　quicquid ibi poteris tangere, tange, mei.
me miserum! monui, paucas quod prosit in horas;
　separor a domina nocte iubente mea.　　　　　　　60
nocte uir includet; lacrimis ego maestus obortis,
　qua licet, ad saeuas prosequar usque fores.
oscula iam sumet, iam non tantum oscula sumet;
　quod mihi das furtim, iure coacta dabis.
uerum inuita dato (potes hoc) similisque coactae:　　65
　blanditiae taceant sitque maligna Venus.
si mea uota ualent, illum quoque ne iuuet opto;
　si minus, at certe te iuuet inde nihil.
sed quaecumque tamen noctem fortuna sequetur,
　cras mihi constanti uoce dedisse nega.　　　　　　70

Notes

1–10 *Having to watch the physical intimacies you and your lover share at the dinner party will drive me crazy with jealousy.*

1 **Vir**: the narrator's rival.
The hissing of the alliterated *s* immediately communicates the narrator's animosity. The chiasmus *Vir tuus . . . / . . . tuo . . . uiro* (2) and the bracketing of the couplet with *uir . . . / . . . uiro* underscore the object of that animosity, the man with legitimate rights.
nobis: dative of reference, with *easdem*.

2 **sit precor**: = *precor (ut) sit*. Verbs of asking, ordering, etc. that introduce indirect commands often take the subjunctive clause <u>without</u> *ut*. Cf. also *precor* (3.1), where the narrator prays to be allowed to love the *puella*.

3 **dilectam . . . puellam**: The perfect passive participles that describe the girl here and in line 5 (*subiecta*) together with the active agency of the two males (*aspiciam*, 4—narrator, *iniciet*, 6—*uir*) reinforce the idea that the *puella* is an object to be controlled.
conuiua: in apposition to *ego*, "I . . . (as) a guest."

4 **aspiciam? tangi**: The deliberate juxtaposition and contrast of seeing and touching, known rhetorically as antithesis (see the glossary), draw attention not only to the opposition between the narrator and the *uir*, but also to the separation of the narrator from his *puella* despite their physical proximity. Enjambment of *aspiciam* sets up the juxtaposition.
tangi quem iuuet: The impersonal verb *iuuet* takes the accusative/infinitive construction *quem + tangi* as its subject. Understand *a te* with *tangi*: " whom being touched (by you) will delight." Only here and in the following line (*fouebis*) does the narrator suggest that the *puella* will play an even remotely active role.
quem: a relative pronoun whose antecedent is *alter*; cf. 1.24.

5 **subiecta** < *subiectus, -a, -um*: here, "lying up under," i.e., "snuggling up close (to)"; also note the double entendre.

6 **iniciet . . . manum** < *inicere manum*, "to embrace," but also "to lay legal claim (to)" (with reference to legal ownership rights). The narrator inverts reality by presenting himself as the one with rights over the *puella*.

7 **posito . . . uino**: Drunkenness obviously was a factor in the Centaurs' attack.
quod: "that," after verbs of perceiving such as *scio, credo, uideo*, and even *miror*.

8 **Atracis**: Greek nominative feminine singular, "woman of Atrax," i.e., Hippodamia. The narrator claims to understand the behavior of the Centaurs at the wedding of King Pirithous and Hippodamia, princess of Atrax. The drunken Centaurs tried to carry off the bride by force, so inflamed were they by her beauty. With this *exemplum*, the narrator reinforces the active/passive relationship between himself and his *puella*. While the female Hippodamia is the catalyst for action (*traxit in arma*), men are the truly active players. The narrator brings home the point when he declares that he will not be able to resist manhandling her (*a te . . . tenere manus*, 10).

Atracis . . . traxit: another example of the wordplay the love poets so enjoyed; cf. 2.9.

ambiguos . . . uiros: i.e., centaurs (half-men, half-horses).

9 **silua domus**: *Domus* is predicate nominative. The narrator explains that he is not an uncivilized beast prone to uncontrolled acts.

10 **a te**: ablative of separation.

10–11 *So this is how you have to act to assure my peace of mind.*

11 **quae**: Understand *ea*, neuter plural; for the omission of forms of *is, ea, id*, see *qui* (2.18).

Euris / . . . Notis (12): datives of indirect object with *da mea . . . uerba*, or perhaps datives of agent with *ferenda*.

13–14 *Get to the party before he does.*

13 **ante . . . quam**: The division of a compound into two parts is called "tmesis." Translate as *antequam*, which is often split in this way, after *ueni*.

ueni: imperative singular. So also *tange* (16), *specta* (17), *excipe*, and *refer* (18), etc. The carefully placed repetition of *ante ueni . . . ueneris ante / . . . ante ueni* (14), emphasizes both the narrator's urgency and his impotence.

quid / . . . possit agi (14): indirect question introduced by *uideo*. The pointlessness of the narrator's instructions becomes evident since he can give no good reason why his mistress should carry them out.

15–28 *Brush against me when you can, and let us share our thoughts by exchanging secret signals.*

15 A Roman dinner party (*cena*) lasted several hours. The guests, both men and women, ate reclining on large couches, each of which held as many

Amores 1.4   55

as three people. They stretched out on their left sides and propped themselves up on one elbow. Usually three couches were arranged around a low square table, one side of which was left open so that the servants could deliver and remove the individual courses (usually seven). The guests ate from the table using their fingers, which required frequent hand washing. (Carcopino 2003: 264–71)

cum: governs both *premet ille* and *ipsa . . . / ibis*.

comes: in apposition to the subject "you" in *ibis* (16), "you (as) a . . ."

17–20 Writing messages with wine and signaling a lover through an assortment of gestures appear in both Tibullus (e.g. 1.2.21ff.) and Propertius (3.8.25ff.).

19 **uerba . . . / uerba . . . uerba**: Anaphora and asyndeton highlight the secret and unspoken communications to be shared by narrator and *puella*.

superciliis . . . / . . . digitis (20): Understand *meis* with both; ablatives of means.

21 **Veneris**: = "lovemaking" as a substitute for Venus, the embodiment of sexual love (see "metonymy" in the glossary).

23 **quid**: Cf. 2.5; *quid* is the antecedent of *quod*.

26 **usque**: "continuously," i.e., "round and round."

27 **tangunt**: Understand *mensam* as direct object by ellipsis or, better, *aram*.

quo more: "in the way that/just as."

28 **optabis . . . cum**: Cf. 1.21.

29–34 *Allow no meeting of the "mouths" through food and drink.*

29 **sapias**: "Be wise/act sensibly," second-person singular, jussive subjunctive (as a "polite command").

bibat . . . iubeto: *Iubeo* generally takes the accusative/infinitive construction, but here the construction is replaced by the subjunctive without *ut*; cf. *sit precor* above (2).

iubeto: second-person singular, future imperative. The future imperative is the language of Roman law and religion. It differs from the present imperative just as "Answer the phone" differs from "Thou shalt not covet thy neighbor's goods." The first is a directive; the second a long-term injunction. The narrator enjoins the *puella* three times in the future imperative not to do things that are not in accord with his laws. (J. T. Davis 1992: 65–66)

30 **puerum . . . posce (id) quod ipsa uoles**: Some verbs of asking (like *poscere*) may take a double accusative, one of "person," *puerum* (direct object), and the other of the "thing desired," *id* (secondary object).

56 Amores 1.4

      leuiter: "quietly."
31 **quae**: What is the antecedent of this relative pronoun? (Cf. 1.24.)
      reddideris: The final syllable *-ris* is short by nature, but metrically long (see "diastole" in the glossary); so also in *biberis* (32).
32 **qua . . . , hac . . . parte**: Both are ablatives of place from which, with *ex* understood.

35–40 *Avoid all above-the-waist physical contact, especially kissing.*

    35 **premat . . . sinito**: For the omission of *ut* in indirect commands, see *sit precor* above (2).
          impositis . . . tua colla lacertis: The chiastic word order creates a compact word picture in which the girl's neck is encircled by the *uir*'s arms. One manuscript has *indignis* instead of *impositis*, a reading that McKeown prefers because it sends an unmistakably critical message.
          sinito: future imperative; cf. *iubeto* above (29).
    36 **mite** < *mitis, mite*.
          nec . . . pone: = *et ne pone*. The present imperative with *ne* is an archaic construction that has legal and religious overtones, "It is incumbent upon you (to) . . . " So also *nec . . . committe, nec cohaere*, and *nec . . . iunge* (43–44).
    37 **sinus . . . habilesue papillae**: Both are subjects of *admittat*, which is singular in agreement with the subject nearest to it.
    39 **manifestus**: a legal term, equivalent to "caught in the act."
    40 **iniciam . . . manum**: The narrator, acting as "praetor," twists the Roman law of property to include kisses (J. T. Davis 1992: 66); cf. *iniciet manum* above (6).

41–50 *As for covert below-the-waist activity (which panics me most because I am an expert in this area), remove your coverlet so that I can see I have nothing to fear.*

    44 **tenerum duro . . . pede . . . pedem**: Chiasmus reflects the "mingling" the narrator seeks to prevent. His description of his *puella*'s feet and those of his rival also plays on terms reflecting genre and style that distinguish elegy from epic; cf. *pedem* in *Amores* 1.4. Words like *tener* and *mollis* represent the soft and the delicate nature of both love elegy and the style of Callimachus and the Roman elegists, as opposed to the harshness (*durus*) associated with war and epic. *Mite* and *rigido* in line 36 above illustrate this same opposition. For other stylistic terminology, see *tenuis* (1.18 and 2.7), *leuis* and *grauis* (1.1 and 1.19, 2.9).

45   **multa ... multa**: repetition for emphasis; the alliteration of *m* may be meant to replicate moaning.
47   **mihi dominaeque meae**: datives of reference.
48   **dulce ... opus**: a euphemism for sexual intercourse (Adams 1982: 157). The narrator quickly passes from imaginary foreplay to the act itself.
49   **puteris** < *puto, putare*.

51–58 *Get him drunk; then, when the party breaks up, find me in the crowd and brush against me.*

51   **bibat ... roga**: cf. 2.
53   **somno uinoque**: In hendiadys, two independent nouns join together to create a single image, "in a drunken sleep."
55   **cum**: governs both *surges* and *surgemus*.
       et: = *etiam*.
56   **fac ... eas**: "See to it that you go ... " The imperatives *dic* and *fac* often take the subjunctive without *ut*. (There is not an ellipsis of *ut*; these are simply old idiomatic expressions.)
57   **agmine ... in illo**: Note how word order mirrors the scene at the end of the party (word picture): the narrator and his *puella* are found in the middle of the crowd.
       inuenieris: Future perfect active or future passive? How can you tell?
58   **mei**: partitive genitive, with *quicquid*.

59–62 *My control over the situation ends soon. I shall be shut out, and he will have my mistress for the night.*

59   **me miserum**: accusative of exclamation; cf. 1.25.
       monui ... quod: "I have given advice that ... "; cf. *quod* above (7).
       paucas ... in horas: accusative of duration of time.
61   **uir includet**: Understand *eam* (= *puellam*) by ellipsis.
62   **qua**: = *qua uia*, "by which route."
       saeuas ... fores: The doors are heartless because they shut out the narrator and keep him separated from his mistress. He becomes an *exclusus amator* ("locked-out lover"), a favorite scenario for the poet-lover in elegy.

63–70 *Submit to him grudgingly. Let there be no pleasure in it. And no matter what happens, say IT didn't happen.*

63   **oscula ... non tantum oscula**: Even as he advises his girl to reject and resist the sex he imagines she will have with her *uir* at home, the narrator cannot help but take a prurient interest in the details.

58 Amores 1.4

64 **furtim, iure coacta**: juxtaposition and antithesis. By this opposition, the narrator suggests that stolen (*furtim*) kisses are given freely, whereas kisses given out of legal obligation (*iure coacta*) are not. Thus, in the world of elegy, illicit behavior is morally superior to lawful, and the traditional Roman value system is turned on its head. (P. Miller 2002: 253)
coacta: nominative singular (< *cogo, cogere*), modifying the subject "you" in *dabis*. Understand the indirect object, *ei* (= *uiro*), with *dabis*.
65 **uerum**: "but."
dato: Perfect passive participle or future imperative? Use the context to decide.
66 **Venus**: cf. *Veneris* above (21).
67 **iuuet**: The subject, *Venus*, is drawn from the preceding line (ellipsis).
68 **si minus**: = *si non*.
nihil: neuter singular, used as an adverb; cf. 1.21.
70 **dedisse**: here, in the sense of "give in/grant sexual favors"; understand *te* as the accusative subject in indirect statement.

For Further Reading

Ford, G. B. 1966. "An Analysis of *Amores* 1.4." *Helikon* 6: 645–52.
James, S. L. 2005. "A Courtesan's Choreography." In *Defining Gender and Genre in Roman Elegy: Essays Presented to William S. Anderson on his Seventy-fifth Birthday,* ed. W. Batstone and G. Tissol, 269–99. New York: Peter Lang.
Miller, P. A. 2004. *Subjecting Verses: Latin Erotic Elegy and the Emergence of the Real,* 169–83. Princeton, N.J.: Princeton University Press.

Amores 1.5

At last Corinna arrives by name and in person in this fifth poem of the collection, and Ovid uses the first eight lines to set the scene with care. It is past the middle of the day, and the narrator is in the middle of the bed. The window shutters are in midposition, making the room more like twilight or dawn than midafternoon. The lighting of the room is reminiscent of the dappled light of a wooded grove, also a suitable environment for erotic encounters. Just as the narrator notes the appropriateness of the setting for modest girls, Corinna bursts into the room, dressed, or rather undressed, for action. A skirmish over her tunic ensues; Corinna surrenders, and the victorious narrator joyfully describes the perfection of her naked body. The final lines of the poem are anticlimactic, literally and metaphorically. The narrator abruptly breaks off his sensuous description and leaves their lovemaking to the imagination of the audience. His final wish for many such midday encounters returns us to the beginning of the poem when he was readying himself for a midday respite.

This poem is a sexual encounter that combines love and war as the two lovers contend for the same result. It also has been read as a depersonalization and objectification of Corinna (Cahoon 1988: 296; Greene 1998: 83). The narrator's detached cataloguing of Corinna's body parts may also serve a literary purpose. Because it mimics a critical examination of a very fine work of art (think of an ancient statue), Ovid may be using Corinna's body to represent his own work of art, his poetic text (Keith 1994: 31). The enjoyment, then, that the narrator takes in his mistress would equal the satisfaction that Ovid takes in creating a perfect literary work.

Aestus erat mediamque dies exegerat horam;
   apposui medio membra leuanda toro.

Amores 1.5

pars adaperta fuit, pars altera clausa fenestrae,
   quale fere siluae lumen habere solent,
qualia sublucent fugiente crepuscula Phoebo   5
   aut ubi nox abiit nec tamen orta dies.
illa uerecundis lux est praebenda puellis,
   qua timidus latebras speret habere pudor.
ecce, Corinna uenit tunica uelata recincta,
   candida diuidua colla tegente coma,   10
qualiter in thalamos formosa Semiramis isse
   dicitur et multis Lais amata uiris.
deripui tunicam; nec multum rara nocebat,
   pugnabat tunica sed tamen illa tegi,
cumque ita pugnaret tamquam quae uincere nollet,   15
   uicta est non aegre proditione sua.
ut stetit ante oculos posito uelamine nostros,
   in toto nusquam corpore menda fuit:
quos umeros, quales uidi tetigique lacertos!
   forma papillarum quam fuit apta premi!   20
quam castigato planus sub pectore uenter!
   quantum et quale latus! quam iuuenale femur!
singula quid referam? nil non laudabile uidi,
   et nudam pressi corpus ad usque meum.
cetera quis nescit? lassi requieuimus ambo.   25
   proueniant medii sic mihi saepe dies.

Notes

1–8   *A hot afternoon, I am on the bed, the room is veiled in half light.*

  1   **aestus**: On one level, this is describing the weather. What sexual connotations could *aestus* also have?
      mediam . . . / . . . medio (2): Word order reinforces the sense of balance in the scene. *Dies* stands between *mediam* and *horam* in line 1, and in line 2 *membra* is framed by *medio* and *toro*.
  2   **medio . . . toro**: dative of end of motion.
      membra leuanda: For the gerundive as a simple participle, see 1.30.
Membra, if read as a plural for a singular (*membrum*), has a sexual sense and hints at the erotic encounter to come.

Amores 1.5   61

3   **pars ... pars altera**: i.e., the window has two shutters. The placement of *pars, pars, fenestrae* at equal intervals in the line supports the picture of a half-opened window.
4   **quale ... lumen**: neuter singular, accusative.
5   This elaborate five-word line, with the alliteration of *l*, the assonance of *u* and *a*, and interlocked order of adjectives and nouns, reflects the languorous richness of the image of the setting sun. Ovid also uses meter adeptly in his description: the spondaic *sublucent* gives way to a series of dactyls as the sun departs.
    qualia ... crepuscula: subject of *sublucent*.
8   **qua**: relative pronoun (ablative of means) whose antecedent is *lux* (7).

9–12 *Corinna suddenly appears, loosely clad and enticing.*

9–10 Scan the lines to see which final *a*'s are long and which are short. Note that the assonance of *a* well represents our awe (or Ahh!) at Corinna's dramatic entry.
 9   **ecce, Corinna uenit**: Corinna unexpectedly appears, seeming somewhat less shy than we have been led to expect. The suddenness of her appearance resembles the epiphany of deities, who tend to reveal themselves to mortals around midday. Writers often use *ecce* and *uenit* to mark such sacred events (Nicoll 1977: 42ff.).
    Corinna: the narrator's mistress. Her name recalls a famously beautiful Greek poet known for the complexity of her poetry. It may also have been created from κόρη ("maiden"), the Greek equivalent of *puella*.
    tunica: the basic garment for Roman men and women. A woman's *tunica* reached to her ankles, could be long-sleeved, short-sleeved or sleeveless, and was belted at the waist. A *tunica* made of a delicate transparent material would require an over-garment to make the outfit suitable for mixed company. (Sebesta and Bonfante 2001: 221, 226)
10 **candida diuidua colla**: *candida ... colla* is the object of *tegente*; poetic plural. Ovid's cleverly juxtaposed adjectives *candida diuidua* play on Catullus's description of his mistress as a *candida diua*, "radiant goddess," *c*. 68.70 (Hinds 1987: 8).
    coma: A Roman woman bound her hair up on her head with bands made from wool. She veiled her head whenever she left the house as a sign of her modesty. Even a courtesan's hair was gathered up and secured by a band. (Sebesta and Bonfante 2001: 48–49)
11 **formosa Semiramis / ... Lais amata** (12): Both are Greek nominatives, singular feminine.
    Semiramis: an Assyrian queen famed for her beauty and her military conquests, who, as legend has it, was the daughter of a Syrian goddess.

12 **Lais**: a popular Corinthian courtesan. Is Corinna a goddess or a harlot? Catullus soon bemoaned the need his "radiant goddess" had for other lovers (*c.* 68.135–40). Ovid's narrator, on the other hand, seems to celebrate Corinna's aggressive sexuality by comparing her to a powerful queen and a popular courtesan.

uiris: dative of agent is common with perfect passive participles, as here; in poetry, it can be used with almost any passive verb.

13–16 *She feigned resistance as I removed her clothing.*

13 **deripui . . . nocebat / pugnabat . . . tegi** (14): What is the effect of bracketing these two lines with verbs?

multum: neuter singular, used as an adverb modifying *nocebat*; cf. *nihil* (4.68).

rara: The adjective describes the delicacy of Corinna's tunic, but is also a stylistic catchword of the Roman love poets signifying their exquisite and meticulous craftsmanship.

14 **pugnabat**: military imagery in an erotic context (*militia amoris*). Here, the terms *pugnare*, *vincere*, and especially *proditio* may suggest that Corinna is being likened to a city under siege (McKeown). Once again Ovid is equating love and war.

tegi: present passive infinitive, complementary with *pugnabat*.

15 **cumque**: *cum*-causal.

tamquam quae: Understand *puella* as the antecedent of *quae*.

16 **non aegre**: suggests both "without difficulty" on the narrator's part and "without hesitation" on Corinna's part (Barsby).

17–22 *How completely perfect her body was from top to toe!*

18 **menda**: McKeown has pointed out that Ovid is the only poet to use this word to mean "a physical blemish." For other authors, and later Ovid as well, the word refers to literary faults.

19 **quos . . . quales . . . / . . . quam** (20): Anaphora highlights a series of three exclamations, each longer than the preceding (an example of tricolon crescens; see "tricolon" in the glossary). Continuing anaphora *quam* (21) . . . / *quantum et quale . . . quam* (22) reverses the series. The narrator describes his mistress's body from top to bottom, with emphasis on the charms of her middle section.

uidi tetigique: the objectification of Corinna. Corinna's arrival and pseudo-resistance are virtually her only independent actions in the poem. The narrator looks, the narrator touches, and later he looks and embraces (*uidi . . . pressi*, 23–24). Even her breasts have no existence apart from his touch (20).

20 **quam**: the exclamation "how," modifying the adjective *apta*. See also *quam* in 21 and 22. Ovid's structure echoes Propertius 2.15 here: *quam . . . / quantaque* (3–4) and *quam . . . / . . . quantum* (9–10). Propertius's exclamations, however, represent a sharing of intimacy with his mistress: "How many words we spoke in the lamplight, / and how great a struggle ensued when the lights went out! / . . . / How entangled our arms became when we were embracing! How long / my kisses lingered on your lips!" Our narrator's exclamations are all about himself.

premi: present passive; epexegetic infinitive with *apta*. In poetry, an adjective may use an infinitive to complete or explain its meaning, imitating the Greek usage: "suitable (*apta*) for . . ."

23–26 *She was perfection, and I made her mine. Afterward, I wished for many such afternoons.*

23 **singula quid referam?**: *quid* = "why"; *referam* is deliberative subjunctive. Here, the narrator happily indulges in mock-*praeteritio* (the rhetorical "passing over" of certain information) to tease us, asking this question only after he has mentioned the important pieces of Corinna.

nil non laudabile: an excellent example of litotes; cf. 2.43.

24 **nudam**: What pronoun is understood by ellipsis?

corpus ad usque meum: = *usque ad meum corpus*. Hyperbaton puts emphasis on *corpus*.

25 **cetera quis nescit?**: The narrator is coy when it comes to describing their lovemaking, and moves directly to its aftermath. The use of parallel questions in initial position, here and in line 23 *(singula quid referam?)* is an effective means to bring the poem to a sudden end.

requieuimus ambo: In the final two lines, Ovid returns us directly to the poem's beginning. His description of their now mutual rest contrasts with the narrator's earlier solo nap (2), and the time of day in line 1 *(mediam dies . . . horam)* is recalled by his wish for many such midday diversions *(medii . . . dies*, 26). This is a good example of ring composition (see the glossary).

26 **proueniant**: *Prouenire* means "sprout" or "spring up" when used of plants (cf. 3.20), and thus provides the final line of the poem with a sexual double entendre.

mihi: The narrator craves these pleasurable diversions only for himself!

For Further Reading

Huntingford, N. P. C. 1981. "Ovid, *Amores*1.5." *Acta Classica* 24: 107–15.
Keith, A. M. 1994. "*Corpus Eroticum*: Elegiac Poetics and Elegiac *Puellae* in Ovid's *Amores*." *Classical World* 88: 27–40.

There are a number of readings that cover *Amores* 1.1–5, Ovid's introductory poems. See, in particular:

Buchan, M. 1995. "*Ovidius Imperamator*: Beginnings and Ends of the Love Poems and Empire in the *Amores*."*Arethusa* 28.1: 53–85.
Hinds, S. 1987. "Generalising about Ovid." *Ramus* 16: 4–31.
Hardie, P. 2002. *Ovid's Poetics of Illusion*: 30–45. Cambridge: Cambridge University Press.

Amores 1.6

Now that he has won the object of his affection (1.5) and looks forward to more such occasions, the narrator turns to a topic that besets lovers and love poets alike—rejection. He becomes the *exclusus amator*, the shut-out lover, left to lament his exclusion and beg for admittance to his *puella*. In 1.6 Ovid is giving us a *paraclausithyron*, a song sung in front of the locked door of his mistress (see the introduction). In the opening lines, he announces the situation and immediately establishes his innovation: the narrator will plead his case not to the door but to the doorkeeper, a lowly slave, and he uses this innovation to set up his first joke. The doorkeeper need open the door only a crack because the metaphor of "wasting away with love" has become literal, making the narrator gaunt enough to slip in through a mere slit (5–6). To gain this favor and the doorkeeper as an ally, the narrator uses flattery and charm, various appeals to pity and reciprocity, and other techniques of persuasion that in the world of elegy are doomed to failure. He even intimates that the doorkeeper is a god.

When these initial attempts to persuade fail, he begins a more emphatic series of arguments, and, to dramatize the narrator's efforts, Ovid introduces a refrain, a structural feature suggestive of a magical incantation. Magic charms work no better for the narrator than do verbal ploys, however. At every point the doorkeeper remains silent, and his silence drives the narrator to greater frustration and frenzy.

As the poem ends and night has passed, the narrator finds himself in exactly the same place he began—suffering on a threshold, alternately begging and cursing a doorkeeper who refuses to heed him. His persuasion is a magnificent failure and as such fits a pattern seen throughout the *Amores*. We have witnessed similar failures in

Amores 1.1 and 1.4. These failures, however, are always tinged with humor and wit, and in this poem much of the humor lies in the incongruity of the circumstances: a lover is forced to cajole his mistress's lowly slave, a lowly slave is supplicated as a god, and a doorkeeper is as rigid and nonresponsive as the door he guards.

Ianitor (indignum!) dura religate catena,
   difficilem moto cardine pande forem.
quod precor exiguum est: aditu fac ianua paruo
   obliquum capiat semiadaperta latus.
longus amor tales corpus tenuauit in usus   5
   aptaque subducto corpore membra dedit;
ille per excubias custodum leniter ire
   monstrat, inoffensos derigit ille pedes.
at quondam noctem simulacraque uana timebam;
   mirabar, tenebris quisquis iturus erat: 10
risit, ut audirem, tenera cum matre Cupido
   et leuiter 'fies tu quoque fortis' ait.
nec mora, uenit amor: non umbras nocte uolantes,
   non timeo strictas in mea fata manus:
te nimium lentum timeo, tibi blandior uni;   15
   tu, me quo possis perdere, fulmen habes.
aspice (uti uideas, immitia claustra relaxa)
   uda sit ut lacrimis ianua facta meis.
certe ego, cum posita stares ad uerbera ueste,
   ad dominam pro te uerba tremente tuli.   20
ergo, quae ualuit pro te quoque gratia quondam,
   heu facinus! pro me nunc ualet illa parum?
redde uicem meritis: grato licet esse, quod optas.
   tempora noctis eunt; excute poste seram.
excute: sic umquam longa releuere catena,   25
   nec tibi perpetuo serua bibatur aqua.
ferreus orantem nequiquam, ianitor, audis:
   roboribus duris ianua fulta riget.
urbibus obsessis clausae munimina portae
   prosunt: in media pace quid arma times?   30

quid facies hosti, qui sic excludis amantem?
   tempora noctis eunt; excute poste seram.
non ego militibus uenio comitatus et armis:
   solus eram, si non saeuus adesset Amor;
hunc ego, si cupiam, nusquam dimittere possum: 35
   ante uel a membris diuidar ipse meis.
ergo Amor et modicum circa mea tempora uinum
   mecum est et madidis lapsa corona comis.
arma quis haec timeat? quis non eat obuius illis?
   tempora noctis eunt; excute poste seram. 40
lentus es, an somnus, qui te male perdat, amantis
   uerba dat in uentos aure repulsa tua?
at, memini, primo, cum te celare uolebam,
   peruigil in mediae sidera noctis eras.
forsitan et tecum tua nunc requiescit amica: 45
   heu, melior quanto sors tua sorte mea!
dummodo sic, in me durae transite catenae.
   tempora noctis eunt; excute poste seram.
fallimur, an uerso sonuerunt cardine postes
   raucaque concussae signa dedere fores? 50
fallimur: impulsa est animoso ianua uento.
   ei mihi, quam longe spem tulit aura meam!
si satis es raptae, Borea, memor Orithyiae,
   huc ades et surdas flamine tunde fores.
urbe silent tota, uitreoque madentia rore 55
   tempora noctis eunt; excute poste seram,
aut ego iam ferroque ignique paratior ipse,
   quem face sustineo, tecta superba petam.
nox et Amor uinumque nihil moderabile suadent:
   illa pudore uacat, Liber Amorque metu. 60
omnia consumpsi, nec te precibusque minisque
   mouimus, o foribus durior ipse tuis.
non te formosae decuit seruare puellae
   limina: sollicito carcere dignus eras.
iamque pruinosos molitur Lucifer axes, 65
   inque suum miseros excitat ales opus.

68 *Amores* 1.6

at tu, non laetis detracta corona capillis,
dura super tota limina nocte iace;
tu dominae, cum te proiectam mane uidebit,
temporis absumpti tam male testis eris. 70
qualiscumque uale sentique abeuntis honorem,
lente nec admisso turpis amante, uale.
uos quoque, crudeles rigido cum limine postes
duraque conseruae ligna, ualete, fores.

Notes

1–6 *The narrator addresses the doorkeeper of his mistress's house: "I ask a small favor, that you open the door just a little bit.*

1 **Ianitor (indignum!) dura religate catena**: The narrator is indulging in a rhetorical practice known as *captatio beneuolentiae*, a technique of flattery used by public speakers to win the goodwill of their audiences. He begins his appeal in high style, with a five-word hexameter in interlocked word order. This elegantly presented address contrasts sharply with its lowly recipient.
indignum: neuter singular accusative; cf. 1.25.
religate: perfect passive participle < *religo* (1); vocative case, modifying *ianitor*. It was customary for the doorkeeper to be chained in position. The task of guarding the door at night, though important, was a most degrading assignment, given to a household slave of very low status.

2 **difficilem . . . / exiguum, . . . paruo** (3): The narrator uses language to contrast the toughness of the door with the minuscule favor he is about to ask (3).
pande forem: The lover's address to the locked door of his beloved is found in some detail as early as Aristophanes' *Ecclesiazusae* (952ff.). It is a common theme in Hellenistic epigram and later finds its way into Roman comedy (e.g., Plautus's *Curculio*, 147ff.). Both Tibullus and Propertius take up the *paraclausithyron*: Tibullus curses and cajoles the door in Tibullus 1.2, whereas in Propertius 1.16 the door itself complains about the lovers who abuse it and kiss up to it.
forem / . . . ianua (3): Words for doors and entranceways often have a sexual double entendre in elegiac poetry, and physical access to the house and the mistress are linked. Other examples are *porta*, *limen*, and *ostium*. (Adams 1982: 89)

Amores 1.6   69

3   **fac ianua . . . capiat** (4): "see to it that the door admits (my) . . . "; for the omission of *ut* with *fac* and a subjunctive, see *fac . . . eas* (4.56).
4   **semiadaperta**: a five-syllable word for meter's sake: read the -i- as a consonant. The length of the word contrasts humorously with the small opening requested.
5   **tales . . . in usus**: cf. 1.22.
    amor . . . tenuauit: For *tenuitas* as a poetic ideal, see 1.18 and 2.7.

7–16 *It is Love who guides me, Love who makes me fearless—well, almost fearless.*

7   **ille . . . / . . . monstrat . . . derigit ille** (8): Repetition, chiasmus, and asyndeton reinforce the narrator's claim. Ironically, the narrator's argument that *amor* defeats doorkeepers is itself defeated through an implicit contrast with the reality of the current situation.
    ire / monstrat (8): the construction of *monstrare* with an infinitive ("show how to . . . ") is largely confined to poetry.
9   **simulacraque uana**: i.e., ghosts. The description of the narrator's former nighttime fears (see also 13–14) recalls descriptions of visits to the Underworld, and this is especially humorous when we realize that *this* "underworld" consists of nocturnal visits to his beloved.
10 **mirabar**: Understand *eum*.
    tenebris: "through the dark."
11 **risit . . . Cupido**: We are reminded of Cupid's mischievousness in *Amores* 1.3, *risisse Cupido*, and the narrator's sudden and coerced transformation into a love poet.
12 **leuiter . . . fortis**: *Leuiter* recalls 1.19, *numeris leuioribus* and the unmasculine nature of love and love poetry. And *fortis* suggests that Cupid has transformed the narrator into a soldier, but a soldier in Cupid's army (*militia amoris*), fighting in the world of love.
13 **nec mora**: ellipsis of *erat*. Note the wordplay between *mora* and *amor*.
    non (timeo) umbras . . . / non timeo . . . manus / te . . . timeo (15): Repetition and asyndeton emphasize the narrator's newfound bravery; chiasmus highlights the irony of the contrast.
15 **te . . . tibi . . . / tu** (16): For the significance of the anaphora of the pronoun *tu*, see 2.33 and 3.16. And, as Barsby points out, the narrator's expressed fears of the doorkeeper end with an arresting pun (*fulmen habes*, 16) by which the slave with a deadbolt is cast as a Jupiter with his thunderbolt.

17–26 *Let me suggest that, since I once did a favor for you, doorkeeper, you should do a favor for me.*

Amores 1.6

17–64 The narrator continues to apply varied techniques of persuasion in a *suasoria* (cf. *Amores* 3.5ff.) intended to persuade the doorkeeper to let him in.

17 **uti**: = *ut*, introducing a purpose clause.
relaxa: imperative singular. The narrator's one attempt at tears (*lacrimis . . . meis*, 18) becomes an opportunity for humor as he tries to trick the doorkeeper into opening the door.

18 **ut**: "how," in an indirect question introduced by *aspice* (17).
sit . . . facta: hyperbaton.

20 **pro**: "on behalf of"; so also *pro* in 21 and 22. The appropriateness of reciprocal favors is underscored through the repeated parallel phrases *pro te . . . / . . . pro te . . . (21) / . . . pro me . . .* (22).

21 **gratia**: For antecedents attracted into their own relative clauses, see *puella* (3.1).

23 **meritis**: dative of reference, "for (my) services."
grato: Understand *tibi*; read *licet (tibi) grato esse, quod (libertatem) optas*, which expresses the doorkeeper's willingness to do a favor for the narrator, who in turn will work for the doorkeeper's freedom.
quod: Relative pronoun or conjunction?

24 **tempora noctis eunt; excute poste seram**: This is the first occurrence of what turns out to be a refrain repeated every eight lines (see also 32, 40, 48, and 56). Such a repetition may call to mind a magical incantation, used here by the narrator to somehow "charm" the *ianitor* into opening the door. In *Idyll* 2 of Theocritus (the possible originator of mime), the witch Simaetha attempts to draw her lover back with a magic brew and an incantation repeated as a refrain. Her plight and her reactions are similar to those of the narrator of this poem insofar as she is experiencing rejection and attempting to counter that rejection (and will fail). The refrain may be a deliberate allusion to Simaetha and her powerless magic, and its introduction halfway through the poem may induce the audience to recognize that the narrator, despite all his many and varied techniques, also will fail.

25 **sic umquam longa releuere catena**: a second attempt at *captatio beneuolentiae*; note the echo to line 1.
umquam: here, "at some time (in the future)."
longa . . . catena: not only "of great length," but also "endured for a long time"; ablative of separation.
releuere: alternate second-person singular (*-re* instead of *-ris*) passive, optative.

26 **tibi**: For the dative of agent with passive voice verbs, see *uiris* (5.12).

27–40 *I am a lover, not a fighter. There is no need to react to me as an enemy army. I am armed only with Love . . . and a little wine.*

27 **ferreus orantem**: Understand *tu* and *me*, respectively.
29 **urbibus obsessis . . . / . . . arma . . .** (30) **/ . . . hosti . . .** (31): The narrator disassociates himself from real warfare and claims to be a man of peace (*pace*, 30) and love (*amantem*, 31); cf. note 12 above.
31 **qui**: relative pronoun whose antecedent is the subject "you" in *facies*, as the verb *excludis* confirms.
33 **militibus . . . et armis**: a possible hendiadys, "armed soldiers." Again the narrator denies his association with real warfare, but the description of his escort *Amor* as *saeuus* (34) hints at the potential for violence. We are reminded of the narrator's epithet for Cupid in *Amores* 1.1, *saeue puer* (5), which the god later fulfilled by attacking him with bow and arrow.
34 **eram, si . . . adesset**: When expressing something that was "intended" or "likely," the indicative (here, *eram*) replaces the subjunctive in the apodosis of a contrary-to-fact condition.
35 **hunc ego**: The narrator's attitude toward *Amor* has changed from resistance (*Amores* 1.1) and capitulation (*Amores* 1.2) to wholehearted welcoming of Love as part of himself. The juxtaposition of pronouns reinforces the union of narrator and god, whereas the separation of *meis* from *membris* (36) aptly represents the separation the narrator rejects.
si cupiam: with concessive force; *si* = *etsi*.
36 **diuidar**: potential subjunctive.
38 **comis**: ablative of place where or cause, rather than separation.
39 **arma**: i.e., *Amor, uinum,* and *corona*, the equipment of love, not the military *arma* of 30 and 33; the narrator again emphasizes his peaceful intentions.
timeat . . . eat: Cf. *diuidar* above (36).

41–48 *Since I am getting no response from you, doorkeeper, I fear that you may be sleeping—sleeping, that is, with a girl of your own.*

41 **qui . . . perdat**: optative subjunctive, "may it (= *somnus*) . . ."
42 **aure . . . tua**: ablative of separation.
44 **in**: here, "up until (the appearance of)."
46 **quanto**: ablative of degree of difference, with *melior*; cf. 2.17.
47 **dummodo sic**: The subjunctive verb has been omitted; read *dummodo sic (res se habeat)*, "provided that this is the case," i.e., that the doorkeeper has a girl (*amica*) sleeping with him.
durae . . . catenae: vocative plural. The chains that the narrator bemoaned (*dura . . . catena*, 1) and that he wished the *ianitor* to be free of (*longa . . . catena*, 25) are the very chains he now asks to

bear. The metaphorical *seruitium amoris* becomes literal: the narrator offers to become a real slave in exchange for what the real slave may have, an *amica* (a ludicrous notion since the *ianitor* is a slave and chained up).

49–56 **Wishful thinking leads me to misinterpret the creaking of the door.**

50 **raucaque concussae**: The interlocked word order (or synchesis), with the harsh-sounding participles first and the nouns second, allows us to hear the rattling of the doors. The alliteration of *c* provides sound effects.
dedere: a syncopated third-person plural, perfect active, common in colloquial speech and poetry. For other verb syncopation, see 3.4 and 3.6.
52 **quam**: "how," modifying the adverb *longe*.
53 **Borea ... Orithyiae**: *Borea* is a Greek vocative singular. *Orithyiae* has four long syllables (*yi* = the diphthong *ui*). Boreas, the blustery North Wind, having failed in his wooing, forcibly carried off Orithyia, princess of Athens, to be his lover and wife.
54 **ades**: < *adeo, adire*; imperative singular, as *tunde* confirms.
55 **silent**: impersonal use of the verb: "things are silent/there is silence." Barsby interprets the silence as emphasizing the solitude of the narrator; McKeown, as emphasizing the failure of the narrator's plea to Boreas.

57–64 **I will attack—that's the state of mind I'm in! I am growing desperate.**

57 **ferroque ignique**: the weapons of an army on the rampage. The narrator's high-flown threat of armed violence contradicts his earlier claim to be unarmed and a man of peace (30ff.). The metaphorical *militia amoris* becomes literal; cf. 47 above.
58 **quem**: relative pronoun whose antecedent is *igni* (57).
face: < *fax, facis*.
60 **illa**: *Nox* is understood by ellipsis.
Liber: a name for Bacchus, god of wine, emphasizing his "freeing" effect.
62 **ipse**: Understand *tu*, vocative case.

65–74 **Day is dawning. I give up. I am leaving a bitter memento for you, my mistress, and I bid farewell to both of you, doorkeeper and door.**

65 **Lucifer**: "bearer of light" = the Morning Star, i.e., dawn.
66 **suum**: "their," reflecting *miseros*, not the subject *ales*.
ales: here, "cock/rooster."

67 **corona**: vocative singular.
capillis: dative of disadvantage, with *detracta*.
69 **dominae**: dative of reference.
71 **qualiscumque**: Understand *ianitor*, vocative case; so also *lente* and *turpis* in 72.
honorem: here, "a compliment" from the narrator as he departs, sincere or ironic—you decide. (The doorkeeper has performed his task well. He has not disgraced himself by letting the narrator in.)
74 **duraque . . . ligna**: in apposition to *fores*. Throughout the poem, the narrator carefully draws attention to the doorkeeper's intransigence (*lentum*, 15; *ferreus*, 27; *lentus*, 41; *foribus durior . . . tuis*, 62; and *lente*, 72), a characteristic that keeps him closely connected with the door he guards (*roboribus duris ianua . . . riget*, 27–28; *dura . . . limina*, 67–68; *crudeles rigido cum limine postes*, 73) and, perhaps by implication, with the beloved, who may in fact be a *dura* (hard-hearted) *puella*.
conseruae: here, used as an adjective, modifying *fores*.

For Further Reading

Copley, F. O. 1956. *Exclusus Amator: A Study in Latin Love Elegy*, 125ff. Madison, Wis: American Philological Association.
Watson, L. C. 1982. "*Amores* 1.6: A Parody of a Hymn?" *Mnemosyne* 35: 92–102.
Yardley, J. C. 1978. "The Elegiac Paraclausithyron." *Eranos* 76: 19–34.

Amores 1.7

The narrator has struck his *puella*. In an opening worthy of the most melodramatic scenes of tragedy—and it is tragedy that Ovid means to invoke—the narrator demands physical restraint. The shackles he requests have nothing to do with the *seruitium amoris* imposed upon him by his *puella* (1.3) or the *ianitor*'s physical enslavement (1.6). They are to prevent a repeat of his violence. The narrator expresses horror at his deed but confronts it with evasion, first by separating himself from it and, second, by exaggeration. He claims his hands, not he, perpetrated the crime, and madness (*furor*) was the cause. He equates his crazed assault with attacks on gods and parents, the most shocking transgressions a Roman could commit. He then conjures up two great heroes of tragedy, Ajax and Orestes, whose deluded minds prompted them to commit acts of slaughter and sacrilege. Their crimes, however, do not seem on par with the narrator's, and when he finally specifies the nature of his violence—he attacked his *puella*'s hairdo—we are surprised by the banality of the offense. We suspect that he is trivializing his crime, and this suspicion is confirmed when he comments that her disheveled hair actually increases her attractiveness. As the poem progresses, we see that the narrator attempts to focus on his *puella* and her feelings and fails. He always returns attention to himself and keeps an emotional distance from her suffering. Finally, her beauty and vulnerability seem to move him to real emotion and remorse, and he attempts reconciliation. In the closing couplet of the poem, however, the narrator absolves himself of all wrongdoing. He blithely orders his mistress to clear away any traces of his crime. From beginning to end, even as he engages in the most dramatic remorse and self-abuse, the narrator avoids any real responsibility for his actions.

Adde manus in uincla meas (meruere catenas),
   dum furor omnis abit, si quis amicus ades:
nam furor in dominam temeraria bracchia mouit;
   flet mea uesana laesa puella manu.
tunc ego uel caros potui uiolare parentes   5
   saeua uel in sanctos uerbera ferre deos.
quid? non et clipei dominus septemplicis Aiax
   strauit deprensos lata per arua greges,
et uindex in matre patris, malus ultor, Orestes
   ausus in arcanas poscere tela deas?   10
ergo ego digestos potui laniare capillos?
   nec dominam motae dedecuere comae:
sic formosa fuit; talem Schoeneida dicam
   Maenalias arcu sollicitasse feras;
talis periuri promissaque uelaque Thesei   15
   fleuit praecipites Cressa tulisse Notos;
sic, nisi uittatis quod erat, Cassandra, capillis,
   procubuit templo, casta Minerua, tuo.
quis mihi non 'demens', quis non mihi 'barbare' dixit?
   ipsa nihil: pauido est lingua retenta metu.   20
sed taciti fecere tamen conuicia uultus;
   egit me lacrimis ore silente reum.
ante meos umeris uellem cecidisse lacertos;
   utiliter potui parte carere mei:
in mea uesanas habui dispendia uires   25
   et ualui poenam fortis in ipse meam.
quid mihi uobiscum, caedis scelerumque ministrae?
   debita sacrilegae uincla subite manus.
an, si pulsassem minimum de plebe Quiritem,
   plecterer, in dominam ius mihi maius erit?   30
pessima Tydides scelerum monimenta reliquit:
   ille deam primus perculit; alter ego.
et minus ille nocens: mihi quam profitebar amare
   laesa est; Tydides saeuus in hoste fuit.
i nunc, magnificos uictor molire triumphos,   35
   cinge comam lauro uotaque redde Ioui,

76 Amores 1.7

quaeque tuos currus comitantum turba sequetur,
   clamet 'io, forti uicta puella uiro est!'
ante eat effuso tristis captiua capillo,
   si sinerent laesae, candida tota, genae. 40
aptius impressis fuerat liuere labellis
   et collum blandi dentis habere notam.
denique si tumidi ritu torrentis agebar
   caecaque me praedam fecerat ira suam,
nonne satis fuerat timidae inclamasse puellae 45
   nec nimium rigidas intonuisse minas
aut tunicam a summa diducere turpiter ora
   ad mediam (mediae zona tulisset opem)?
at nunc sustinui raptis a fronte capillis
   ferreus ingenuas ungue notare genas. 50
astitit illa amens albo et sine sanguine uultu,
   caeduntur Pariis qualia saxa iugis;
exanimis artus et membra trementia uidi,
   ut cum populeas uentilat aura comas,
ut leni Zephyro gracilis uibratur harundo 55
   summaue cum tepido stringitur unda Noto;
suspensaeque diu lacrimae fluxere per ora,
   qualiter abiecta de niue manat aqua.
tunc ego me primum coepi sentire nocentem;
   sanguis erat lacrimae, quas dabat illa, meus. 60
ter tamen ante pedes uolui procumbere supplex;
   ter formidatas reppulit illa manus.
at tu ne dubita (minuet uindicta dolorem)
   protinus in uultus unguibus ire meos;
nec nostris oculis nec nostris parce capillis: 65
   quamlibet infirmas adiuuat ira manus.
neue mei sceleris tam tristia signa supersint,
   pone recompositas in statione comas.

Amores 1.7   77

Notes

1–6 ***I need to be restrained. In a fit of anger, I struck my mistress, a crime equal to abusing parents or gods.***

1 **adde . . . ades** (2): The narrator opens dramatically with an imperative, calling upon some friend—any friend—to restrain him. Note the bracketing and wordplay.
uincla . . . catenas: *Vinc(u)la* is a general term for restraints, and *catenae* refers more specifically to heavy chains (McKeown).

3 **in dominam . . . bracchia mouit**: Propertius emphatically refuses to engage in rough physical contact with his mistress (2.5.21–26); Tibullus condemns the man who strikes his mistress, but he is not adverse to tearing off her clothes, messing up her hair, and making her cry, so long as it does not get rough (1.10.51–66). Though Ovid plays with the ideas and language of the other love poets, his narrator is the only one to actually raise a violent hand to his mistress. *Dominam* suggests the *seruitium amoris* relationship, but here the slave has dared to strike his master.

7–11 ***Even great heroes have acted with crazed violence. Did this justify my actions?***

7 **Aiax . . . Orestes** (9): two important figures of tragedy whom, according to the narrator, temporary madness drove to shocking transgressions. Ajax, son of Telamon, was a great hero in Homer's *Iliad*, second only to Achilles. His standard epithet is "bulwark (ἕρκος) of the Achaeans" because of his enormous size, strength, and stamina, and he carried a huge shield of sevenfold ox hide. After the Trojan War, he was enraged that the Greek commanders unfairly (in his view) deprived him of his just due, the weapons of the deceased Achilles. His anger drove him to delusion, and he trapped and slaughtered a flock of sheep, believing them to be the Greek commanders from Troy. Sophocles dramatizes these events in his play *Ajax*, as does Ovid later in the *Metamorphoses*. Orestes, son of the Greek commander Agamemnon and his wife, Clytemnestra, killed his mother in vengeance because she had murdered his father. In the version presented by Aeschylus in his *Choephoroi* (*Libation Bearers*), after her murder Orestes was pursued and tormented by her avenging Furies, goddesses of bloodguilt.

78 *Amores* 1.7

9   **patris**: objective genitive, with *uindex*.
10 **arcanas deas**: periphrasis for the Furies.
11 **ergo . . . ?**: introducing a rhetorical question, which is often used ironically and anticipates a negative reply.

12–18 *Yet my mistress, even in her disarray, looked as beautiful as a mythological heroine.*

13 **Schoeneida**: Greek accusative singular. Atalanta, identified by the patronymic "daughter of Schoeneus," was a young and beautiful huntress in Boeotia. The active, aggressive Atalanta, with her naturally windblown hair, seems the very opposite of the battered *puella*, but the comparison suggests that the narrator is titillated by the way his roughed-up mistress looks.
14 **Maenalias**: "of Maenalus," a mountain in Arcadia. One version of the Atalanta legend makes the huntress a Boeotian, another an Arcadian. Ovid conflates the two.
15 **Thesei**: The synizesis ("collapsing") of *-ei* to one syllable results in a two-syllable word, *The-sei* (see the glossary). Theseus was an Athenian hero and faithless lover who abandoned Ariadne, princess of Crete, on a deserted island after she had helped him overcome the Minotaur. For the story, see Catullus, *c.* 64.58ff.
16 **Cressa**: "the maiden from Crete," i.e., Ariadne, maiden daughter of King Minos. Ariadne, her hair disheveled in grief, is portrayed at the point of betrayal and abandonment by Theseus, and the reference to her may reflect the *puella*'s passivity and vulnerability.
17 **nisi . . . quod**: "except for the fact that . . ."
    uittatis . . . capillis: ablative of description.
    Cassandra: maiden daughter of King Priam of Troy, who was dragged by the Greeks from the statue of Minerva (Athena), where she had taken refuge after the destruction of Troy, and raped. She was also a prophet of Apollo who was fated never to be believed. Ovid seems to follow Vergil's account of the tale, *Aeneid* 2.403ff., in which Cassandra is shown moments before she is sexually violated. Cassandra's hair, bound with a sacred headband, signals her sacred virginity and, as the narrator himself notes, puts her at odds with the previous two maidens. The *exempla*, however, move progressively from positive to negative, and the focus on the beauty and hair slowly devolves into a focus on beauty and violation.
18 **casta Minerua**: Direct address of an imaginary audience, known as apostrophe (see the glossary), raises the emotional tone.

19–22 *She condemned me not aloud, as others did, but with her eyes.*

20 **ipsa nihil**: Understand *dixit*. Her silence stands in stark contrast to the narrator's dramatic outcries of blame and guilt.

22 **egit . . . reum** < *reum agere*, "to put on trial/accuse."

23–34 *Oh hands, I curse you for your role in this sinful deed. I deserve severe punishment, for my crime was that of a slave who attacked a master, of a mortal who attacked a goddess.*

23 **ante**: here, an adverb.
uellem cecidisse lacertos: = *utinam lacerti cecidissent*. *Vellem* with an infinitive or subjunctive is often equivalent to an optative subjunctive; *uellem* itself, in this case, is a potential subjunctive.
lacertos . . . manus (28): The narrator reproaches himself in exaggerated ways that recall his opening lines (1–4): he blames his arms and hands as if they have an identity separate from his own.

24 **mei**: partitive genitive, used with *parte*. *Mei* is the pronoun here, not the possessive adjective.

25 **in mea . . . dispendia**: "for my own loss," i.e., "at a cost to myself."
habui: here, "I employed."

26 **ualui** < *ualeo, ualere*, with *in* + accusative, "to have power to achieve (x)."

27 **quid mihi uobiscum**: "What have I to do with you?" (literally, "What [is there] for me with you?")

28 **sacrilegae . . . manus**: vocative plural.

29 **an, si pulsassem . . . / plecterer, . . . mihi . . . erit?** (30): "Is it true that, if I had struck . . . , I would be beaten, but when it comes to . . . I shall have . . .?" (Barsby). It was a hallmark of Roman society that male citizens as a class were protected from physical assault, but women and slaves and foreigners were not. By attacking his *puella*, even though the attack is represented as relatively trivial, the narrator is upholding a Roman cultural standard: males dominate.
Quiritem: an archaic legal term for "a Roman citizen with full civil rights." The term was derived from the name of a Sabine town that had become part of the Roman state at a very early date.
dominam: The narrator invokes *seruitium amoris* once again to call attention to his outrageous violation of the slave-master relationship; cf. *dominam* above (3). See *deam* below (32) for a similar transgression, mortal against deity.

31 **Tydides**: i.e., Diomedes as identified by the patronymic "son of Tydeus." He was the Greek hero who wounded Venus (Aphrodite) as she tried to protect her son Aeneas from his attack during the Trojan War (*Iliad*

80 *Amores* 1.7

5.330ff.). The narrator compares himself now, perhaps more appropriately, to a hero who knowingly chose to attack a goddess.
32 **ille ... primus ... alter ego**: Chiasmus highlights the antithesis.
33 **mihi**: Cf. 5.12.

35–42 *Celebrate your victory with a triumphal parade, oh mighty conqueror of one wretched girl. She should not bear wounds of war, but marks of lovemaking.*

35 **i nunc ... victor**: The narrator is addressing himself, using irony, as if he were a Roman general celebrating a major military victory. For a description of a Roman triumph, see the notes and introduction at *Amores* 1.2. The repetition of *c*, *t,* and *qu* underline the narrator's heavy sarcasm.
molire: deponent imperative singular.
37 **quae ... turba**: Cf. *puella* (3.1).
40 **candida tota**: an apodosis, in which "she would be ... " is implied.
41 **aptius ... fuerat (collum) livere**: a past contrary-to-fact condition. In the apodosis, the indicative (here, *fuerat*) is used in place of the subjunctive to denote necessity, propriety, and the like; the protasis (the *si*-clause) is implied in the subject infinitive (*collum livere*): "It would have been more fitting if her neck had been black and blue." *Collum* is the accusative subject of both *liuere* and *habere* (42).
labellis: the diminutive of *labrum*, to heighten the sense of intimacy.

43–50 *Even in my rage, I should have had more control over my actions: there are alternatives to physical violence.*

43 **denique**: "at least."
45 **satis fuerat ... inclamasse**: See *aptius ... fuerat* above (41); "it would have been enough if I had ... "
47 **turpiter**: implies shame for the *puella*, but also disgraceful behavior on the part of the narrator.
48 **mediae**: dative of end of motion.
49 **at nunc**: "but as it is," introducing a fact contrary to previous possibilities.
sustinui ... notare (50) < *sustinere* + infinitive, "to be able/to allow oneself to ... " This construction occurs first in Ovid and Livy.

51–60 *She stood there, pale, lifeless, trembling, and when she finally broke into tears, I began to feel her pain.*

51–58 The narrator provides a more extensive description of the girl's reaction to his abuse. He keeps his emotional distance from her suffering, however, by comparing her outward appearance—paleness, trembling, and tears—to the inanimate world of nature. Her beauty and vulnerability eventually push him to empathy.

51 The assonance of *a* accentuates her shock and anguish.
52 **Pariis ... iugis**: The island of Paros (one of the Cyclades near Greece) was known for the translucent luster of its white marble. The suggestion of white marble brings to mind statues, which can be beautiful objects of art but are also inanimate and voiceless (Greene 1998: 89).
56 **summaue**: = *summa* + the enclitic *-ue*.
58 **abiecta de niue manat aqua**: The simile of melting snow moves us naturally toward the narrator's change of heart.
59 **ego me . . . / . . . illa meus** (60): The focus on the narrator at the beginning of the couplet and the shift to the conjunction of *puella* and narrator at the end succinctly represent his transition from self-indulgence to fellow feeling. He now seems overwhelmed by real remorse.
60 **erat**: singular, in agreement with the predicate nominative *sanguis;* the subject is *lacrimae*.

61–66 *I begged her forgiveness but was rebuffed. "Go at me then," I bid her; "retaliation will make you feel better."*

61 **ter . . . / ter** (62): The narrator's attempt at reconciliation recalls an emotional reunion scene in the great epic poems of Homer (Odysseus with this mother, Antikleia, *Odyssey* 11.206ff.) and Vergil (Aeneas with his wife Creusa, *Aeneid* 2.792ff.; Aeneas with his father, Anchises, in the Underworld, *Aeneid* 6.700ff.), where the grieving hero tries in vain to embrace the insubstantiality of his loved one.
63 **at tu**: The narrator addresses his mistress for the first time.
ne dubita: For the legal connotation of *ne* with the imperative, see *nec pone* (4.36).
66 **quamlibet**: adverb, modifying *infirmas*.

67–68 *And, so that we can forget about this unfortunate incident, fix your hair.*

67 The alliteration of the harsh *t* and *s* sounds underscores the violence of the assault and sets the reader up for the abrupt and unexpected ending.
68 **recompositas in statione**: On a secondary level, Ovid may be having some fun with military imagery here. *Recompositas* < *recompono, recomponere,* a combination created by Ovid, can recall *compono* in its military sense, "to draw up/arrange (troops)," thus taking on a meaning such as "having regrouped." *In statione* also has a military connotation, "on alert/at one's post."

For Further Reading

Greene, E. 1999. "Travesties of Love: Violence and Voyeurism in Ovid, *Amores* 1.7." *Classical World* 92: 409–18.

Morrison, James V. 1992. "Literary Reference and Generic Transgression in Ovid, *Amores* 1.7: Lover, Poet, Furor." *Latomus* 51: 571–89.

Khan, H. Akbar. 1966. "*Ovidius Furens*: A Revaluation of *Amores* 1,7." *Latomus* 25: 880–94.

Amores 1.8

An aged hag instructs a pretty young girl to accept a rich man as her lover while the penniless narrator eavesdrops on the conversation. The roots of this scenario are in mime and comedy as well as elegy, and Ovid's hag combines the features of a *lena* (a madam or brothel owner) with an old nurse giving advice and a witch whose magical powers include the ability to transform natural phenomena, change her shape, and raise the dead. She is operating here as a *praeceptor amoris* ("a teacher of love"), instructing a younger woman in arts of love that, in fact, amount to prostitution. Her topics include the desirability of love and lovers, the girl's beauty and her undeserved lack of material possessions, the attractiveness of her potential lover, and the uselessness of true modesty and chastity.

    These arguments could be considered trite, but Ovid instills in them an amusing materialism that becomes blatant as the *lena* turns to instructing the girl in how to take a lover *and* how to take a lover for everything he's got. Her advice is practical, witty, and offensive to anyone who thinks love should not involve monetary profit. It is especially telling that, in her instructions, the *lena* mirrors the traditional complaints made by poet-lovers concerning their own mistresses. A poet-lover is never happy with a *puella* who begs for gifts, with the presence of a rival or husband, or with any circumstance that hinders his access to his girl. The *lena*'s view here, therefore, directly opposes the interests of the poet-lover, and she pointedly denigrates the poetry he offers his *puella* in place of money and gifts. The poem ends as it begins, in the context of comedy and mime: the narrator, fearing impending discovery, abruptly departs with a curse, and the outcome of the *lena*'s attempted persuasion remains a mystery.

Est quaedam (quicumque uolet cognoscere lenam,
    audita), est quaequam nomina Dipsas anus.
ex re nomen habet: nigri non illa parentem
    Memnonis in roseis sobria uidit equis.
illa magas artes Aeaeque carmina nouit   5
    inque caput liquidas arte recuruat aquas;
scit bene quid gramen, quid torto concita rhombo
    licia, quid ualeat uirus amantis equae.
cum uoluit, toto glomerantur nubila caelo;
    cum uoluit, puro fulget in orbe dies.   10
sanguine, si qua fides, stillantia sidera uidi;
    purpureus Lunae sanguine uultus erat.
hanc ego nocturnas uersam uolitare per umbras
    suspicor et pluma corpus anile tegi.
suspicor, et fama est; oculis quoque pupula duplex   15
    fulminat et gemino lumen ab orbe uenit.
euocat antiquis proauos atauosque sepulcris
    et solidam longo carmine findit humum.
haec sibi proposuit thalamos temerare pudicos;
    nec tamen eloquio lingua nocente caret.   20
fors me sermoni testem dedit; illa monebat
    talia (me duplices occuluere fores):
'scis here te, mea lux, iuueni placuisse beato?
    haesit et in uultu constitit usque tuo.
et cur non placeas? nulli tua forma secunda est;   25
    me miseram! dignus corpore cultus abest.
tam felix esses quam formosissima uellem:
    non ego te facta diuite pauper ero.
stella tibi oppositi nocuit contraria Martis;
    Mars abiit; signo nunc Venus apta suo.   30
prosit ut adueniens, en aspice: diues amator
    te cupiit: curae, quid tibi desit, habet.
est etiam facies, qua se tibi comparet, illi:
    si te non emptam uellet, emendus erat.
erubuit! decet alba quidem pudor ora, sed iste,   35
    si simules, prodest; uerus obesse solet.

cum bene deiectis gremium spectabis ocellis,
   quantum quisque ferat, respiciendus erit.
forsitan immundae Tatio regnante Sabinae
   noluerint habiles pluribus esse uiris;   40
nunc Mars externis animos exercet in armis,
   at Venus Aeneae regnat in urbe sui.
ludunt formosae: casta est quam nemo rogauit;
   aut, si rusticitas non uetat, ipsa rogat.
has quoque, quae frontis rugas in uertice portant,   45
   excute, de rugis crimina multa cadent.
Penelope iuuenum uires temptabat in arcu;
   qui latus argueret corneus arcus erat.
labitur occulte fallitque uolatilis aetas,
   ut celer admissis labitur amnis aquis.   50
aera nitent usu, uestis bona quaerit haberi,
   canescunt turpi tecta relicta situ:
forma, nisi admittas, nullo exercente senescit;
   nec satis effectus unus et alter habent.
certior e multis nec tam inuidiosa rapina est;   55
   plena uenit canis de grege praeda lupis.
ecce, quid iste tuus praeter noua carmina uates
   donat? amatoris milia multa leges.
ipse deus uatum palla spectabilis aurea
   tractat inauratae consona fila lyrae.   60
qui dabit, ille tibi magno sit maior Homero;
   crede mihi, res est ingeniosa dare.
nec tu, si quis erit capitis mercede redemptus,
   despice: gypsati crimen inane pedis.
nec te decipiant ueteres circum atria cerae: 65
   tolle tuos tecum, pauper amator, auos.
qui, quia pulcher erit, poscet sine munere noctem,
   quod det amatorem flagitet ante suum.
parcius exigito pretium, dum retia tendis,
   ne fugiant; captos legibus ure tuis.   70
nec nocuit simulatus amor: sine credat amari
   et caue, ne gratis hic tibi constet amor.

86 Amores 1.8

saepe nega noctes: capitis modo finge dolorem;
  et modo, quae causas praebeat, Isis erit.
mox recipe, ut nullum patiendi colligat usum   75
  neue relentescat saepe repulsus amor.
surda sit oranti tua ianua, laxa ferenti;
  audiat exclusi uerba receptus amans;
et quasi laesa prior nonnumquam irascere laeso:
  uanescit culpa culpa repensa tua.   80
sed numquam dederis spatiosum tempus in iram:
  saepe simultates ira morata facit.
quin etiam discant oculi lacrimare coacti,
  et faciant udas illa uel illa genas;
nec, si quem falles, tu periurare timeto: 85
  commodat in lusus numina surda Venus.
seruus et ad partes sollers ancilla parentur,
  qui doceant apte quid tibi possit emi,
et sibi pauca rogent: multos si pauca rogabunt,
  postmodo de stipula grandis aceruus erit.   90
et soror et mater, nutrix quoque carpat amantem:
  fit cito per multas praeda petita manus.
cum te deficient poscendi munera causae,
  natalem libo testificare tuum.
ne securus amet nullo riuale caueto: 95
  non bene, si tollas proelia, durat amor.
ille uiri uideat toto uestigia lecto
  factaque lasciuis liuida colla notis;
munera praecipue uideat quae miserit alter:
  si dederit nemo, Sacra roganda Via est.   100
cum multa abstuleris, ut non tamen omnia donet,
  quod numquam reddas, commodet ipsa roga.
lingua iuuet mentemque tegat: blandire noceque;
  impia sub dulci melle uenena latent.
haec si praestiteris usu mihi cognita longo   105
  nec tulerint uoces uentus et aura meas,
saepe mihi dices uiuae bene, saepe rogabis
  ut mea defunctae molliter ossa cubent—'

uox erat in cursu, cum me mea prodidit umbra;
  at nostrae uix se continuere manus 110
quin albam raramque comam lacrimosaque uino
  lumina rugosas distraherentque genas.
di tibi dent nullosque Lares inopemque senectam
  et longas hiemes perpetuamque sitim!

Notes

1–18 *Let me tell you about a procuress, named Dipsas: she is old, a drunk, and practiced in the arts of witchcraft.*

1 **lenam**: The "procuress" or "madam" who profits financially from arranging sexual relationships for men with young women is a figure from mime and comedy further developed by the elegists. Other female comic characters, such as the *ancilla* ("maidservant") in Plautus's *Mostellaria*, performed similar services. By Ovid's time, characteristics of the *lena* had become standard: she is old, avaricious, alcoholic, and completely without moral principle.

2 **Dipsas**: a name taken from a small snake (διψάς) known to cause extreme thirst in its victims. This works on two levels: first, it indicates the poisonous nature of the *lena* who makes the *puella* "thirsty" for monetary rewards, and, second, it points to the condition of alcoholism often associated with old women (McKeown).

3 **ex re**: "based on fact/reality."
  nomen habet: Cf. *nomen habent* (3.21).
  nigri ... parentem / Memnonis in roseis ... equis (4): a periphrasis for Dawn, the mother of Memnon, king of Ethiopia.

5–18 The magical powers of Ovid's *lena* recall those of similar characters in Tibullus and Propertius. The *saga* ("witch") of Tibullus 1.2 possesses powers almost identical to the *lena*'s in this poem, but there she uses them to help the poet in his love affair. The *lena* of Tibullus 1.5 and the *anus* of Tibullus 1.8 are both associated with witchcraft, but the aim of the former is to supplant the poet with a wealthy rival, while the latter seems to have cast a spell of love over a young man. In Propertius 4.5, the *lena* is a conflation of the procuress and the witch, and her powers and unethical intentions are remarkably similar to those of Ovid's *lena*.

5 **Aeaea**: "of Aea," i.e., Circe, the divine inhabitant of the island Aea, who used her magic herbs and spells to transform Odysseus's men into animals (*Odyssey* 10).

6 **in caput**: "toward their source."

88   Amores 1.8

7   **quid ... quid .../ ... quid** (8): Anaphora and the repetitions *cum uoluit ... (9) / cum uoluit ... (10), sanguine ... (11) / ... sanguine (12), suspicor ... (14) / suspicor* (15) and even *proauos atauosque* (17) give an incantatory flavor to the narrator's description of Dipsas's magical powers.

   torto concita rhombo / licia (8): The *rhombus* was a disk-shaped instrument with two holes in its center through which a string was passed. By alternating between increasing and relaxing the tension of the string, the instrument was made to spin first in one direction, then in the other. The magical force released from the whirling *rhombus* was said to be useful as an aphrodisiac.

8   **quid ... ualeat**: "what power (x) has."

   uirus amantis equae: i.e., a secretion from a mare in heat (used as a love charm).

9   **toto caelo**: ablative of place where; *in* is often omitted when ablatives of place where are modified by *totus, -a, -um*.

10 **orbe**: "the vault of heaven."

11 **si qua fides**: For the same claim to credibility, see 3.16.

13 **uersam** < *uerto, uertere*, modifying *hanc*, the accusative subject of *uolitare*. The repetition of *u* suggests onomatopoetically the whoosh of the witch flying swiftly through the night.

15 **oculis**: ablative of place where without *in*, as is common in poetry.

16 **orbe**: "eyeball."

19–22   *She was giving my mistress advice, persuasively—to my detriment. (I accidentally overheard.)*

19 **haec sibi proposuit**: "she intended (to) ... "

20 **tamen**: Translate with *nocente*, "however harmful (it may be)."

21 **me ... dedit**: "gave me the opportunity (to be) ... " The seven initial long syllables of the line lend authority to the narrator's right to eavesdrop.

22 **occuluere**: Cf. *dedere* (6.50).

23–34   *"A rich young man has fallen for you. His wealth could ensure you (and me) a lifestyle on par with your great beauty. The stars are aligned for love, and he is quite good looking."*

23 **here**: a colloquial form of *heri*.
    mea lux: a term of endearment, addressed to the *puella*, similar to English "light of my life."
    beato: "wealthy." The rival is a common character in love poetry (see *Amores* 1.4); in both elegy and comedy he is typically rich. One of the narrator's common complaints is that although he himself is a devoted lover and talented poet, he cannot always compete successfully with the rival and his gifts.
25 **cur non placeas**: deliberative subjunctive, expressing indignation.
26 **me miseram**: Cf. 1.25.
    corpore: ablative with both *dignus* and *abest*.
27 **esses ... uellem**: = *utinam esses;* for *uellem* and the optative, see 7.23.
28 The juxtaposition of the pronouns *ego te* and the adjectives *diuite pauper* combine with the use of chiasmus to solidify the bond between the *lena* and the girl.
    diuite: ablative sing.; *diues* is one of a few third-declension adjectives that is not an i-stem.
29 **oppositi ... Martis / ... Venus apta** (30): Astrologically speaking, the planet Mars, god of war, is on the wane, and the planet Venus, which is appropriate for love, has entered one of her favorable Zodiac signs *(signo ... suo)*, either Taurus or Libra. Note the chiasmus to emphasize the contrast.
30 **signo ... suo**: Cf. *oculis* above (15); understand *est* by ellipsis.
31 **prosit ut**: indirect question (*ut* = "how"), with *aspice*; the subject of *prosit* is Venus.
    diues amator: Cf. *beato* above (23). Ovid may be recalling Tibullus here, *quod adest huic diues amator, / uenit in exitium callida lena meum*, "Because a wealthy lover is available and interested, a clever procuress comes to destroy me" (1.5.47–48).
32 **curae**: dative of purpose.
33 **est etiam facies ... illi**: i.e., the new *amator* is also quite handsome.
34 **si te non emptam uellet, emendus erat**: a present contrary-to-fact condition. *te non emptam* = *te non emere*; for the indicative (here, *erat*) used in the apodosis in place of the subjunctive, see *aptius ... fuerat* (7.14).

35–38 *Modesty, when feigned, can be a useful tool in getting what you want from a man.*

35 **erubuit!**: spoken as an aside by Dipsas.
    pudor: i.e., the blushing that accompanies modesty.
    iste: Understand *pudor* by ellipsis both here and with *uerus*.

90 Amores 1.8

37 **ocellis**: diminutive of *oculus*.
38 **quantum**: Understand a corresponding *tantum* with *respiciendus erit*: "Each one will have to be considered in accordance with how much (money) he brings."

39–48 *Chastity is old-fashioned and ill suited to modern times. Even seemingly virtuous women harbor secret infidelities.*

39 **immundae**: The uncultured simplicity of Rome's early women was often contrasted, to their benefit, with the sophistication of modern women. For Dipsas, however, modern women live in materialistic times and should have little use for such an old-fashioned notion as chastity.
Tatio regnante: Tatius was the king of the Sabines at the time that Romulus was establishing Rome.
40 **habiles ... esse**: "to accommodate/to be accommodating (to)."
41 **Mars ... / Venus** (42): The implication is that, while the husbands wage war abroad, the women enjoy lovemaking at Rome. The simultaneous occurrence of these activities is reinforced by parallel structure: deity as subject, active voice verb, *in* + the ablative.
43 **ludunt**: "play around (sexually)."
nemo: the final *-o* is short (systole).
rogauit / ... rogat (44): *rogare* in the sense of "to proposition (sexually)."
45 **has ... quae ... portant**: i.e., the Roman *matronae*; the wrinkled brow is a sign that they are high-class and, thus, prim and proper.
46 **excute**: = *si excusseris*; a disguised condition in which the protasis (*si*-clause) is expressed as a command.
crimina: "improprieties / improper activities or thoughts."
47 **Penelope**: Homer presents Penelope in *Odyssey* 19 as the virtuous wife of Odysseus, intent on waiting faithfully for her husband to return from the Trojan War. In the twentieth year of his absence, however, she can put off her suitors no longer. She devises a contest with herself as the prize: she will marry the man who can string and shoot Odysseus's mighty bow. Unknown to all, Odysseus himself is already present, in disguise.
47 **uires ... arcu / ... latus ... corneus arcus** (48): All of these words have sexual overtones.

49–56 *Use it or lose it: youth and beauty are fleeting. Take as many lovers as possible.*

49–50 The metrical balance of these two lines and the repetition of *labitur* emphasize the imperceptible yet inevitable passage of time. The structurally balanced golden line (50) completes the picture of steady and smooth progression.

49 **occulte**: "without being noticed."
fallit: "sneaks by."
50 **ut . . . amnis aquis**: Some manuscripts have *et . . . annis equis*, which merely repeats the thought of the previous line; with *ut . . . amnis aquis*, the narrator develops that thought by comparing the swift passage of time to an uncontrolled torrent of water. *admissis* gives the suggestion of horses that have been given free rein.
51 **haberi**: "to be worn."
52 How are the sound effects appropriate to the sense in this line?
53 **admittas**: Understand *amatorem* as the direct object.
54 **effectus**: partitive genitive, with *satis*.
unus . . . alter: What noun is understood by ellipsis?
56 **canis** < *canus, -a, -um*.

57–62 *Your poet offers you only poems; a wealthy man offers you gifts and money. Choose a wealthy man.*

57 **iste tuus . . . uates**: The narrator and the girl are lovers, a complication we realize now for the first time. At this point, we begin to understand that the narrator is more than a casual observer, and that the lines with which he introduced the *lena* may contain genuine rancor based on personal feelings. Lines 57–62, therefore, become a turning point in the poem. The harsh sounds of *s* and *t* and the pejorative sense of *iste* underline the *lena*'s scornful attitude. For the *lena*'s dismissal of the narrator with the pretentious designation *uates*, cf. Cupid in 1.1.24.
58 **amatoris milia multa leges**: There are two possible interpretations: (1) *amatoris* refers to the narrator *(iste tuus . . . uates)* and *carminum* is to be understood with *milia multa*, i.e., "All you will get from a poet-lover is a bunch of poems to read"; or (2) *amatoris* refers not to the narrator, but to a rich man *(diues)*, and *nummorum* is to be understood with *milia multa*, i.e., "You will collect a lot of money if your lover is a rich man, not a poor poet."
59 **ipse deus uatum**: i.e., Apollo, god of music and poetry, prophecy, archery (to name a few of his areas of influence). The point may be that Apollo, patron of poets and himself the source of poetry, has wealth because he is a god.
aurea: synizesis of *-ea* into one syllable; cf. *Thesei* (7.15).

Amores 1.8

- 61 **qui dabit**: i.e., the lover who will give gifts and money.
  tibi: dative of reference, expressing point of view.
- 62 **dare**: subject infinitive of *est*.

63–68 *Choose a freedman who is rich over a poor man who is aristocratic or good-looking.*

- 63 **erit . . . redemptus**: "has bought his freedom from slavery" (and thus become a freedman).
- 64 **gypsati . . . pedis**: At auctions, one could identify a foreign-born slave by his feet, which were marked with chalk.
  crimen inane: *inane* is the predicate adjective.
- 65 **ueteres . . . cerae**: i.e., the *imagines maiorum*. The aristocratic families of Rome proudly displayed the "wax death masks of their ancestors" in their homes. In Ovid's time, many such families had aristocratic status but had lost their fortunes.
- 66 **tolle tuos tecum**: The *lena* dismisses the *pauper amator* just as she did the penniless poet above (57)—with harsh, attention-drawing alliteration.
  amator: As the *lena* gives pointers on how to attract and keep a lover, it is remarkable how often the "love" word appears: *amator* (68), *amor* (71, 72, and 76), *amari* (71), and *amans* (78). This emphasis on love provides an ironic counterpoint to the *lena*'s lessons in manipulation and deception.
- 68 **flagitet**: a verb that takes a double accusative (cf. 4.30), "press (x) = *amatorem . . . suum* for (y) = *quod det*."

69–86 *Treat a potential lover gently. Once he is caught, use the standard tricks of the love trade: be passionate, then indifferent, demand gifts, make him jealous, get angry, then relent, cry, and lie when necessary.*

- 69 **parcius**: adverb or adjective?
  exigito: the language of Roman law and religion (cf. 4.29); *legibus . . . tuis* (70) continues the metaphor.
- 70 **captos legibus ure tuis**: *Seruitium amoris* combined with the image of love as fire is subverted since the materialistic *lena* does not promote a relationship of love between mistress and narrator, but a one-sided game of profit between prostitute and client.
- 71 **nocuit**: a gnomic perfect. The perfect is sometimes used (especially with a negative) of a gnome, i.e., a general truth, to indicate that what has been true in the past is always true (see the glossary). Translate as a present or present perfect.

sine credat: *sine* < *sino, sinere*; for the omission of *ut*, see 4.2.
amari: Understand *se* (= *amatorem*) as the accusative subject in indirect statement.

72 **caue**: with a short *–e* due to iambic shortening, a feature of colloquial speech; cf. *puto* (2.5).
gratis . . . tibi constet: "be worth nothing to you," i.e., "cost your lover nothing." *Gratis* is ablative plural (syncopated), used adverbially.

73 **capitis . . . dolorem**: "headache."

74 **Isis**: the Egyptian goddess Isis, whose worship was popular in Rome and required an annual period of sexual abstinence of her followers.
surda . . . oranti . . . laxa ferenti: Dipsas is drawing a contrast between the treatment of a lover who offers nothing but words and a lover who brings gifts.

78 **exclusi**: For the *exclusus amator*, see *Amores* 1.6 and the introduction.

79 **quasi laesa prior . . . laeso**: This is an example of the "offense is the best defense" strategy: if you have wronged your lover (*laeso*), act as if you were wronged by him first (*quasi laesa prior*). Note how the separation of *laesa . . . laeso* marks the contrast.
irascere: deponent imperative; cf. *molire* (7.35).

80 **culpa culpa**: Repetition and juxtaposition at the *diaeresis* connect the *culpa* of the girl with the *culpa* of her lover. Scan the line to see which *a*'s are long and which are short.

81 **numquam dederis**: perfect subjunctive, jussive (polite command).

83 **coacti**: "on demand" (literally, "having been compelled/forced [to]").

84 **illa uel illa**: i.e., other women. Most manuscripts have *ille uel ille*, which refers to the eyes: the girl is urged to be adept at shedding tears from one eye or the other; *illa uel illa* provides an explanation for the directive of the previous line, namely, that the girl should pretend that her lover's other (supposed) affairs are causing her grief.

87–94 *Trick him out of gifts, and let others in the family take advantage of him also.*

87 **servus . . . sollers ancilla**: The "clever slave" was a stock figure in Roman comedy who successfully fulfilled the wishes of his master, generally the *adulescens*, by means of trickery.
partes: "roles (in a dramatic production)."

88 **doceant**: Understand *amantem* as the direct object.

89 **multos . . . pauca**: a double accusative with *rogabunt;* cf. 4.30.

90 **de stipula grandis aceruus**: a harvest metaphor. *Carpat* (91) continues this imagery.

92 **fit cito**: "quickly accumulates."

94 **natalem**: Understand *diem.*
testificare: Cf. 7.35.

94 *Amores* 1.8

95–100 **Let him know he has a rival. This will increase his passion and hopefully his gift giving.**

- 95 **nullo riuale**: ablative absolute; there is no present participle for *esse*.
- 98 **factaque . . . colla**: Understand *esse* in indirect statement introduced by *uideat* (97).
     lasciuis . . . notis < *lasciua nota*, "a love bite."
- 99 **miserit**: future perfect indicative.
- 100 **Sacra . . . Via**: The *Sacra Via* was lined with shops, where a girl could go to purchase tokens of an "imaginary" lover's affection.

101–104 **Seduce him out of all he's worth.**

- 101 **ut non tamen**: "yet not with the result that . . ."
- 103 **noceque**: = *et noce*, < *noceo, nocere*.

105–108 **Follow my advice, and you will thank me eternally."**

- 107 **dices . . . bene** < *benedico, -ere*, "to commend / praise" + dat.
- 108 **defunctae**: "when I am dead"; literally, "of (me) dead." Remember that *mei*, the genitive of the personal pronoun *ego*, cannot be used to express possession and so must be understood from *mea*.

109–14 **Midsentence, my presence was revealed, and I struggled not to inflict upon Dipsas the punishment she deserved. Let the gods do that.**

- 109 **uox erat in cursu**: i.e., she was still running at the mouth.
- 110 **nostrae uix se continuere manus**: The narrator reacts angrily to the *lena*'s advice, but with restraint.
- 111 **quin . . . / . . . distraherent** (112): a clause of hindrance, "from tearing to pieces." A subjunctive clause with *quin* is used after verbs of hindering and refusing, when these verbs are negated. *Se continuere* (110) indicates hindering, and *uix* (110) carries the idea of negation.
- 113 **tibi**: i.e., Dipsas.
     -que . . . -que . . . / et . . . -que (114): polysyndeton reflects the all-inclusive nature of the narrator's curse on the *lena*.

For Further Reading

Myers, K. S. 1996. "The Poet and the Procuress: The *Lena* in Latin Love Elegy." *Journal of Roman Studies* 86: 1–21.

Gross, N. 1995–96. "Ovid *Amores* 1.8: Whose Amatory Rhetoric?" *Classical World* 89: 197–206.

Amores 1.9

In *Amores* 1.9, Ovid actually "solves" the problem of love poets, who rebel against society's expectations and commit to love rather than war, by merging these two opposing aspects into one lover-soldier. The either/or situation becomes a both/and consolidation: love is war, and the lover is a warrior. The narrator emphasizes this union with a series of arguments designed to show that although the soldier and the lover operate in different contexts, their functions are identical. They keep watch, they journey far (although the lover, perhaps, journeys farther than the soldier), they endure extremes of weather, they spy, they besiege, they invade. Throughout, the narrator is careful to support his parallel functions with a balanced structure, but equally careful not to extend the balance into monotony. As a result, his presentation comes across as convincing, both aesthetically and rhetorically.

He brings home his own triumph when he rejects any imputation of laziness to the lover and tells us point-blank that *Amor* takes risks. In support of his claim, he lists four famous warriors—Achilles, Hector, Agamemnon, and Mars—who are also lovers. Even though their role as lovers competes with their role as warriors in some ways (for example, Achilles' love for Briseis causes him to withdraw from war), the *exempla* can demonstrate that because of love these men take risks as great as the risks that soldiers take (for example, Achilles' love for Briseis causes him to draw his sword against his own commander). When the narrator turns to himself as the final example, he claims that before he fell in love, he was lazy and soft, but love has driven out all slothfulness on his part and filled him with energy. Each of the three final couplets describes a stage in his metamorphosis from idle lay-about to active soldier—a soldier, that is, under Love's command.

Militat omnis amans, et habet sua castra Cupido;
  Attice, crede mihi, militat omnis amans.
quae bello est habilis, Veneri quoque conuenit aetas:
  turpe senex miles, turpe senilis amor.
quos petiere duces animos in milite forti, 5
  hos petit in socio bella puella uiro:
peruigilant ambo, terra requiescit uterque;
  ille fores dominae seruat, at ille ducis.
militis officium longa est uia: mitte puellam,
  strenuus exempto fine sequetur amans. 10
ibit in aduersos montes duplicataque nimbo
  flumina, congestas exteret ille niues,
nec freta pressurus tumidos causabitur Euros
  aptaue uerrendis sidera quaeret aquis.
quis nisi uel miles uel amans et frigora noctis 15
  et denso mixtas perferet imbre niues?
mittitur infestos alter speculator in hostes,
  in riuale oculos alter, ut hoste, tenet.
ille graues urbes, hic durae limen amicae
  obsidet; hic portas frangit, at ille fores. 20
saepe soporatos inuadere profuit hostes
  caedere et armata uulgus inerme manu.
sic fera Threicii ceciderunt agmina Rhesi,
  et dominum capti deseruistis equi.
nempe maritorum somnis utuntur amantes 25
  et sua sopitis hostibus arma mouent.
custodum transire manus uigilumque cateruas
  militis et miseri semper amantis opus.
Mars dubius, nec certa Venus: uictique resurgunt,
  quosque neges umquam posse iacere, cadunt. 30
ergo desidiam quicumque uocabat amorem,
  desinat: ingenii est experientis Amor.
ardet in abducta Briseide maestus Achilles
  (dum licet, Argeas frangite, Troes, opes);
Hector ab Andromaches complexibus ibat ad arma, 35
  et galeam capiti quae daret, uxor erat;

summa ducum, Atrides uisa Priameide fertur
   Maenadis effusis obstipuisse comis.
Mars quoque deprensus fabrilia uincula sensit:
   notior in caelo fabula nulla fuit. 40
ipse ego segnis eram discinctaque in otia natus;
   mollierant animos lectus et umbra meos;
impulit ignauum formosae cura puellae,
   iussit et in castris aera merere suis.
inde uides agilem nocturnaque bella gerentem: 45
   qui nolet fieri desidiosus, amet.

Notes

1–2 *A lover is a soldier, and Cupid his commander.*

   1 **militat omnis amans**: *amans* = *amator*. The first couplet reads as a jingle, beginning and ending with this phrase. The two verbal forms *militat* and *amans* reflect the merger of lover and soldier, and *omnis* emphasizes its universality. The soothing alliteration of *m* and *n* underscores the similarity and makes the phrase stand out against the harsh *c* sounds of the words in between.
   sua castra: Ovid reintroduces Cupid as a general; cf. Cupid's camp (2.32). *Castra* implies also "army/warfare" (metonymy).
   2 **Attice**: vocative singular; Atticus, to whom the poem is addressed, is not identifiable, but his name has a military ring to it. The Senate sometimes honored a conquering general by conferring upon him an additional name (*agnomen*) to celebrate his achievement. The *agnomen* was created by adding *-icus* to the name of the country the general had subdued (e.g., *Britannicus*, "conqueror of Britain"; or *Dacicus*, "conqueror of Dacia"). Therefore, *Atticus* can mean "conqueror of Greece." If the narrator can convince a soldier of his claim, it seems, his claim has real validity.

3–16 *Both must be young, hardy, and persevering in adversity.*

   3–4 Ovid emphasizes the blending of the lover into the soldier by purposeful word choice and word placement. In the hexameter, *bello* and *Veneri* are in

98   *Amores* 1.9

parallel position and case, and they are linked even more closely by bracketing the line with *quae . . . aetas*. The pentameter's word arrangement is carefully balanced, A *turpe* B *senex* C *miles* / A *turpe* B *senilis* C *amor*: *turpe* is repeated, the synonyms *senex* and *senilis* follow, and *miles* (person) is matched by *amor* (function).

4   **turpe**: "a shameful thing," neuter singular adjective used as a noun; understand *est*.
   senilis amor: = *senex amator*.

5–6   Ovid continues to use carefully chosen words and word placement to equate the lover and the soldier. This couplet is balanced by initial monosyllables (*quos . . . / hos*) that modify *annos*, and rhyme (*-os -os -os*) emphasizes the parallel. Generals (*duces*) replace war, and the *puella* replaces love through interlocked word order: A *petiere* B *duces* / A *petit* B *puella*. Though preserving the analogy, Ovid now varies the word order and placement of the corresponding phrases, *in milite forti / . . . in socio . . . uiro*, to artful effect. He also indulges in clever wordplay by juxtaposing two words with military echoes, real (*socio*) and imagined (*bella*), an arrangement that also places the *bella puella* in the "embrace" of her *uir*.

5   **animos**: Some manuscripts have *annos* for *animos*. *Annos* restates the point made previously in 3–4; *animos* introduces what follows—a list of duties and deeds that require courage on the part of both the soldier and the lover.
   petiere: for syncopated forms, see 3.4. For the gnomic perfect, see *nocuit* (8.71).

6   **bella** < *bellus, -a, -um*, not *bellum, -i*, n.

7–10   Ovid supports the parallel functions of lover and soldier with a balanced structure: *ambo* and *uterque* (7), *ille . . . ille* (8), and *militis* and *amans* bracketing lines 9–10.

9   **uia**: = *iter* (in military context).
   mitte puellam: For a disguised condition, see *excute* (8.46).

10   **exempto fine**: = *sine fine* (literally, an ablative absolute).

14   **aptaue**: the negation in *nec* (13) also affects this clause.
   uerrendis . . . aquis: dative with *apta*.

16   **et denso mixtas**: The five heavy syllables appropriately represent the onerous weather conditions described.

17–30   *Their missions are similar, their strategies the same. They both take risks and deal with uncertainty.*

17   **speculator**: in apposition to *alter*, "as a . . . "
18   **oculos . . . tenet**: identical to the English "keeps his eyes (on) . . . "

Amores 1.9   99

19   **ille ... hic ... / ... hic ... ille** (20): Chiasmus marks a reversal: *hic* = the lover in the first set, but in the second set *hic* = the soldier.
  limen ... / ... fores (20): For the sexual meaning of entryways, see 6.2.
21–26   The parallel is stretched thin here, for despite the narrator's clever analogy, taking advantage of slumbering enemies to slaughter them (21–22) is much more gruesome than taking advantage of a sleeping husband to have sex with his wife (25–26).
21   **profuit**: For the gnomic perfect, cf. 8.71.
23   **Threicii ... Rhesi**: Rhesus had brought his troops from Thrace to help the Trojans win the war against the Greeks. In *Iliad* 10.469ff., a brutal scene, his camp is raided at night by the Greek heroes Diomedes and Odysseus; he and twelve of his men are slain as they sleep, and his famous white horses are stolen.
24   **capti ... equi**: vocative pl. Apostrophe has a mock-tragic effect here; cf. *casta Minerua* (7.18).
26   **sua ... arma mouent**: Don't miss the sexual double entendre here and below, *opus* (28); cf. 1.1 and 1.24.
27   **manus**: masculine accusative plural, "bands (of men)."
28   **militis ... opus**: Understand *est*, "It is the work of a soldier ... " (+ infinitive).
  miseri: may describe both *amantis* and *militis*.
29   **Mars ... Venus**: The uncertainty of both war and love is a given.
  -que ... -que (30): "both ... and," an epic convention; cf. 2.37. The epic flavor makes a clever contrast with the sexual overtones of the couplet: *resurgent* (29) / ... *cadunt* (30). For a similar sexual reference, see 1.27.
30   **neges**: potential subjunctive.

31–40   *So don't say the lover's life is an idle one. Even great heroes on the battlefield have been lovers, so too the god of war.*

31   **desidiam**: a predicate accusative; *uocare* takes a double accusative, "to call (x) a (y)."
32   **ingenii ... experientis**: genitive of description, used in place of a predicate adjective.
33   **Briseide ... Achilles**: *Briseide* is a Greek ablative singular. The basis of Homer's *Iliad* is the anger and grief of Achilles, who withdrew from the fighting because the captive girl Briseis was taken from him by the Greeks' commander in chief, Agamemnon—a grave insult. *Ardet* represents both his anger at Agamemnon and his passion for Briseis.

35 **Hector ... Andromaches**: *Andromaches* is a Greek genitive singular. In the final scene of *Iliad* 6 Hector, having left the battlefield to return to Troy, briefly reunites with his beloved wife, Andromache, and their son. In a very touching and human scene, they make their farewells; Hector never returns. (In Homer's version, Andromache does not place the helmet on Hector's head.)
36 **uxor erat**: Understand *Hectori* (dative of possession).
37 **summa**: neuter plural adjective used as a noun, "the foremost."
Atrides ... Priameide: *Atrides* is a Greek nominative singular patronymic; for *Priameide*, another patronymic, see *Briseide* above (33). When Troy fell, Agamemnon, son of Atreus and commander in chief of the Greeks, won Cassandra, daughter of Troy's king Priam, as a prize. Because of her wild, unbound hair, Cassandra is compared to a maenad, or Bacchante (a female adherent of the cult of Bacchus). For Cassandra with bound hair, see 7.17.
39 **Mars**: According to Homer's *Odyssey* 8.266ff., Mars and Venus were captured in bed together by her husband, Vulcan, who had set a net of chains as a trap to catch them in the act. Vulcan then summoned all the Olympian gods to witness their humiliating predicament.
fabrilia ... fabula (40): Wordplay, in spelling and sound, link the cause and result of Mars's entrapment.

41–46 *I used to be idle, but now as a lover I am on active duty.*

41 **ipse ego**: The narrator deals with himself last, placing himself in a position of importance following three epic heroes and a war god.
segnis ... discincta: As he portrays the narrator's inclination to *otium*, Ovid seems to make a strong distinction between lover and soldier by using words whose military sense he can play against. For example, *discincta* can mean "without a sword belt," and *segnis*, according to McKeown, can refer to *segnitia*, a behavior punishable under Roman military law. See also *animos* (42) with its military meaning "courage/fighting spirit."
discincta: a transferred epithet, i.e., an adjective logically referring to *ipse ego*, but grammatically attached to *otia* (see the glossary).
42 **lectus et umbra**: hendiadys.
mollierant: This verb of inaction is offset by subsequent verbs of action, *impulit* (43) and *iussit* (44). For *mollire* as a term of genre and style that distinguishes elegy from epic, see 4.44.
43 **ignauum**: Understand *me*, here, and again as the accusative subject of *merere* (44).
cura: a signal of the merging of the narrator as a lover and a soldier, since it is used often by the elegists to refer to "love" but can also mean "command (of an army)."

44 **in castris aera merere suis**: Both soldier and prostitute can apply here. *Aera merere* can mean not only "to serve in the army" but also "to make a living as a prostitute." The metaphor solidifies the merger of lover and soldier, and it returns the reader to the first line of the poem, *et habet sua castra Cupido* (ring composition).

45 **uides**: The verb in the second-person singular also brings us full circle—back to the addressee, Atticus, in line 2.

agilem . . . gerentem: Cf. *ignauum* above (43). Note how *agilem* answers *segnis* (41) and *ignauum* (43).

nocturna bella gerentem: This military action neatly parallels the lack of action in line 41, *discinctaque in otia natus*, although both McKeown and Murgatroyd (1999: 571) observe that real battles were rarely fought at night.

bella: Ovid reverses the wordplay in line 6.

For Further Reading

Olstein, K. 1980. "*Amores* 1.9 and the Structure of Book 1." *Studies in Latin Literature and Roman History* (Collection Latomus) 2: 286–300.

McKeown, J. C. 1995. "*Militat omnis amans.*" *Classical Journal* 90: 295–304.

Murgatroyd, P. 1999. "The Argumentation in Ovid, *Amores* 1.9." *Mnemosyne* 52: 569–72.

Amores 1.10

The poem opens with a series of comparisons in which the narrator measures his mistress against three desirable mythological maidens: Helen, the most beautiful woman in the world, carried off by Paris and the cause of a deadly war; her mother, Leda, whose bizarre seduction by Jupiter is cited in *Amores* 1.3; and Amymone, whom Neptune seduced and then rewarded. Our first impression is that the narrator is tormented by jealousy and the fear of losing his girl to another. When, however, he turns from the mythic past to the present, the true subject of the poem emerges. The narrator has lost all desire for his girl because she has requested gifts. Once he has established the situation, he defends his position with carefully crafted arguments. He appeals to (1) logic (love has no need for money), (2) analogy (prostitutes give love for money, whereas animals give love freely), (3) fairness (why should only men pay?), (4) decency (money ruins relationships), and finally (5) history and mythology (Tarpeia and Eriphyle).

Two underlying themes arise in this poem: materialism and filth. Somehow, as he moves though his arguments, the narrator transforms his *puella*'s request for gifts into a rant about the greed of humans for filthy lucre. Unexpectedly, the narrator qualifies his position and allows that it might be acceptable to ask a rich lover for presents. A poor poet, he claims, has nothing to offer but love, poetry, and immortality, and he will give all three to a mistress who is deserving. This must be the point, and we can now imagine the scene. The narrator's hapless *puella* had the audacity to ask for a gift, and he responded with a poem, which indeed is all he has to give, but his poem is a defensive invective, as a greedy girl deserves. Perhaps a simple refusal would have been better.

Nevertheless, the narrator is able to make his real point, one that he introduced in *Amores* 1.3 and that anticipates the final poem of the book. Poetry immortalizes. Poetry is better than any material gift. That said, the narrator backtracks and promises a gift. Does this mean his anger is not to be taken seriously? Or, now that he has established control over a situation that was momentarily and monetarily not his, can we assume that he is he able and willing to appear generous?

Qualis ab Eurota Phrygiis auecta carinis
   coniungibus belli causa duobus erat,
qualis erat Lede, quam plumis abditus albis
   callidus in falsa lusit adulter aue,
qualis Amymone siccis errauit in Argis,   5
   cum premeret summi uerticis urna comas,
talis eras: aquilamque in te taurumque timebam
   et quicquid magno de Ioue fecit Amor.
nunc timor omnis abest animique resanuit error,
   nec facies oculos iam capit ista meos.   10
cur sim mutatus quaeris? quia munera poscis:
   haec te non patitur causa placere mihi.
donec eras simplex, animum cum corpore amaui;
   nunc mentis uitio laesa figura tua est.
et puer est et nudus Amor, sine sordibus annos   15
   et nullas uestes, ut sit apertus, habet.
quid puerum Veneris pretio prostare iubetis?
   quo pretium condat, non habet ille sinum.
nec Venus apta feris Veneris nec filius armis:
   non decet inbelles aera merere deos.   20
stat meretrix certo cuiuis mercabilis aere
   et miseras iusso corpore quaerit opes;
deuouet imperium tamen haec lenonis auari
   et, quod uos facitis sponte, coacta facit.
sumite in exemplum pecudes ratione carentes: 25
   turpe erit, ingenium mitius esse feris.
non equa munus equum, non taurum uacca poposcit,
   non aries placitam munere captat ouem.

sola uiro mulier spoliis exultat ademptis,
   sola locat noctes, sola licenda uenit   30
et uendit, quod utrumque iuuat, quod uterque petebat,
   et pretium, quanti gaudeat ipsa, facit.
quae Venus ex aequo uentura est grata duobus,
   altera cur illam uendit et alter emit?
cur mihi sit damno, tibi sit lucrosa uoluptas,   35
   quam socio motu femina uirque ferunt?
nec bene conducti uendunt periuria testes
   nec bene selecti iudicis arca patet.
turpe reos empta miseros defendere lingua,
   quod faciat magnas, turpe tribunal, opes;   40
turpe tori reditu census augere paternos
   et faciem lucro prostituisse suam.
gratia pro rebus merito debetur inemptis;
   pro male conducto gratia nulla toro:
omnia conductor soluit mercede soluta;   45
   non manet officio debitor ille tuo.
parcite, formosae, pretium pro nocte pacisci:
   non habet euentus sordida praeda bonos.
non fuit armillas tanti pepigisse Sabinas
   ut premerent sacrae uirginis arma caput;   50
e quibus exierat, traiecit uiscera ferro
   filius, et poenae causa monile fuit.
nec tamen indignum est a diuite praemia posci:
   munera poscenti quod dare possit habet;
carpite de plenis pendentes uitibus uuas,   55
   praebeat Alcinoi poma benignus ager.
officium pauper numeret studiumque fidemque;
   quod quis habet, dominae conferat omne suae.
est quoque carminibus meritas celebrare puellas
   dos mea: quam uolui, nota fit arte mea.   60
scindentur uestes, gemmae frangentur et aurum;
   carmina quam tribuent, fama perennis erit.
nec dare, sed pretium posci dedignor et odi;
   quod nego poscenti, desine uelle, dabo.

Notes

1–8 *You used to be as desirable as the heroines of mythology, whom heroes and gods seduced because of their beauty.*

1–8 One single long sentence is a rarity in the *Amores*. Ovid is intentionally recalling Propertius here, whose poem 1.3 opens with an extended comparison of his sleeping Cynthia to three mythological maidens, desirable in their vulnerability (1–10): "Like Ariadne lying limp on deserted shores, unaware of Theseus's departing ship; like Andromeda, released now from the rocks, laying her limbs to rest in first sleep; and just like the Thracian maid collapsing in the grass, worn out by Bacchic revelry; so she seemed to breathe in gentle sleep—Cynthia—resting her head on hands askew." Propertius soon learns that his first impression of a "gentle Cynthia" is incorrect. Like him, we are in for a surprise.

1 **Qualis . . . auecta . . .** : Understand *ea*, i.e., Helen, wife of Menelaus, the king of Sparta. She was considered the most beautiful woman in the world and was carried away (both literally and figuratively) by Paris, a prince of Troy. When the Trojans refused to return her, Menelaus and his brother Agamemnon led the Greeks against them. The ensuing Trojan War lasted ten years, ending in the defeat and total destruction of Troy. The destructive side of Helen is given prominence here.

ab Eurota Phrygiis . . . carinis: The Eurotas River ran through Sparta; Phrygia was a territory in Asia Minor and the poetic equivalent to Troy. The juxtaposition of the two is purposeful: Sparta signifies manliness, whereas Phrygia implies effeminacy.

2 **coniugibus duobus**: i.e., Menelaus of Sparta and Paris of Troy.

3 **Lede**: Greek nominative singular feminine. The beautiful Leda, wife of Sparta's king Tyndareus, was seduced by Jupiter in the guise of a swan (cf. 3.22) and subsequently gave birth to four children from two eggs: Helen and Pollux from one, Clytemnestra and Castor from the other. (Pollux and Castor were also known as the Dioscuri; Clytemnestra murdered her husband, Agamemnon, upon his return from the Trojan War.)

4 **callidus . . . adulter**: i.e., Jupiter; cf. 3.22.

5 **Amymone**: Greek nominative singular feminine. Amymone, one of the fifty daughters of Danaus, king of Argos, was sent by her father in search of water and happened upon a satyr who attempted to seduce her. Neptune rescued her but then seduced her himself. As a reward (or as payment for services rendered), he struck a rock with his trident and caused a spring to gush forth, to be known thereafter as the Spring Amymone. The Danaids ("daughters of Danaus") were better known for murdering their husbands on their wedding night.

7 **talis eras**: The narrator is speaking to his *puella* and placing her in the same category as the three mythological heroines (described above), who inflamed the desire of males both mortal and divine.

aquilamque . . . taurumque: That Jupiter assumed different forms to seduce attractive young women and men is well documented in classical literature. Jupiter's most famous abduction in the shape of an eagle was of the youth Ganymede. As a bull, he carried off the princess Europa; cf. 3.23–34.

8 **quicquid**: "whatever form."

9–14 *I am no longer blinded by love for you. Why? Because you ask for gifts. Your true nature makes you undesirable.*

9 **timor omnis**: i.e., that her beauty would lead to her abduction.
animi . . . error: i.e., the "blindness" of love.

10 **nec facies oculos iam capit ista meos**: a striking echo to the first line of Propertius's first poem: *Cynthia prima suis miserum me cepit ocellis*; cf. 1.25. *Capit* also has a figurative sense, "charm/captivate."

11 **cur sim mutatus**: The slow spondaic meter of the indirect question contrasts with the quickening meter of the response. The chiastic alliteration of *mutatus quaeris quia munera* further highlights the opposition.

13 **simplex**: "innocent/lacking in guile."

15–20 *Love should be pure and innocent. There is no place for money in matters of the heart.*

15 **nudus Amor**: both "naked" and "without material possessions"; cf. 2.38.
sine sordibus annos / . . . habet (16): i.e., he is young and innocent.

16 **sit apertus**: i.e., "has nothing to hide." What use of the subjunctive?

17 **pretio**: ablative of price. To highlight "materialism," the narrator stresses price (*pretium*, 17, 18, 32, 47) and payment (*aera*, 20, *aere*, 21), buying and selling (*mercabilis*, 21, *mercede*, 45, *uendit*, 31 and 34, *emi*, 34, *empta*, 39), and profit and loss (*damno, lucrosa*, 35). Underlying this emphasis is the suggestion that all relationships involving money amount to prostitution of one sort or another.

18 **quo pretium condat . . . sinum**: There is surely a great deal of humor in this "logical" statement that naked Cupid can have no use for money because he has no place to carry it. The humor increases when we remember that *sinum* can be a euphemism for vagina (Adams 1982: 90).

19   **nec Venus apta feris . . . armis**: Yet another reference to Love as an antiwar, peacetime activity.
20   **aera merere**: This phrase can mean both "to serve in the army" and "to make a living as a prostitute"; cf. 9.44. In the present context, the former sense is meant. However, it is clear from the deliberate verbal echo in the following line *(meretrix . . . aere)* that the narrator intends to play on the latter sense so he can compare the girl's behavior with that of a low-class prostitute.

21–28   *You are worse than a common prostitute. She is forced to sell love for money; you do it willingly. Learn how to have a proper relationship by observing the natural behavior of simple beasts.*

21   **certo . . . aere**: ablative of price. The fixed rate that prostitutes charged for their services points to prostitution as a simple and standard business deal.
22   **iusso corpore**: "by being forced to sell her body" (literally, an ablative absolute).
24   **sponte**: The elegant chiastic arrangement of *facitis sponte, coacta facit* emphasizes the contrast between the willing *puella* and the unwilling prostitute.
25   **sumite in exemplum**: an introduction that smacks of a pomposity worthy of the law courts. However, what follows—*pecudes ratione carentes*—takes us from the sublime to the silly. The narrator's pretty picture of horses, oxen and rams courting their "girlfriends" without the benefit of gifts (27–28) is comical.
26   **turpe**: The "filth" theme comes into play as the narrator emphasizes how very vulgar his *puella*'s request is. He implies that animals would never engage (never mind could!) in such disgusting practices (27–28).
     mitius: neuter singular comparative adjective, modifying *ingenium*. Understand *quam uobis*, "than you have."
     feris: dative of possession.
27   **non . . . non . . . / non** (28): Anaphora highlights a series of three examples, each increasing in length (tricolon crescens). The anaphora *sola . . . / sola . . . sola* (29–30) reverses the series. This chiastic arrangement effectively emphasizes the contrast between irrational beasts and rational humans. (Note, however, that according to the narrator only the female human, *sola*, sees sex as a commodity.)
     munus equum: double accusative with *poposcit*, "demand (x) from (y)." So also *(munus) taurum*.
     popsocit: cf. 8.71.
28   **placitam**: "(erotically) pleasing (to him)."
     captat: "woos/courts."

108 *Amores* 1.10

29–36 *A woman makes a man pay for what they both enjoy equally. Why this inequity when it comes to love and sex?*

29 **uiro**: dative of disadvantage, with *ademptis*.
30 **licenda** < *liceor, liceri*.
   uenit: = *est*. So also *uentura est* below (33) = *futura est*.
31 **quod utrumque iuuat, quod uterque petebat**: Parallel structure reinforces the mutual satisfaction described.
32 **pretium ... facit** < *pretium facere*, "to set a price."
   quanti gaudeat ipsa: = *quanti gaudium suum aestimet*. *quanti*: "for how much/according to how much"; genitive of value.
33 **Venus**: Take with both *quae* and *illam* (34).
   Venus ... uentura ... / ... uendit (34): wordplay on the goddess's name.
   ex aequo: = *aeque*. Ovid often uses *ex* + an adjective in place of an adverb.
35 **mihi ... damno**: double dative construction. The use of legal language, *damnum* and *lucrosus*, underscores the moral illegality of charging money for mutually satisfying sex.
36 **socio motu**: i.e., sexual intercourse.

37–46 *Selling what should never be sold is despicable, whether it is in the law court or in the bedroom. It destroys natural relationships between people.*

37 **nec bene**: = *male*, "wrongfully" (litotes). Again, the narrator plays the "filth" card. (See *turpe* above, 25.) His disgust and indignation over other forms of unethical mercenary behavior are accentuated by the anaphora *nec bene ... / nec bene* in initial position and his use in three consecutive lines (39–41) of the word *turpe*, with its spitting *t* and *p* sounds.
38 **selecti iudicis**: Judges (= jurors) were chosen for a case by the *praetor urbanus*.
   arca patet: i.e., in order to receive bribe money.
39 **turpe**: ellipsis of *est*. So also *turpe* (40) and *turpe* (41).
   empta ... lingua: Advocates, such as Cicero, provided their legal services at no charge. Since the second century BCE, it had been forbidden by law for an advocate to accept payment for defending clients in court.
41 **census ... paternos**: The mention of inherited wealth suggests that the class of women the narrator is referring to here is "freeborn women."

This makes the crassness of *prostituisse* in the following line (42) stand out all the more.

44 **male**: "with base intent," i.e., to exchange sex for money.

45 **omnia . . . soluit**: "has dissolved all (obligations)," i.e., what should be a personal and emotional connection between two people has become an impersonal business transaction—no strings attached.

mercede soluta: "when the fee has been paid."

46 **debitor**: predicate noun; translate after *manet*.

officio tuo: "for services rendered by you."

47–52 ***Womanly greed brings only disaster, as history has shown.***

47 **formosae**: The dramatic apostrophe raises the emotional level of the narrator's plea.

49 **tanti**: genitive of value.

50 **sacrae uirginis**: i.e., Tarpeia, the Vestal virgin who, greedy for gold, had made an agreement to betray Rome to the Sabine enemy in return for what they wore on their arms *(armillas)*, meaning their gold bracelets. After the capture, they crushed her to death with their shields *(arma)*, which they also wore on their left arms.

52 **filius**: i.e., Alcmaeon, who took vengeance upon his mother, Eriphyle, for the death of his father, Amphiaraus. Eriphyle had accepted a bribe from Polynices—the golden necklace *(monile)* of Harmonia. In return, she persuaded her husband Amphiaraus to join the expedition against Thebes, even though she knew it would mean his death. *Filius* receives special emphasis through enjambment.

53–58 ***Asking for money from wealthy lovers is fine; a poor lover can provide payment of a different kind. Let each lover give what he can to his mistress.***

54 Read in the following order: *habet quod possit dare (mulieri) poscenti munera.*

quod: "something (that)."

56 **Alcinoi . . . ager**: Alcinous, the generous king of the wealthy country Phaeacia who entertained Odysseus at the end of his wanderings and returned him to Ithaca (*Odyssey* 7 and 13). He was said to have possessed orchards renowned for their fertility.

57 **numeret**: "count off as payment"; hortatory jussive, as *conferat* (58) corroborates.
58 **quis**: = *quisque*.

59–64 *I can give immortality through my poetry, a reward more lasting than material goods. It's not so much the giving I mind—it's being asked to give.*

59 **quoque**: i.e., in addition to the narrator's other offerings: *officium, studium,* and *fidem* (57).
60 **nota fit**: What noun is understood as subject by ellipsis?
63 **dare**: object of *dedignor et odi*.
   pretium: Take as both the object of *dare* and as the accusative subject of *posci*.
64 **nego**: Final *-o* is shortened (iambic shortening); cf. 2.5.
   poscenti: Understand *tibi*.
   desine uelle: Cf. 8.46.

For Further Reading

Curran, L. C. 1964. "Ovid, *Amores* 10." *Phoenix* 18: 70–87.
James, S. L. 2001. "The Economics of Roman Elegy: Voluntary Poverty, the *Recusatio*, and the Greedy Girl." *American Journal of Philology* 122: 223–53.

Amores 1.11

Amores 1.11 and 1.12 begin a series of paired poems found in the *Amores*, called *diptychs*. The narrator establishes a situation in the first poem of the pair, and in the second, after a dramatic pause in which some sort of change takes place, the narrator reacts. This first poem is addressed entirely to a slave named Nape, and in it the narrator makes a simple request: he wants her to take a message to Corinna. The techniques he uses to gain Nape's assistance work on two levels simultaneously. He begins with a magnificent address to her that rivals the grandest invocation to a goddess or a muse. In a single sentence, eight lines long, he praises her abilities and skill. As a hairdresser, no one is better at the artful arrangement of tresses than Nape, but her talents as a go-between earn her the greatest acclaim. She excels especially in her influence over Corinna and her loyalty to him.

Amid all this praise, however, the narrator inserts significant reminders that Nape is, in reality, a slave and thus there is no real need for him to persuade her. At what is nearly the center of the poem, he shifts perspective and brings two additional players onto the scene: Corinna herself and the tablets that bear his message to her. The focus subtly begins to move away from Nape onto the tablets and then to Corinna, as the narrator pictures her receiving, reading, and replying to his words of love. In the final celebratory scene that he envisions, the tablets return with the answer he has hoped for, and he promises them to Venus, the goddess of love. The poem ends with the words of his dedication, which recall the low status the tablets once had, and, as we shall see in the next poem, predict what they will become.

Amores 1.11

Colligere incertos et in ordine ponere crines
docta neque ancillas inter habenda, Nape
inque ministeriis furtiuae cognita noctis
utilis et dandis ingeniosa notis,
saepe uenire ad me dubitantem hortata Corinnam, 5
saepe laboranti fida reperta mihi,
accipe et ad dominam peraratas mane tabellas
perfer et obstantes sedula pelle moras.
nec silicum uenae nec durum in pectore ferrum
nec tibi simplicitas ordine maior adest; 10
credibile est et te sensisse Cupidinis arcus:
in me militiae signa tuere tuae.
si quaeret quid agam, spe noctis uiuere dices;
cetera fert blanda cera notata manu.
dum loquor, hora fugit: uacuae bene redde tabellas, 15
uerum continuo fac tamen illa legat.
aspicias oculos mando frontemque legentis:
et tacito uultu scire futura licet.
nec mora, perlectis rescribat multa iubeto:
odi, cum late splendida cera uacat. 20
comprimat ordinibus uersus, oculosque moretur
margine in extremo littera rasa meos.
quid digitos opus est graphio lassare tenendo?
hoc habeat scriptum tota tabella 'ueni.'
non ego uictrices lauro redimire tabellas 25
nec Veneris media ponere in aede morer.
subscribam VENERI FIDAS SIBI NASO MINISTRAS
DEDICAT. AT NUPER VILE FVISTIS ACER.

Notes

1–8 *You who are a talented hairdresser and have aided me in the past, Nape, serve again as a go-between and deliver this letter to my mistress with speed.*

> 1 **colligere . . . et . . . ponere**: epexegetic infinitives with the adjective *docta* (2). For an infinitive used to complete or explain the meaning of an adjective, see *premi* (5.20).
> **incertos . . . crines**: object of both *colligere* and *ponere*.

Amores 1.11   113

2 **docta neque ... habenda**: vocatives, modifying *Nape,* as are *cognita* (3), *utilis et ... ingeniosa* (4), *hortata* (5), *reperta* (6), and *sedula* (8). *Docta* receives special emphasis through enjambment. In Catullus, the epithet *doctus* is reserved for talented poets and the *puellae* who share and appreciate their craftsmanship. Ovid's choice here is amusing: on the one hand, *docta Nape* is a stand-in for the talented narrator himself, but, on the other, Nape's skill at artful arrangement pertains to women's hairdos.

ancillas inter: The term for a preposition following its object is "anastrophe" (see the glossary). Although the narrator declares that Nape is not to be considered an *ancilla,* the very statement reminds us that this is precisely what she is.

Nape: a typical Greek name for a female slave; nominative singular. She is the maidservant of Corinna and serves as a go-between in her love affair with the narrator. (The *ancilla* as go-between is a common figure in Roman comedy.)

3 **furtiuae**: a transferred epithet, logically referring to *ministeriis,* but grammatically attached to *noctis.*

cognita: Again the narrator undermines his praise of Nape by reminding her that her competence is as a go-between.

4 **utilis et ... ingeniosa**: predicate adjectives with *cognita* (3), "known (as) ... " *Vtilis* receives special emphasis through enjambment. *Ingeniosa* is an adjective also used to describe a gifted poet (cf. *docta* in line 2), but in this case Nape's "innate talent" is confined to delivering messages, as female slaves often do.

dandis ... notis: dative of reference or purpose.

5 **dubitantem hortata Corinnam**: *Hortor* generally takes an indirect command (cf. 4.2), but in poetry the subjunctive clause is often replaced by an accusative/infinitive construction. Although the narrator suggests with *hortata* that Nape has some influence with Corinna, its placement between *dubitantem* and *Corinnam* suggests rather that it is Corinna who dominates. (Note that *uenire* works with both *hortata* and *dubitantem.*)

6 **laboranti ... mihi**: dative with the adjective *fida.*

fida: predicate adjective with *reperta*; cf. *utilis* (4). Nape (*fida reperta*) is "enclosed" within the words denoting the narrator's power (*laboranti ... mihi*).

7 **accipe et ... / ... perfer et ... pelle** (8): This series of imperatives reminds Nape (and us) that she is a slave and that she should not rise above her station.

mane: Note that this adverb is positioned between *peraratas* and *tabellas,* and thus should be translated with *peraratas* rather than with *perfer* (8).

8   **sedula**: a good example of an adjective used as an adverb.

9–12   *Your nature and your own experience with love should incline you to help me, a fellow lover.*

9   **uenae . . . ferrum / . . . simplicitas** (10): All three nouns are subjects of the verb *adest* (which is singular because it agrees with the one nearest to it); *tibi* (10), dative of possession. The anaphora *nec . . . nec . . . / nec . . .* draws attention to the tricolon crescens.
10   **tibi . . . / . . . te** (11) **. . . / . . . tuae** (12): cf. 2.33.
   ordine: Understand *tuo*; ablative of comparison, with *maior*.
11   **et**: = *etiam*.
12   **in me**: "on my account," i.e., "by helping me" (Barsby).
   militiae signa . . . tuae: The military imagery suggests that Nape also serves in the "army" of love (*militia amoris*) and therefore, as his comrade-in-arms, should help the narrator.
   tuere: Cf. 7.35.

13–18   *Convince her of the urgency of this matter. Then, as she is reading the tablets, watch for her reaction.*

13   **quaeret**: *Corinna* is the understood subject. The arrangement of verbs in this line creates a word picture: the narrator (*agam*) stands between Corinna (*quaeret*) and Nape (*dices*).
   uiuere: What pronoun is understood by ellipsis as the accusative subject in indirect statement?
14   **cera notata**: i.e., the wax tablet he has written on.
15   **dum loquor, hora fugit**: This phrase recalls Horace's famous Leuconoe (*carpe diem*) ode: *dum loquimur, fugerit inuida / aetas*, "While we speak, envious time slips away" (1.11.7–8). It is a mark of the narrator's obsessiveness that, despite this reminder, he continues his instructions unchecked for nine more lines.
   uacuae: Understand *dominae* by ellipsis; dative of end of motion.
16   **continuo**: Translate with *legat*.
   fac . . . legat: Cf. 4.56.
18   **et**: Cf. 11, above.
   tacito uultu: ablative of source or cause.

19–24   *She must write back immediately . . . a long reply. No, one word is enough!*

19   **nec mora**: Understand *sit* (jussive).
   perlectis: Understand *tabellis* by ellipsis.

Amores 1.11 115

rescribat ... iubeto: For *iubeo* with a subjunctive rather than an accusative/infinitive, see 4.29. It is unlikely that Nape, a slave, would give an order to her mistress. She, then, is primarily a vehicle for the narrator's words (Ramsby 2007: 95).

21 **comprimat**: Understand *Corinna* as the subject. Note that the narrator softens his imperatives to jussive subjunctives when speaking of Corinna.

ordinibus: ablative of place where, with *in* understood; cf. *in ordine* (1).

oculos ... meos (22): The extreme hyperbaton corresponds to how long it will take the narrator to read and revel in the lengthy reply he hopes for.

22 **littera rasa**: the much-delayed and unexpected subject of *moretur*. *Rasa* (< *rado, radere*) needs to mean "(having been) inscribed" to fit the context; "having been scratched," a legitimate translation, does not really carry the same force. Therefore, some editors have chosen to mark *rasa* with daggers, signaling that it does not work in this context.

23 **quid ... opus est**: "Why is there a need (for her) ... " (+ infinitive).

24 **'ueni'**: imperative singular, in apposition to *hoc scriptum*. The placement of *hoc* in first position, *scriptum* before the pause, and *ueni* at line's end creates a word picture of what the narrator wants and needs to see inscribed in supersized letters across the tablet.

25–28 *When I see the proof of my success, I shall honor the triumphant tablets and dedicate them to Venus.*

25 **uictrices lauro ... tabellas**: This phrase calls to mind *litterae laureate*, letters crowned with laurel wreaths. Dispatches sent by successful generals to announce military victory to the Senate were wreathed in laurel.

redimire ... / ponere (26): complementary infinitives with *morer* (potential subjunctive); *tabellas* is the object of both infinitives.

26 **Veneris ... in aede**: a double reference to (a) the practice of placing an inscribed votive tablet in the temple of a divinity as a thank offering, and (b) the custom of dedicating the laurel wreath of a triumphant general to Jupiter in his temple on the Capitoline Hill. Ovid again may be thinking of Horace who in *c.* 1.5 describes how he dedicated tablets to Venus because he had escaped love. Our narrator, however, imagines himself as a conquering hero of love (*militia amoris*).

27–28 **VENERI ... / ... ACER**: The elegiac couplet is the most common meter used for inscribed dedications and, therefore, the capital letters reflect the way a real inscription would have appeared. The internal rhyme, *-as ... -as* (27), *-at ... at* and *-er ... -er* (28), effectively highlights the contrast between the tablets' present (27) and past (28).

27 **subscribam**: future indicative, showing the narrator's confidence in the success of his message.
Veneri . . . sibi: *Veneri* is dative with *dedicat,* and *sibi* is dative with *fidas.*
fidas . . . ministras: Note the ironic inversion of line 6, *laboranti fida reperta mihi.* Now the narrator (*sibi Naso*) is enclosed within the power of his "faithful helper," which has become the tablets. Nape is nowhere to be seen.
Naso: = Publius Ouidius Naso; final *-o* is short (systole).
28 **fuistis**: The narrator is addressing the tablets.
acer < *acer, -cris* (with a short *a*).

For Further Reading

Meyer, E. 2001. "Wooden Wit: *Tabellae* in Latin Poetry." In *Essays in Honor of Gordon Williams: Twenty-five Years at Yale,* ed. E. Tylawski and C. Weiss, 201–12. New Haven, Conn.: Henry R. Schwab Publishers.

Amores 1.12

Failure. But whose? While the narrator has not failed in his persuasion of Nape in 1.11, he immediately makes clear in 1.12 that his request to spend time with Corinna has been refused. Part of the blame lies clearly with him, but part also belongs to his mistress. Yet Corinna is markedly absent from the poem, as is any direct condemnation of her. In a masterpiece of projection, the narrator makes first Nape and then the tablets the culprits—and the recipients of his rage. Nape appears only briefly, possibly as a link to the previous poem, and her appearance is completely humorous. The learned and sympathetic abettor of 1.11 has become an ill-omened drunk.

Nape's shortcomings, however, are nothing compared to the tablets', on which the narrator now focuses obsessively. He shifts the blame away from his own words onto the vehicle that transported them, and the tablets receive the full force of his wrath. He brutally attacks and curses them, he declares the craftsman who made them a miasma, he vilifies the tree that begot them. The narrator also accuses the tablets of being two-faced, which indeed they are both literally, since Roman tablets had two facing writing surfaces, and metaphorically, since they proved disloyal by failing to bring him the success he anticipated. Yet for all of his abuse the narrator cannot escape what these tablets signify. They are his request to Corinna for a night of lovemaking; their failure, then, is his failure to persuade, and we can interpret this failure in at least two ways. First, in the elegiac world, as S. L. James suggests (2003: 113), access to the *puella* needs to be difficult so that the narrator's pursuit of her continues to engage both his interest—and ours. And second, by having Corinna give an unfavorable reply to the narrator's carefully wrought love note, Ovid reminds us just how challenging it is for the real-life poet to craft poems of exceptional quality and thus achieve the success and fame he desires.

Flete meos casus: tristes rediere tabellae;
   infelix hodie littera posse negat.
omina sunt aliquid: modo cum discedere uellet,
   ad limen digitos restitit icta Nape.
missa foras iterum limen transire memento   5
   cautius atque alte sobria ferre pedem.
ite hinc, difficiles, funebria ligna, tabellae,
   tuque, negaturis cera referta notis,
quam, puto, de longae collectam flore cicutae
   melle sub infami Corsica misit apis.   10
at tamquam minio penitus medicata rubebas:
   ille color uere sanguinulentus erat.
proiectae triuiis iaceatis, inutile lignum,
   uosque rotae frangat praetereuntis onus.
illum etiam, qui uos ex arbore uertit in usum,   15
   conuincam puras non habuisse manus.
praebuit illa arbor misero suspendia collo,
   carnifici diras praebuit illa cruces;
illa dedit turpes raucis bubonibus umbras,
   uulturis in ramis et strigis oua tulit.   20
his ego commisi nostros insanus amores
   molliaque ad dominam uerba ferenda dedi?
aptius hae capiant uadimonia garrula cerae,
   quas aliquis duro cognitor ore legat;
inter ephemeridas melius tabulasque iacerent,   25
   in quibus absumptas fleret auarus opes.
ergo ego uos rebus duplices pro nomine sensi:
   auspicii numerus non erat ipse boni.
quid precer iratus, nisi uos cariosa senectus
   rodat, et immundo cera sit alba situ?   30

Notes

1–2   *The sequel to I.11: the tablets have not returned victorious.*

1   **Flete ... tristes ... / infelix** (2): Each word of woe holds emphatic first position in its clause. Long *e* and harsh *t* sounds reflect the unhappy scene.
   tristes: i.e., because they have failed in their mission. The personification of the tablets, begun at the end of 1.11, continues.
2   **littera**: See 11.22.
   posse: Expand to *Corinnam uenire posse.*

3–6   *It is Nape's fault, who tripped as she went out.*

3   **aliquid**: "something important/meaningful" (*omina*, not *omnia*!).
   cum ... uellet: i.e., "when she was just about to ..."
4   **ad limen**: Stumbling, especially "at the threshold," was considered a bad omen by the Romans.
   digitos restitit icta: For Latin's equivalent to the Greek middle voice, see *compta ... comas* (1.20). What sound effects enliven the image and actions the narrator describes?
6   **sobria**: The narrator suggests that Nape's stumble may have resulted from a nip too many; cf. *Dipsas* (8.4).

7–12   *It is the fault of the tablets: their wax was made from poison and blood.*

7   **funebria ligna**: vocative, in apposition to *difficiles ... tabellae.* The word is a reminder of death, as is *sanguinolentus* in line 12.
8   **negaturis ... notis**: ablative of means with the adjective *referta;* here, the future active participle indicates intention ("intending to ... ").
9   **quam**: object of *misit* (10); its antecedent is *cera* (8).
   puto: For the distancing effect of *puto,* and iambic shortening, see 2.5.
   longae ... cicutae: The hemlock is a long-stalked plant whose poison was sometimes used to execute criminals (perhaps most famously, Socrates).
   collectam ... misit (10): For a useful English translation of the Latin perfect passive participle and perfect indicative verb, see *possessa ... uersat* (2.8). With *misit,* understand *Romam* (accusative, place to which, with the names of cities, ...).
10   **melle sub infami Corsica ... apis**: The honey exported, along with its honeycomb, from Corsica was notorious for its bitter taste. The honeycomb (i.e., the wax) typically settles at the bottom of the honey.

Amores 1.12

11 **tamquam**: Take with *medicata*.
   minio: *Minium* was an expensive bright red dye produced from mercuric sulfide (cinnabar) and was imported chiefly from Spain.
12 **ille color**: The wax on writing tablets was usually black or dark red; the narrator cleverly associates a tablet of red wax with both shame and bloodshed.

13–20 *Their maker was a criminal, and the wood they were made of came from an ill-omened tree.*

13 **triuiis**: Lying dead "in the crossroads" was a fate reserved for the criminal and the indigent; prostitutes also hung around the crossroads. "The crossroads" of ancient times equal "the gutter" in our time.
   inutile lignum: vocative, in apposition to *tabellae* (implied by *proiectae*).
14 **onus**: here, the "weight" of a cart.
15 **illum . . . / . . . puras non habuisse manus** (16): *Illum* is the accusative subject of *habuisse* in indirect statement. In the narrator's attack on the woodsman, who shaped the tree into tablets, there is an echo to the opening of Horace's *c*. 2.13, in which he abuses both a tree that almost killed him and the man who planted it: *Ille et nefasto te posuit die, / quicumque, primum et sacrilega manu / produxit, arbos . . .* , "That man, whoever he is, planted you on a black day and helped you grow with a cursed hand, O tree, . . . "
17 **suspendia**: i.e., death by hanging, especially suicides.
18 **illa**: Remember, plants and trees are typically feminine in Latin; cf. 1.29.
19 **bubonibus . . . / uulturis . . . et strigis** (20): The horned owl, vulture, and screech owl were all considered to be of ill omen.

21–26 *Why did I use such tablets for love notes!? They are much more suited to menial work, like law or accounting.*

21 **his ego**: The juxtaposition supports the conflation of tablets and narrator.
   insanus: adjective used adverbially; cf. 11.8.
   amores / molliaque . . . uerba (22): Ovid's own love poems are named the *Amores*, and elegy itself is called *mollis;* see *Amores* 2.1.21, in which the narrator asserts that his elegies (*lenia uerba*) soften (*mollierunt*) harsh doors (*duras fores*).
22 **ferenda**: Gerund or gerundive? How can you tell?
23 **capiant**: here, "would contain" (potential).
25 **ephemeridas**: Greek accusative plural.
   tabulas: here, in the business sense, "account books" or "ledgers."

27–30 ***A curse on you, you unlucky, double-dealing duo. May you rot with old age.***

27 **uos . . . duplices**: Understand *esse* by ellipsis (indirect statement introduced by *sensi*). The "double" nature of the tablets contrasts with the *simplicitas* (10) of Nape in poem 11. The description *duplices* is appropriate not only to the tablets but also to the dramatic episodes of poems 11 and 12. The pairing of the poems reinforces the sense of message and then response so characteristic of the use of *tabellae* in the Roman world (Meyer 2001: 209).
rebus: = *re uera*, "in truth/in reality."
pro nomine: "in accordance with your name."

28 **auspicii . . . boni**: genitive of description, used in place of a predicate adjective after *erat*; cf. 9.32. The noun/adjective pair brackets the line, emphasizing the dual nature expressed in the single word *duplices* (27).
numerus . . . ipse: i.e., *duo*.

29 **precer** < *precor, precari*.
nisi: = *nisi (precor) . . . rodat* (30).
cariosa senectus: Just as in poem 11, the narrator ends with a vivid personification of the tablets: in the former, as his "trustworthy assistants" *(fidas . . . ministras)*, here, as persons broken down by extreme old age; cf. *Dipsas* (8.13–14).

For Further Reading

Davis, J. T. 1977. *Dramatic Pairings in Propertius and Ovid. Noctes Romanae* 15: 76–85. Bern.

McCarthy, K. 1998. "*Seruitium Amoris: Amor Seruitii.*" In *Women and Slaves in the Greco-Roman Culture,* ed. S. R. Joshel and S. Murnagham, 174–92. London: Routledge.

Ramsby, T. R. 2007. *Textual Performance. Roman Elegists and the Epigraphic Tradition,* 91–97. London: Duckworth.

Amores 1.13

In a tradition that reaches back to the origins of literature, poets have written poems in praise of deities. In myths reaching back as far as the Homeric epics, deities like Athena in *Odyssey* 23 have been capable of extending the night. Ovid combines these two threads in a distinctive poem in which the narrator asks Aurora, the goddess of Dawn, to extend the night by staying away— because he is in bed with his *puella*. The first half of the poem can be read as a combination of prayer and persuasion. The narrator identifies the god he is addressing (Aurora), presents his first argument for her delay, makes his request, and then lists reasons why she should grant it.

However, he subverts traditional hymnic praise into criticism through unexpected reversals of thought and language. He greets the goddess as "unwelcome," when true suppliants would call her "welcome." He suggests that, in place of the benefits a deity should bring, Aurora brings only hardship to sailors, travelers, soldiers, and farmers. He accuses her of inhumane treatment of schoolboys, litigants, women, and especially lovers like him. The narrator's tone, which begins as relatively mild, grows more indignant, and in the second half of the poem his indignation escalates into full-blown abuse. The narrator attributes Aurora's disregard of lovers to her own pathetic love life: she is sexually frustrated and taking it out on him! Her husband is old and impotent, and she currently has no young lover on the side. If she did, she could identify with him. We are momentarily deceived into believing that the narrator's final rebuke has embarrassed the goddess and stopped her advance. However, we quickly realize that his "prayer" will go unanswered. His poetry cannot counter the course of nature.

Iam super oceanum uenit a seniore marito
  flava pruinoso quae uehit axe diem.
quo properas, Aurora? mane: sic Memnonis umbris
  annua sollemni caede parentet auis.
nunc iuuat in teneris dominae iacuisse lacertis;   5
  si quando, lateri nunc bene iuncta meo est.
nunc etiam somni pingues et frigidus aer,
  et liquidum tenui gutture cantat auis.
quo properas ingrata uiris, ingrata puellis?
  roscida purpurea supprime lora manu.   10
ante tuos ortus melius sua sidera seruat
  nauita nec media nescius errat aqua.
te surgit quamuis lassus ueniente uiator
  et miles saeuas aptat ad arma manus.
prima bidente uides oneratos arua colentes,   15
  prima uocas tardos sub iuga panda boues.
tu pueros somno fraudas tradisque magistris,
  ut subeant tenerae uerbera saeua manus,
atque eadem sponsum cultos ante Atria mittis,
  unius ut uerbi grandia damna ferant.   20
nec tu consulto nec tu iucunda diserto:
  cogitur ad lites surgere uterque nouas.
tu, cum feminei possint cessare labores,
  lanificam reuocas ad sua pensa manum.
omnia perpeterer; sed surgere mane puellas   25
  quis, nisi cui non est ulla puella, ferat?
optaui quotiens ne nox tibi cedere uellet,
  ne fugerent uultus sidera mota tuos!
optaui quotiens aut uentus frangeret axem
  aut caderet spissa nube retentus equus!   30
inuida, quo properas? quod erat tibi filius ater,
  materni fuerat pectoris ille color.   32
Tithono uellem de te narrare liceret: 35
  femina non caelo turpior ulla foret.
illum dum refugis, longo quia grandior aeuo,
  surgis ad inuisas a sene mane rotas;

124 *Amores* 1.13

at si quem manibus Cephalum complexa teneres,
  clamares 'lente currite, noctis equi.' 40
cur ego plectar amans, si uir tibi marcet ab annis?
  num me nupsisti conciliante seni?
aspice quot somnos iuueni donarit amato
  Luna, neque illius forma secunda tuae.
ipse deum genitor, ne te tam saepe uideret, 45
  commisit noctes in sua uota duas.
iurgia finieram. scires audisse: rubebat,
  nec tamen assueto tardius orta dies.

Notes

   1–2 *Dawn is coming.*

     1 **seniore marito**: i.e., Tithonus. Aurora, the goddess of dawn, had fallen in love with this handsome young prince, then abducted and married him. She asked the gods to grant him eternal life but forgot to request eternal youth, and so he grew older and older and, as is suggested here, was no longer much of a companion in bed.
     2 **flaua**: That Aurora has blonde hair here may result from the similarity of her name to *aurum*, "gold," and/or may suggest her continuing youth and attractiveness, especially in contrast to her husband's aging.
       axe: synecdoche; cf. 2.42.

   3–8 *Delay your arrival, Dawn, for I am in the embrace of my mistress.*

     3 **mane** < *maneo, manere*.
       Memnonis . . . / . . . auis (4): Memnon, son of Aurora and leader of the Ethiopians, who was killed by Achilles during the Trojan War. His shade in the Underworld was honored every year by his birds, who flew from Ethiopia to his gravesite and fought one another to the death. The narrator may be making a witty reference to this strange ritual, given that Memnon's name is similar to the Greek verb μιμνει, "wait, stay." In which case, if Aurora waits (i.e., "does a Memnon") she will be honoring her son. The repetition of *m* both harmonizes with Memnon and reminds us of mourning. The birds that sacrifice themselves as a comfort to Memnon anticipate the beautiful birds that enhance the sleep of the narrator and his mistress (7–8).
     4 **annua**: neuter plural used as an adverb.

5 **nunc ... / ... nunc ...** (4) / **nunc** (5): Anaphora and tricolon crescens underscore the pleasant involvements that prompt the narrator's protest to Aurora.
   teneris ... lacertis: For *tener* as a catchword of the elegiac poets, see 4.44. The narrator's complaint, on a poetic level, may indicate his unwillingness to disengage from elegy, which the coming of Aurora, the epic goddess, urges.
   iacuisse: subject infinitive with the impersonal verb *(me) iuuat*.
6 **quando**: indefinite after *si*.
   iuncta ... est: What noun is understood by ellipsis?
7 **pingues et frigidus**: *Pingues* is the predicate adjective of *somni*, and *frigidus* is the predicate adjective of *aer*.
8 **liquidum**: "clearly/melodiously"; cf. 4.68.
   tenui: The sleek and refined nature of the poetic verses of elegy is appropriately applied here to the singing of a songbird; cf. 1.18.

9–24 *Delay your arrival, for no mortal is ever happy to see you and the hardships you bring—not sailors, travelers, soldiers, farmers, students, litigants and advocates, or women.*

9 **ingrata uiris, ingrata puellis**: In a clever reversal of the traditional encomium (= hymn of praise) of a deity's benevolence to mankind, Aurora is criticized instead of being praised.
10 **roscida ... manu**: a golden line, whose artistry is most appropriate for an address to a deity. The request, however, is unexpected. Again the characteristics of a hymn are reversed—this time, the kletic hymn, in which a suppliant beseeches a deity to come to him in person and bring aid. The whole of this section is structured with a chiastic focus on *manus* that begins with Aurora's rosy fingers (10), ends with the work-worn hands of the Roman *matrona* (24), and encompasses the battle-scarred hands of the soldier (14) and rod-scarred hands of the schoolboy (18).
12–24 The reversal of the traditional formula in the encomium continues: the narrator lists all the poor mortals (and beasts) whose hardships are increased, rather than lessened, by the arrival of Dawn. The narrator's *exempla* encompass all humankind, beginning with the whole world and narrowing to the country, the city, and finally the home.
13 **surgit ... lassus ... uiator**: Ovid adds humor to the description of the traveler with sexual vocabulary that suggests that the goddess not only rouses but arouses him. For the sexual implication of *surgit*, see *Amores* 1.17 and 27; for that of *lassus*, see *Amores* 5.25, and Adams 1982: 196. Similar innuendo is used of the soldier, *aptat ad arma manus* (14) (cf. 9.26) and the farmer, *bidente* and *arua colentes* (15)

(cf. 1.10). Unlike the narrator, these men—with hard lives, in occupations generally rejected by the love elegists—have a positive sexual response to the attractive goddess from epic poetry.

15 **prima ... uides**: "you are the first to see"; another hymnic formula typically used in praising a deity as the first to offer a specific benefit to mankind.
arua colentes: periphrasis for *agricolas*.
17 **somno**: ablative of separation.
19 **eadem**: a coordinate with *tu*, "you are the same one who . . ."
sponsum: accusative supine, expressing purpose with *mittis*.
cultos: "people dressed in their best."
ante Atria: i.e., the praetor's court near the *Atrium Vestae*, the shrine of Vesta.
20 **unius ... uerbi**: "due to one word"; subjective genitive. That word was "agreed" *(spondeo)*. By responding in this formal way, a litigant entered into a binding contract, known as a *sponsio*, whereby he offered to pay a certain sum of money if his claim proved false in the subsequent court hearing.
21 **nec iucunda**: another reversal of the encomium; cf. *ingrata* (9).
consulto ... diserto: referring to two distinct legal professions, the jurisconsult *(consultus)*, an expert in the law itself, and the orator in the court of law *(disertus)*, who was highly skilled in delivering speeches.
23 **possint**: potential subjunctive in a temporal *cum*-clause. This suggests that the women have already worked through most of the night.
24 **sua**: reflexive to *manum*; cf. 1.16.

25–30 *Most unforgivable is that you separate lovers, which has often made me wish for a way to stop you from coming.*

25 **surgere ... puellas**: accusative-infinitive construction, introduced by *ferat* (26).
mane: adverb or imperative?
27–30 The extraordinary parallelism between the two couplets recalls magic incantations (McKeown): ***optaui quotiens ne** nox . . . / **ne** fugerent . . . / **optaui quotiens aut** uentus . . . / **aut** caderet . . .*
30 **spissa nube**: Translate with *retentus*.

31–45 *Delay your arrival, Dawn. Don't take the misfortunes of your own love life out on me. You would do as I ask if, like Luna and Jupiter, you found a sweet young thing to love.*

31 **inuida, quo properas?**: the repetition of this question (see 3 and 9) emphasizes the narrator's increasing desperation; cf. the refrain of *Amores* 1.6 at lines 32, 40, 48, and 56. The startling vocative, *inuida*, signals that his persuasion is failing, that Aurora continues to approach, and that serious abuse is beginning.
quod: "as to the fact that."
32 **fuerat**: i.e., even before she gave birth to Memnon.
ille color: signifying evil and, as we are soon to learn, adulterous behavior.
35 **uellem ... liceret**: Cf. 7.23; *Tithono* is dative with *liceret*.
36 **foret**: = *esset*.
37 **longo ... aeuo**: ablative of degree of difference.
38 **a sene**: ablative of place from which, but because of its position, *a sene* can also be construed as ablative of agent with *inuisas*.
rotas: synecdoche.
39 **Cephalum**: Cephalus is a young Athenian hero whom Aurora once carried off for a love affair. The narrator suggests that Aurora would identify with his plight if she were sexually engaged. (He uses the same argument in his attempted persuasion of the *ianitor* in 1.6 and of Nape in 1.12.)
40 **lente currite, noctis equi**: Note how the narrator's proposed cry recalls his own sound bite, *quo properas*, and promotes Aurora's identification with him and his situation.
43 **somnos**: "(nights of) sleep."
iuueni ... amato / Luna (44): After Luna, goddess of the moon, glimpsed the handsome young shepherd Endymion, she lay beside him every night as he slept. In fulfillment of her wishes, Jupiter granted him eternal sleep along with eternal youth. Thus Luna could lie with her beloved in the day and would not have to neglect her nighttime duties to be with him.
44 **illius**: = *Lunae*.
secunda: predicate adjective, modifying *forma*.
tuae: Understand *formae* by ellipsis, dative with *secunda*.
45 **deum**: syncopated genitive plural.
ne te ... uideret: The narrator cleverly tucks in one last insult.
46 **in sua uota**: i.e., "to fulfill his wishes." To extend his lovemaking with Alcmena, future mother of Hercules, Jupiter doubled the length of the night. (Plautus created his comedy the *Amphitruo* around this myth.)

47–48 *I ended my rant, and Dawn reddened.*

47 **audisse**: Understand *eam* (= *Auroram*) as the accusative subject in indirect statement.

128   *Amores* 1.13

> **rubebat**: The narrator would have us believe that Aurora was turning red with shame and embarrassment in the face of his reproaches. In reality, Aurora was reddening because she represents the natural process of the day dawning.
>
> 48   **assueto**: ablative of comparison, with *tardius*.
>
> **dies**: The final word of the poem returns us straightaway to its beginning, *diem* (2) (ring composition).

For Further Reading

Parker, D. 1969. "The Ovidian Coda." *Arion* 8: 80–97.
Elliot, A. G. 1973. "*Amores* 1.13. Ovid's Art." *Classical Journal* 69: 127–32.

Amores 1.14

The narrator laments the loss of his *puella*'s hair due to excessive chemical coloring. Personification allows him both to praise the hair in its natural state and to criticize the girl for torturing it to death. At the same time, he suggests that he is as much a victim as the hair, and he reproaches his mistress for her cruel treatment. The dearly departed hair takes on a life of its own, and the narrator indulges in what becomes a eulogy that combines praise of the dead with his emotional reactions as the chief mourner.

He begins by extolling the physical appearance of the hair and its pleasing personality. His praise leads him to recall how very sexy the hair made his girl. This last thought appears to cause him much anguish, and he turns to very passionate expressions of grief. He ends with a lament, a solemn pronouncement that is characteristic of death poems, and immediately raises the deceased hair to the level of the divine. While the narrator mourns, he denounces the girl for the hair's destruction. He is particularly harsh when he declares that she has no right to mourn her own loss, and he considers other possible causes for the hair's death only to show unequivocally that *she* alone is responsible. Unexpectedly, the narrator proposes a solution, a wig, but immediately undermines it so that his apparent supportive suggestion becomes yet another means of blaming his mistress.

Thus, it is both surprising and not surprising that in the final lines of the poem, the narrator steps back from his strong condemnation and attempts to comfort her. His words of solace seem to contradict his former abuse, and it may be that his reaching out to her signifies his awareness of and sympathy for her plight. But he never loses sight of himself. He sees her reaction only in terms of the upset it causes him, and his final consolation, that she will be attractive again once her hair grows back, comforts him as much as her. After all, who will be doing the looking?

Dicebam 'medicare tuos desiste capillos';
   tingere quam possis, iam tibi nulla coma est.
at si passa fores, quid erat spatiosius illis?
   contigerant imum, qua patet, usque latus.
quid, quod erant tenues et quos ornare timeres,   5
   uela colorati qualia Seres habent,
uel pede quod gracili deducit aranea filum,
   cum leue deserta sub trabe nectit opus?
nec tamen ater erat neque erat tamen aureus ille
   sed, quamuis neuter, mixtus uterque color,   10
qualem cliuosae madidis in uallibus Idae
   ardua derepto cortice cedrus habet.
adde quod et dociles et centum flexibus apti
   et tibi nullius causa doloris erant.
non acus abrupit, non uallum pectinis illos;   15
   ornatrix tuto corpore semper erat;
ante meos saepe est oculos ornata nec umquam
   bracchia derepta saucia fecit acu.
saepe etiam nondum digestis mane capillis
   purpureo iacuit semisupina toro;   20
tum quoque erat neglecta decens, ut Thracia Bacche,
   cum temere in uiridi gramine lassa iacet.
cum graciles essent tamen et lanuginis instar,
   heu, mala uexatae quanta tulere comae!
quam se praebuerunt ferro patienter et igni,   25
   ut fieret torto nexilis orbe sinus!
clamabam 'scelus est istos, scelus, urere crines.
   sponte decent: capiti, ferrea, parce tuo.
uim procul hinc remoue: non est, qui debeat uri;
   erudit admotas ipse capillus acus.'   30
formosae periere comae, quas uellet Apollo,
   quas uellet capiti Bacchus inesse suo;
illis contulerim, quas quondam nuda Dione
   pingitur umenti sustinuisse manu.

quid male dispositos quereris periisse capillos?   35
    quid speculum maesta ponis inepta manu?
non bene consuetis a te spectaris ocellis:
    ut placeas, debes immemor esse tui.
non te cantatae laeserunt paelicis herbae,
    non anus Haemonia perfida lauit aqua,   40
nec tibi uis morbi nocuit (procul omen abesto),
    nec minuit densas inuida lingua comas.
facta manu culpaque tua dispendia sentis;
    ipsa dabas capiti mixta uenena tuo.
nunc tibi captiuos mittet Germania crines;   45
    tuta triumphatae munere gentis eris.
o quam saepe comas aliquo mirante rubebis
    et dices 'empta nunc ego merce probor.
nescioquam pro me laudat nunc iste Sygambram;
    fama tamen memini cum fuit ista mea.'   50
me miserum! lacrimas male continet oraque dextra
    protegit ingenuas picta rubore genas;
sustinet antiquos gremio spectatque capillos,
    ei mihi, non illo munera digna loco.
collige cum uultu mentem: reparabile damnum est: 55
    postmodo natiua conspiciere coma.

Notes

1–12 *Your hair has all fallen out because of too much dyeing. Your tresses had once been long, thick, and silky, and a beautiful shade of auburn.*

   1 **medicare tuos desiste capillos**: Roman elegists sometimes criticize their mistresses for their overly elaborate appearance. In Propertius 1.2, the poet complains that Cynthia's many enhancements—hair ornamentation, perfumed oil, imported materials—spoil her natural beauty, claiming *nudus Amor formae non amat artificem*, "Love in his nakedness hates artificial beauty" (1–8), and in 2.18b he specifically condemns women who change the color of their hair: *illi sub terris fiant mala multa puellae, / quae mentita suas uertit inepta comas*, "May many evils befall that girl in the Underworld, who in her foolishness dyes her hair" (5–6).

Amores 1.14

3   **passa fores**: = *passa esses*; cf. *foret* (13.36).
      erat: For the indicative in place of the subjunctive in the apodosis of a contrary-to-fact condition, see *eram* (6.34).
4   **qua patet**: "where it (*latus*) spreads out," i.e., the fullness of the hips.
5   **quid, quod**: "what of the fact that . . ."
      tenues: Cf. 1.18.
      quos: "the sort which . . ."; relative clause of characteristic.
6   **uela**: here, "cloth/fabric."
      Seres: i.e., the Chinese. Even in the Augustan period, the Romans made little distinction between the peoples of India, Ethiopia, and China, all of whom were regarded as dealing in silks and luxury goods.
7   **aranea**: The spider was an image for the "new poets," including Catullus (Poliakoff 1985: 249). Like the *Seres* and the *aranea*, the elegiac poets take great pains to create delicate and finely crafted material (*uela . . . / pede . . . gracili . . . filum*, 6–7); cf. *rara (tunica,* 5.13).
8   **leue** < *leuis, leue*; cf. 1.19.
9   **ater erat . . . erat . . . aureus**: chiasmus and wordplay underscore the contrast of the hair's colors.
11   **qualem**: Understand *colorem* by ellipsis.
12   **ardua . . . cedrus**: Because "cedars" do not grow on Mount Ida (near Troy), what the narrator describes is probably the juniper. Nevertheless, the color is only suggestive—perhaps auburn. The dark-haired Roman women seemed to favor a reddish tint, achieved in early times through a concoction of ashes and later through dyes from Gaul and Germany (Barsby).

13–18   *For the hairdresser, your hair had been a dream: she could style it in many different ways, nor did she ever need fear that you would fly into a rage over some hair mishap.*

13   **quod**: "the fact that . . ."
      et . . . et . . . et (14): In addition to anaphora, what other rhetorical devices does Ovid use to emphasize the amenable personality of the hair?
      dociles et centum flexibus apti: language that can be applied to lovers as well as to love poetry. The former are teachable and physically flexible; in the latter, the love poets value the flexibility of the elegiac couplet, which makes it adaptable to many different generic styles.
      flexibus: "curls/waves."
16   **tuto corpore**: ablative of description, used in place of a predicate adjective; cf. 9.32.
17   **est . . . ornata**: The subject now becomes *domina mea*.
18   **bracchia**: Understand *ornatricis*.

19–22 *And while a good "do" is to be appreciated, there is something to be said for the natural look.*

21 **Thracia Bacche**: *Bacche* is a Greek nominative singular feminine. Thrace was considered the homeland of the god Bacchus (the Greek Dionysus). The women who celebrated his frenzied and exhausting rites were called Bacchantes. This simile, taken together with the suggestive *purpureo* and *semisupina* of line 20, creates a particularly erotic picture of the narrator's *puella*. For a similarly erotic comparison of a *puella* and a Bacchante, see Propertius 1.3.5–6 (*Amores* 10, note 1). For the sexual connotation of *lassa*, see *Amores* 13.13.

23–30 *Oh, the tragedy! Your innocent hair did not deserve to suffer and die as it did.*

23 **cum . . . essent**: with concessive force.
24 **heu . . . uexatae . . . comae**: The cry of grief and the wail of the internal rhyme (*-ae . . . -ae*) add to the tragic tone of the passage.
25 **quam**: "how," modifying the adverb *patienter.*
ferro . . . et igni: "destruction by fire and the sword"; an image of a city destroyed by an invading army (cf. 6.57), but here referring to a heated curling iron. The heavy-handed approach of the *puella* in forcing her hair into elaborate and artificial form may be meant to recall the grandiose and unnatural style and diction of tragedy and epic. *Ferro* and *ferrea* (28) reference these "hard" genres; cf. 4.44 and 13.5.
27 **clamabam**: The "continuous action" imperfect recalls *dicebam* (1) in sound, line placement, and function. This more forceful verb corresponds to the narrator's increased indignation.
28 **sponte decent**: Praise for the hair in its natural condition again suggests the elegists' stance against the unnatural and overdone characteristics of epic and tragedy; cf. the *puella* as *neglecta decens* above (21).
29 **non est**: Understand *capillus* from line 30 as subject (by ellipsis).
qui debeat: relative clause of characteristic.

31–38 *On the contrary, your hair should have been immortal. And you, as accomplice to the crime, have no right to mourn over it.*

31 **Apollo / . . . Bacchus** (32): Both Apollo and especially Bacchus, with their long flowing curls, were regarded as the epitome of youth and beauty. They are also deities associated with poetry; cf. 3.11.
33 **illis contulerim, quas . . .**: Read *illis comis contulerim comas, quas . . .*; *contulerim* is perfect subjunctive, potential.

Dione: a Greek nominative singular feminine, "Venus." The fouth-century-BCE Greek painting "Aphrodite Anadyomene" by Apelles, to which the narrator here refers, was brought to Rome and set up by Augustus in the temple of *Diuus Iulius* ("the divine Julius Caesar").

35 **male dispositis**: i.e., to the degree that it needed to be artificially treated.
quereris: Scansion will help you determine the tense and voice of this verb.

37 **non bene**: Read with *a te spectaris*, "it is not a good thing for you to look at your reflection . . . " Note that Ovid has chosen <u>not</u> to write *te spectas*, thus emphasizing the *puella*'s appearance as reflected in the mirror.
consuetis . . . ocellis: "with eyes accustomed (to looking at you as you used to be)."

38 **ut placeas**: Based on *tui*, understand *tibi*.
tui: "of your (former) self"; genitive with *immemor*.

39–44 *Neither magic nor disease can be blamed for your predicament. Only you.*

39 **non . . . non** (40) **. . . nec** (41) **. . . nec** (42): The series of negatives in first position emphasizes the implausibility of other possible causes, which keeps the focus on the *puella* as solely to blame for her hair disaster.
cantatae: "bewitched."

40 **Haemonia**: = "Thessalian." Thessaly is commonly associated with magic and witchcraft.

41 **abesto**: Third-person singular imperative, with its archaic legal and religious significance, adds authority to his prayer of prevention (for warding off evil).

42 **inuida lingua**: The narrator is referring to *fascinatio*, the casting of evil spells.

43 **manu culpaque tua**: hendiadys.

45–50 *A wig is a possible solution, but it would only bring you disgrace and humiliation.*

45 **captiuos mittet Germania crines**: In Germany, captives were said to have had to cut off their own hair and hand it over as a token of submission. Martial, in 5.68, also refers to hair sent from Germany. Literary sources and portraiture document the use of wigs, hairpieces, and hair extensions by Roman women (and even Roman men). All were made of human hair and meticulously crafted and fashioned. The preferred hair colors appear to have been blonde (from Germany) and jet black (from India). (Bartman 2001: 14)

46 **tuta triumphatae**: The *t* alliteration adds a harsh, mocking tone.
    munere: ablative of means or cause.
48 **empta ... merce**: ablative of cause.
49 **Sygambram**: "a Sygambrian woman"; the Sygambri were considered wild and uncivilized, like all German tribes, and they had recently been subjugated by Augustus.
50 **mea**: predicate adjective to *fama ... ista*.

51–56 *I have been too harsh: she is upset. "Don't worry. It will grow back as beautiful as ever."*

51 **continet**: Supply a subject that fits the context.
52 **picta ... genas**: cf. 1.20.
54 **ei**: synizesis.
    munera: in apposition to *capillos*.
55 **collige cum uultu mentem**: zeugma in which the verb *collige* applies to both nouns but has one meaning with *mentem* and another with *uultu*.
56 **natiua ... coma**: ring composition (*nulla coma*, 1); cf. 5.26. As commentary on natural beauty, cf. *sponte decent* (28).
    conspiciere: infinitive or second-person singular?

For Further Reading

Boyd, B.W. 1997. *Ovid's Literary Loves*, 117–22. Ann Arbor: University of Michigan Press.

Wyke, M. 1994. "Women in the Mirror: The Rhetoric of Adornment in the Roman World." In *Women in Ancient Societies: "An Illusion of the Night,"* ed. L. J. Archer, S. Fischler, and M. Wyke, 134–51. London: Routledge.

Amores 1.15

The focus of *Amores* 1.15 is the world of poetry, Ovid's place in it, and the immortality it brings. As a poet, Ovid seeks to join the ranks of his famous literary predecessors and, like them, to achieve everlasting fame for both himself and his work. The beginning and end of the poem are connected through a vivid personification of *Liuor* ("Envy") whom, he states, his renown will defeat. *Liuor* accuses him of laziness and wasted talent. He counters with a strong and unqualified rejection of military and political life. He declares that the latter is ephemeral, and claims for himself and his poetry the rewards of fame and immortality sought by those devoted to the army and the forum.

In the central section of the poem, Ovid displays his literary virtuosity as he lists the famous Greek and Roman poets whose company he is joining. His choice of poets is significant and suggests much about how he defines both his poetry and himself as a poet. Tibullus and Gallus were Roman elegists, and Ovid is obviously a member of their company. Callimachus, the Hellenistic scholar and poet, wrote mime and elegy, which, along with the comedy of Menander and other comic poets, fed into Latin love poetry, and his emphasis on erudition and shorter poems was greatly admired and imitated by the later Roman poets. The placement of Callimachus directly following Homer and Hesiod demonstrates that his influence over poetry was equally as important as theirs. Homer, of course, was the great and inimitable master, and Hesiod's works, although written in epic meter, provided an alternative to Homeric epic that appealed to the Hellenistic poets. Sophocles, Ennius, Accius, Varro, Lucretius, and Vergil, all of whom had achieved great fame as poets in Ovid's world, also pushed poetry to develop in new and significant ways. Ovid's placement among these serious writers of epic, tragic, and didactic poetry sends the message that love poetry, especially his love poetry, is both an important development of its poetic predecessors and also their equal.

It is significant that at the end of the poem Ovid claims Apollo as his inspiration. This change from Cupid (1.1) to Apollo supports the idea that he places great importance on the subject matter and scope of his poetry. At the same time his assumption of myrtle, a plant associated with Venus, as his triumphant crown and his declaration that his audience will consist of lovers remind us that his poetry is concerned ostensibly with love. Ovid, then, sees the function of the love poet as equal to if not surpassing the functions of what others considered the more exalted forms of poetry. It goes without saying (but we will say it nevertheless) that the exultant proclamation in the poem's final line remains true: Ovid does live on, and a great part of him has survived!

Quid mihi, Liuor edax, ignauos obicis annos
   ingeniique uocas carmen inertis opus,
non me more patrum, dum strenua sustinet aetas,
   praemia militiae puluerulenta sequi
nec me uerbosas leges ediscere nec me   5
   ingrato uocem prostituisse foro?
mortale est, quod quaeris, opus; mihi fama perennis
   quaeritur, in toto semper ut orbe canar.
uiuet Maeonides, Tenedos dum stabit et Ide,
   dum rapidas Simois in mare uoluet aquas;   10
uiuet et Ascraeus, dum mustis uua tumebit,
   dum cadet incurua falce resecta Ceres.
Battiades semper toto cantabitur orbe:
   quamuis ingenio non ualet, arte ualet.
nulla Sophocleo ueniet iactura cothurno;   15
   cum sole et luna semper Aratus erit.
dum fallax seruus, durus pater, improba lena
   uiuent et meretrix blanda, Menandros erit.

Amores 1.15

Ennius arte carens animosique Accius oris
   casurum nullo tempore nomen habent.   20
Varronem primamque ratem quae nesciet aetas
   aureaque Aesonio terga petita duci?
carmina sublimis tunc sunt peritura Lucreti,
   exitio terras cum dabit una dies.
Tityrus et fruges Aeneiaque arma legentur,   25
   Roma triumphati dum caput orbis erit.
donec erunt ignes arcusque Cupidinis arma,
   discentur numeri, culte Tibulle, tui.
Gallus et Hesperiis et Gallus notus Eois,
   et sua cum Gallo nota Lycoris erit.   30
ergo cum silices, cum dens patientis aratri
   depereant aeuo, carmina morte carent:
cedant carminibus reges regumque triumphi,
   cedat et auriferi ripa benigna Tagi.
uilia miretur uulgus; mihi flauus Apollo   35
   pocula Castalia plena ministret aqua,
sustineamque coma metuentem frigora myrtum
   atque a sollicito multus amante legar.
pascitur in uiuis Liuor; post fata quiescit,
   cum suus ex merito quemque tuetur honos.   40
ergo etiam cum me supremus adederit ignis,
   uiuam, parsque mei multa superstes erit.

Notes

1–8   *You should not criticize me for preferring a life of writing poetry to a career in the military or civil government. It is through poetry, not service to the state, that I will attain immortality.*

  1   **Liuor edax**: Callimachus was the first to give poetic prominence to a personified "Envy." In his literary justifications of his poetic style, he used Envy to represent those who criticized his type of poetry (frag. 1: Βασκανίης ὀλοὸν γένος, "the ruinous race of Jealousy," Hymn 2: Φφόνος, "Envy," and frag. 393: Μῶμος, "Reproach"). While Ovid may be indicating his allegiance to Callimachean poetics here,

his Envy does not so much signify criticism of his own poetry as criticism of poetry itself as a worthy pursuit. The qualifying *edax* makes Ovid's Envy gruesome and destructive, and calls to mind the *imber edax* ("gnawing rain") that Horace claims, in his final poem of book 3 of the *Odes*, is unable destroy the immortality that his poetry grants him.

ignauos: The opening couplets may recall *Amores* 1.9 in which the narrator blithely contradicts the Roman view that soldiering and politics are the only worthy vocations. This time, however, he is not attempting to equate a military (and, by association, political) career with a literary one; he firmly rejects the former outright.

obicis: Scan the initial syllable *ob-* as long, as if *obiicis*.

3 **me . . . / . . . sequi** (4): indirect statement, loosely governed by *quid obicis* (1).

5–6 Comment on the meter and its appropriateness to the meaning of the couplet.

6 **ingrato uocem prostituisse foro**: The Forum was the central marketplace where goods and services of *all* sorts were sold for profit; it was also the center of civil and political life in Rome, the place where magistrates made speeches to the people and where advocates publicly prosecuted or defended their clients. The forceful and vulgar *prostituisse* boldly links the self-serving greed of the *lena* (1.10) with the traditional Roman political career and, at the same time, contrasts the worthlessness of these pursuits with the immortality conferred by poetry. The assonance of long *o* suggests the dolefulness of a political or legal career.

7 **mortale . . . perennis**: Bracketing and chiasmus reinforce the contrast.

fama perennis: It was conventional for the poet to claim for himself the everlasting worth of his poetry at the end of a book or collection of poems. Such a poem is called a *sphragis*, a "poem that seals," because it both closes the book and guarantees the achievements of its author.

9–30 *The great poets, Greek and Roman, through their masterpieces will endure forever.*

9 **Maeonides**: patronymic for Homer. Maeon was reputedly Homer's father, and Maeonia was the Homeric name for Lydia, one of the possible birthplaces of the poet Homer, master of epic poetry. (Seven localities claimed Homer as their own!)

Tenedos . . . Ide: Greek nominative singular forms. Tenedos was the nearby island where the Greek fleet anchored immediately before

140 *Amores* 1.15

the sack of Troy; Ida was the mountain overlooking the plains of Troy. Tenedos and Ida are both part of the setting for Homer's great work the *Iliad*.

10 **Simois**: a river of Troy. Like Tenedos and Ida, it signifies the Trojan War.

11 **Ascraeus**: "the man from Ascra," i.e., Hesiod. Ascra was a village in Boeotia, birthplace of the poet Hesiod, who stood in contrast to Homer as a major figure in early Greek epic poetry. The narrator introduces and links his first two *exempla*, Homer and Hesiod, with a pattern of repetition: *uiuet . . . dum . . . / dum . . . / uiuet . . . dum . . . / dum . . .*, and names both poets by their place of birth.

mustis: ablative of material.

uua . . . / . . . Ceres (12): In his famous didactic poem, "Works and Days," Hesiod discusses wine (*uua*) and the harvesting of grain (*Ceres*). These nouns balance *Tenedos, Ide,* and *Simois* above; the narrator alludes to the great literary work of each author rather than naming it outright.

13 **Battiades**: patronymic for Callimachus. Battus was the founder of Cyrene, birthplace of the learned third-century BCE Hellenistic poet Callimachus. Callimachus significantly influenced Roman poetry, and for this reason Ovid has elevated him to a most prominent position, immediately following Homer and Hesiod. He strengthens Callimachus's connection to the two illustrious epic poets by identifying him in the first part of the line with a patronymic that references him by his place of birth.

semper toto cantabitur orbe: The echo to the narrator's claim of immortality for himself in line 7, *in toto semper ut orbe canar*, suggests his poetic affiliation with Callimachus. See also *per totum . . . cantabimur orbem*, his enticement of the *puella* in *Amores* 1.3.25.

15 **Sophocleo . . . cothurno**: Ovid chooses Sophocles (fifth century BCE) as representative of Greek tragedy, and the tragedian is elevated with a golden line. The thick-soled boot worn by tragic actors to increase their height (*cothurnus*) serves as a metonymy for tragedy.

iactura: "loss (of stature)."

16 **Aratus**: the third-century BCE Hellenistic author admired by Callimachus and famous for turning a treatise on astronomy into beautiful poetry, titled *Phaenomena*. It was widely read in the ancient world and was almost as popular as Homer's epics.

18 **Menandros**: Greek nominative singular form. Menander, the fourth-century BCE Athenian playwright, was praised for the realism of his domestic comedies, in which love was always an ingredient. Recurring stock characters (e.g., *seruus, pater, lena, meretrix*), many of which are found in elegy, populate his plays. For Aratus and Menander, Ovid

reverses his previous structural order: he begins with their subject matter and postpones the poets' names to the line's end; he again uses parallelism and emphatic repetition (*Aratus erit* / . . . *Menandros erit*).

19 **Ennius**: a Roman poet of the early second century BCE who undertook the formidable task of adapting the Latin language to epic style, one famous result being the *Annales*, a history of Rome in dactylic hexameter. As the first Roman poet in this catalogue, Ennius is equated with Homer.

arte carens: The innovative changes Ennius wrought on Roman poetry were not always fully appreciated by later poets, who considered his verses rustic and unrefined. Cf. Callimachus and *arte ualet* (14).

Accius: Ovid selects Accius (second century BCE) as representative of Roman tragedians, highlighting his grand rhetorical style (*animosi . . . oris*) with imagery (boisterous wind) and sound (long *o* and *s*).

animosi oris: genitive of description.

20 **casurum** < *cado cadere*, "to fall into oblivion."

21 **Varronem**: Varro Atacinus (first century BCE), who translated Apollonius's *Argonautica* (the tale of Jason, Medea, and the Golden Fleece) from Greek into Latin. (Note that the original work of Apollonius, the famous Hellenistic epic poet, is not part of this catalogue.)

22 **Aesonio . . . duci**: a periphrasis for the hero Jason, son of Aeson.

23 **Lucreti**: Lucretius, the first-century BCE philosopher-poet who composed a successful didactic poem based on Epicurean philosophy, *De rerum natura* ("On the Nature of Things").

24 **exitio . . . una dies**: This line purposefully echoes Lucretius's own declaration that the world will, in truth, come to an end: *una dies dabit exitio* (5.95).

25 **Tityrus . . . fruges . . . Aeneia . . . arma**: Ovid sets Vergil's fame and influence apart by citing him not by name nor patronymic nor place of birth, but by reference to his three great works, the *Eclogues* (*Tityrus*), the *Georgics* (*fruges*), and the *Aeneid* (*Aeneia . . . arma*).

27 **arma**: predicate nominative.

28 **Tibulle**: the first of the two first-century BCE elegists in the catalogue whose love poems preceded and influenced the *Amores*. Tibullus authored sixteen poems, with a focus on peace and the beauty of the Italian countryside (see the introduction). Apostrophe adds a personal tone.

29 **Gallus**: the second elegist, Cornelius Gallus, who is actually Tibullus's predecessor despite his placement after Tibullus in the catalogue. He was a political and military figure as well as a love poet, and, though his poems have been lost to us, he is given credit for establishing

142 *Amores* 1.15

love-elegy as a worthy literary genre (see the introduction). Ovid reaches a poetic climax with mention of Gallus, whose name appears three times in two lines, 29–30. Line 29 is divided essentially into two metrically identical halves because of the positioning of the second *et* (much like a pentameter). *Gallus* thus stands out as the first word of each set of three words, and the geographical locations (*Hesperiis* and *Eois*) stand out as the last. This word order reinforces the notion that Gallus's fame will reach the ends of the earth.

30 **sua**: For reflexive adjectives not related to the subject, see 1.16.
Lycoris: refers to Gallus's poetic mistress and thus evokes the poetry he wrote about her.

31–42 **With time, things that seem indestructible perish, things that seem important lose value, but through my poetry, I will continue on.**

31 **cum ... depereant** (32): Cf. 14.23.
34 **Tagi**: The Tagus was a river in Spain whose gold mines provided Romans with great wealth. The riches of the gold-bearing Tagus River were proverbial.
35 **Apollo / ... Castalia ... aqua** (36): a combination of two traditional metaphors of poetic inspiration, the god Apollo and the poetic spring of the Muses. (The font of Castalia was located on Mt. Parnassus above Delphi, the home of the Muses).
37 **metuentem frigora myrtum**: Ovid's garland is myrtle, not laurel, as is appropriate for a poet devoted to Venus; cf. 1.29. Myrtle, by nature, cannot tolerate cold temperatures; however, the reference must also suggest the warmth associated with erotic love.
38 **multus**: Cf. 11.8.
39 **pascitur ... Liuor ... quiescit**: Note the central position of *Liuor* and the chiastic structure and antithesis of this line as the poem comes full circle with the personification of the destructive emotion; cf. *Liuor edax* above (1).
41 **supremus ignis**: i.e., the funeral pyre, the symbol of death that Ovid will overcome through his poetry.
adederit: future perfect indicative, as *uiuam* and *erit* (42) confirm.
42 **uiuam, parsque mei multa superstes erit**: In the last poem of his first book, Ovid again purposefully echoes the final poem of Horace's third book of Odes, *non omnis moriar multaque pars mei / uitabit Libitinam*, "I will not wholly die, and a considerable part of me will avoid Libitina [the goddess of corpses and funerals]" (6–7). *Viuam*, which recalls *uiuet* in lines 7 and 9, and *superstes erit* are much more confident and optimistic claims than are Horace's parallel *non omnis moriar* and *uitabit Libitinam*.

For Further Reading

Vessey, D. W. T. 1981. "Elegy Eternal: Ovid, *Amores* 1.15." *Latomus* 40: 607–17.
Giangrande, G. 1981. "Hellenistic *topoi* in Ovid's *Amores*." *Museum Philologum Londoniense* 4:25–51, esp. 25–33.

Vocabulary

A

a, interj., *ah!*
ā/ab, prep. + abl., *from, away from; by; as a result of*
abdō, -dere, -didī, -ditum, *to conceal, cover*
abdūcō, -dūcere, -duxī, -ductum, *to lead away, carry off*
abeō, -īre, -iī, -itum, irreg., *to go away*
abiciō, -icere, -iēcī, -iectum, *to throw away, discard, set aside*
abrumpō, -rumpere, -rūpī, -ruptum, *to break, break off*
absum, -esse, āfuī, irreg., *to be far away (from), be absent or lacking*
absūmō, -sūmere, -sūmpsī, -sūmptum, *to take away; to use up; to waste*
accendō, -cendere, -cendī -cēnsum, *to kindle, set afire; to make hotter, intensify*
accipiō, -cipere, -cēpī, -ceptum, *to receive, take, welcome*
Accius, -ī, m., *Accius, a second-century* BCE *Roman tragedian*
accumbō, -cumbere, -cubuī, -cubitum, *to lie down next to*
acer, -cris, n., *the maple tree; the wood of the maple*
ācer, -cris, -cre, *sharp, fierce, harsh*
aceruus, -ī, m., *a heap, pile*
Achillēs, -is, m., *Achilles, Greek hero of the Trojan War*
acus, -ūs, m., *a needle, a pin; a hairpin*
acūtus, -a, -um, *sharp, pointed*
ad, prep. + acc., *to, toward, at, near*
adaperiō, -aperīre, -aperuī, -apertum, *to open fully*
addō, -dere, -didī, -ditum, *to give to, bring to; to add, join, put*
adedō, -edere, -ēdī, -ēsum, *to eat up, consume*
adeō, -īre, -iī, -itum, irreg., *to come to, approach, be at hand*
adimō, -imere, -ēmī, -emptum, *to remove forcefully, take away*
aditus, -ūs, m., *an entrance, access*
adiungō, -iungere, -iūnxī, -iūnctum, *to join to, connect; to yoke, harness*
adiuuō, -iuuāre, -iūuī, -iūtum, *to help, benefit*
admittō, -mittere, -mīsī, -missum, *to let in, give access to; to let loose, give rein to*
admoueō, -mouēre, -mōuī, -mōtum, *to move (to), apply (to); (mil.) to move up (into position)*
adsum, -esse, -fuī, irreg., *to be present*
adueniō, -uenīre, -uēnī, -uentum, *to come to*
aduersus, -a, -um, *opposite, facing, opposing, turned toward*
adulter, -erī, m., *an adulterer*
Aeaeus, -a, -um, *of the island Aea, where Circe lived*
aedēs, -is, f., *a dwelling place; temple, shrine*
aegrē, adv., *with difficulty; hardly, scarcely*

Aenēās, -ae, m., *Aeneas, hero of Trojan War, founder of the Roman race*
Aenēius, -a, -um, *of Aeneas*
aequus, -a, -um, *even, equal; fair*
āēr, āeris, m., *air*
aes, aeris, n., *copper, bronze; money, pay*
Aesonius, -a, -um, *descended from Aeson, father of Jason*
aestus, -ūs, m., *boiling, seething; heat*
aetās, -ātis, f., *age, time of life, one's lifetime*
aeuum, -ī, n., *time, period of time, age*
affectō (1), *to strive for, go after*
ager, -grī, m., *a field; estate, farm*
agilis, -e, *nimble, quick, active*
agmen, -inis, n., *an army on the march, an army; a crowd, throng*
agō, -ere, ēgī, actum, *to do, drive; to carry*
Aiax, -ācis, m., *Ajax, son of Telamon*
āiō, defective, *to say, affirm*
albus, -a, -um, *white; fair-skinned, pale*
Alcinous, -ī, m., *Alcinous, king of Phaeacia*
āles, -itis, m./f., *a large bird, bird of prey; a cock*
aliquandō, adv., *at any time, sometimes, ever*
aliquis, aliquid, pron., *someone, something;* adj., *some, any*
alter, -era, -erum, *the one, the other (of two), another, a second;* alter . . . alter, *the one . . . the other*
altus, -a, -um, *high, on high; deep*
amāns, -ntis, m./f., *a lover*
amātor, -ōris, m., *a lover*
ambiguus, -a, -um, *of double nature; uncertain*
ambitiōsus, -a, -um, *ambitious, self-seeking*
ambō, -ae, -ō, *two together, both*
āmens, -ntis, *out of one's mind, distraught*
amīca, -ae, f., *a friend, girlfriend*
amīcus, -ī, m., *a friend*
amō (1), *to love, like*
amor, -ōris, m., *sexual passion, love;* pl., *the object of love, a lover; a love affair*
Amor, -ōris, m., *Cupid, god of love*
Amȳmōnē, -ēs, f., *Amymone, a daughter of Danaus*
an, conj., *or, whether, if*
ancilla, -ae, f., *a maidservant; female slave*
Andromachē, -ēs, f., *Andromache, wife of Hector*
anīlis, -e, *of an old woman*
animōsus, -a, -um, *bold, spirited; proud; violent*
animus, -ī, m., *the mind, spirit;* pl., *courage, fighting spirit*
annus, -ī, m., *a year;* pl., *age (in years)*
annuus, -a, -um, *of the year, yearly*
ante, prep. + acc., *before, in front of;* adv., *before, earlier, first*
antequam, conj., *before*
antīquus, -a, -um, *old, former; ancient*
ānulus, -ī, m., *a ring*
anus, -ūs, f., *an old woman, hag; sorceress*
Äonius, -a, -um, *Aonian, of Aonia, a part of Boeotia*
aperiō, -īre, aperuī, apertum, *to open, reveal, lay bare*
apertus, -a, -um (pple. of aperiō), *open, accessible, bare, exposed*
apis, -is, f., *bee*
Apollō, -inis, m., *Apollo, god of music and poetry, prophecy, medicine, etc.*

appōnō, -pōnere, -posuī, -positum, *to place nearby, set next to; to put on, set down*
aptō (1), *to fit, fix*
aptus, -a, -um, *tied, bound, fitted together;* + dat., *suitable, useful, fitted (to/for)*
aqua, -ae, f., *water*
aquila, -ae, f., *an eagle*
arānea, -ae, f., *a spider's web; a spider*
arātrum, -ī, n., *a plow*
Arātus, -ī, m., *Aratus of Cilicia, third-century* BCE *poet*
arbor, -oris, f., *a tree*
arca, -ae, f., *a money chest, coffer*
arcānus, -a, -um, *secret, mysterious*
arcus, -ūs, m., *a hunting bow*
ardeō, -ēre, arsī, *to burn, blaze; to burn with passion*
arduus, -a, -um, *tall, lofty, high; steep*
Argēus, -a, -um, *of Argos, Argive, Greek*
Argī, -ōrum, m. pl., *Argos, an important city of the Peloponnese*
arguō, -ere, arguī, argūtum, *to reveal, prove*
ariēs, -etis, m., *a ram*
arma, -ōrum, n. pl., *arms, weapons; equipment; fighting, war*
armilla, -ae, f., *an armband, bracelet*
armō (1), *to provide with weapons*
ars, -tis, f., *a skill; artistic skill*
artus, -ūs, m., *a body joint; a limb*
aruum, -ī, n., *a plowed field, field*
Ascraeus, -a, -um, *of Ascra, birthplace of Hesiod*
asper, -era, -erum, *rough, harsh; wild, uncultivated*
aspiciō, -spicere, -spexī, -spectum, *to notice, look at, observe; to consider, think about*
assiduus, -a, -um, *continual, constant*
assuētus, -a, -um, *usual, customary*
astō, -stāre, -stitī, *to stand still*
at, conj., *but*
atauus, -ī, m., *a grandfather*
āter, -tra, -trum, *dark, black*
atque, conj., *and, also*
Atracis, -idis, f., *a woman of the town Atrax in Thessaly, i.e., Hippodamia*
Atrīdēs, -ae, m., *a son of Atreus, i.e., Agamemnon*
ātrium, -ī, n., *the first main room in a Roman house*
Ātrium, ī, n., *the Atrium Vestae, the temple of Vesta*
attenuō (1), *to make thin; to weaken*
Atticus, -ī, m., *Atticus; an inhabitant of Attica in Greece*
auārus, -a, -um, *greedy, miserly*
auctor, -ōris, m., *the originator, progenitor*
audeō, -ēre, ausus sum, *to dare*
audiō, -īre, audīuī, audītum, *to hear*
āuehō, -uehere, -hexī, -uectum, *to carry off;* pass., *to depart*
auferō, -ferre, abstulī, ablātum, *to take away*
augeō, -ēre, auxī, auctum, *to increase, enrich*
auis, -is, m./f., *a bird*
aura, -ae, f., *a breeze, wind, air*
aureus, -a, -um, *golden*
aurifer, -era, -erum, *gold-bearing*
auris, -is, f., *the ear*
aurō (1), *to overlay with gold*
Aurōra, -ae, f., *Aurora, goddess of dawn; dawn*
aurum, -ī, n., *gold, riches*
auspicium, -ī, n., *an omen, sign*
aut, conj., *or;* aut . . . aut, *either . . . or*
axis, -is, m., *an axle; a chariot*

B

Bacchē, -ae, f. *a female worshipper of Bacchus, Bacchante*
Bacchus, -ī, m., *Bacchus, god of vegetation and of wine*
barbarus, -a, -um, *foreign, savage*
Battiadēs, -ae, m., *offspring of Battus; an inhabitant of Cyrene, founded by Battus; Callimachus*
beātus, -a, -um, *happy, fortunate; wealthy*
bellum, -ī, n., *war, warfare*
bellus, -a, -um, *beautiful, charming*
bene, adv., *well, morally well, satisfactorily, approvingly*
benignus, -a, -um, *generous; abundant*
bibō, -ere, bibī, *to drink*
bidens, -ntis, *a two-pronged hoe*
blandior, -īrī, blandītus sum, + dat., *to flatter, charm, coax with endearments*
blanditia, -ae, f., *flattery, endearment,* often pl. with sg. meaning
blandus, -a, -um, *seductive, coaxing*
bonus, -a, -um, *good, morally good; healthy, sound*
Boreās, -ae, m., *Boreas, god of the north wind*
bōs, bouis, m./f., *an ox, bull; a cow*
brācchium, -ī, n., *the forearm (elbow to hand), arm*
Brīsēis, -idos, f., *Briseis, the war prize of Achilles*
būbō, -ōnis, m., *an owl*

C

cadō, -ere, cecidī, cāsūrum, *to fall; to fall in battle, die*
caecus, -a, -um, *blind*
caedēs, -is, f., *a cutting down, slaughter; slaughter for a sacrifice*
caedō, -ere, cecīdī, caesum, *to beat, slaughter; to hew, quarry*
caelum, -ī, n., *the heavens, sky*
Caesar, -aris, m., *Caesar (a cognomen of the gēns Iulia); Caesar Augustus*
callidus, -a, -um, *clever, crafty, cunning*
campus, -ī, m., *a field, plain*
candidus, -a, -um, *shining white; fair-skinned*
cānescō, -ere, *to grow white or gray*
canō, -ere, cecinī, cantum, *to sing, chant; to sing about, celebrate*
cantō (1), *to continually sing; sing about, celebrate in song; to bewitch with a spell*
cānus, -am -um, *gray*
capillus, -ī, m., *the hair*
capiō, -ere, cēpī, captum, *to take, capture; to take on*
captīuus, -a, -um, *captured, captive*
captō (1), *to try to catch or take hold of*
caput, -itis, n., *the head; leader; one's status as a free man*
carcer, -eris, n., *jail, prison*
cardō, -inis, m., *a hinge*
careō, -ēre, caruī, caritum, + abl., *to be lacking, be without, be free from*
carīna, -ae, f., *the hull of a ship; ship, boat*
cariōsus, -a, -um, *decayed, rotten*
carmen, -inis, n., *a ritual utterance, chant, hymn; a song, poem, poetry*
carnifex, -ficis, m., *an executioner*
carpō, -ere, carpsī, carptum, *to pluck, pick the fruit of*
cārus, -a, -um, *dear, beloved*
Cassandra, -ae, f., *Cassandra, daughter of Priam, a prophet fated not to be believed*

Castalius, -a, -um, *associated with Castalia, the fountain of Apollo and the Muses on Mount Parnassus; Castalian*
castīgātus, -a, -um, *controlled; firm*
castra, -ōrum, n. pl., *a military camp*
castus, -a, -um, *pure, untouched, chaste*
cāsus, -ūs, m., *misfortune, downfall*
catēna, -ae, f., *a chain*
caterua, -ae, f., *a crowd*
caueō, -ēre, cāuī, cātum, *to be on one's guard, beware*
causa, -ae, f., *judicial proceedings, a case; cause, reason, origin, source*
causor (1), *to plead a case; to plead as an excuse, allege*
cautē, adv., *in a cautious manner, carefully*
cēdō, -ere, cessī, cessūrum, *to go, proceed;* + dat., *to yield, surrender; to be inferior (to)*
cedrus, -ī, f., *the cedar or juniper tree*
celebrō (1), *to sing the praises of*
celer, -ris, -re, *swift*
celō (1), *to hide, conceal; to cover; to keep in the dark, deceive*
cēna, -ae, f., *a meal, dinner*
census, -ūs, m., *one's fortune, wealth*
centum, indecl., *a hundred; a large number*
Cephalus, -ī, m., *Cephalus, a young and attractive Athenian hero*
cēra, -ae, f., *wax; writing tablet coated with wax; wax bust or figure*
Cerēs, -eris, f., *Ceres, goddess of grain; grain*
certus, -a, -um, *certain, fixed, sure, on the mark*
cessō (1), *to be idle, do nothing; to cease, stop*
cēterī, -ae, -a, pl., *other, the rest*

cibus, -ī, m., *food*
cicūta, -ae, f., *the hemlock plant (used for poison)*
cingō, -ere, cīnxī, cīnctum, *to surround, encircle*
circā, prep. + acc., *around*
circum, prep. + acc., *around*
cito, adv., *quickly*
clam, adv., *secretly*
clāmō (1), *to shout*
claudō, -ere, clausī, clausum, *to close*
claustrum, -ī, n., *a bolt, bar*
clipeus, -ī, m., *a round shield*
clīuōsus, -a, -um, *hilly, steep*
coepī, -isse, coeptum, *to begin*
cognātus, -ī, m., *a kinsman, relative*
cognitor, -ōris, m., *an attorney, lawyer*
cognōscō, -nōscere, -nōuī, -nitum, *to find out, find to be, learn, come to know; to hear about*
cōgō, -gere, -ēgī, -āctum, *to compel, force*
cohaereō, -haerēre, -haesī, -haesum, *to cling to, adhere to*
colligō, -ligere, -lēgī, -lectum, *to gather (together); to compose, recover; to arrange; to acquire (over a period of time)*
collum, -ī, n., *the neck*
colō, -ere, coluī, cultum, *to till; to worship*
color, -ōris, m., *color, tint, hue*
colōrātus, -a, -um, *colored; sunburnt, tanned*
columba, -ae, f., *a dove*
coma, -ae, f., *the hair; foliage*
comes, -itis, m./f., *a companion*
comitō (1), *to accompany*
commendō (1), *to recommend*
committō, -mittere, -mīsī, -missum, *to bring together;* + dat., *to entrust (to)*

commodō (1), *to lend, provide*
commodum, -ī, n., *an advantage, benefit*
commodus, -a -um, *pleasant*
cōmō, -ere, cōmpsī, cōmptum, *to make beautiful, adorn; to dress, arrange, comb*
comparō (1), *to compare, put oneself in the same class (with)*
complector, -plectī, -plexus sum, *to embrace, clasp*
complexus, -ūs, m., *an embrace*
compōnō, -pōnere, -posuī, -positum, *to compose, settle*
comprimō, -primere, -pressī, -pressum, *to squeeze; to pack tightly*
conciliō (1), *to bring together; to recommend, be favorable*
concitō (1), *to set in rapid motion*
concutiō, -cutere, -cussī, -cussum, *to shake, wave; to stir up*
condō, -dere, -didī, -ditum, *to put (into), put away*
condūcō, -dūcere, -dūxī, -ductum, *to hire; to bribe*
conductor, -ōris, m., *the one who pays, hirer*
conferō, -ferre, -tulī, collātum, *to compare; to bestow*
confiteor, -fitērī, -fessus sum, *to admit, confess*
congerō, -gerere, -gessī, -gestum, *to gather together, collect; to pile up*
coniunx, -iugis, m./f., *a spouse, husband, wife*
cōnscius, -a, -um, *having common knowledge with another; conspiratorial, conspiring; aware*
conserua, -ae, f., *a fellow slave*
cōnsilium, -ī, n., *a plan*
consonus, -a, -um, *harmonious*

conspiciō, -spicere, -spexī, -spectum, *to catch sight of, see, notice*
constāns, -ntis, *steady, firm, unchanging*
cōnstō, -stāre, -stitī, *to take up a position, stand upon, stand firmly, stand still; to cost, go for*
consuescō, -suescere, -suēuī, -suētum, *to be accustomed, be used (to)*
consuētus, -a, -um (pple. of consuescō), *usual, customary*
consultus, -ī, m., *a juristconsult, expert in the law*
consūmō, -sūmere, -sūmpsī, -sūmptum, *to use up, employ, exhaust*
contineō, -tinēre, -tinuī, -tentum, *to hold back, restrain*
contingō, -tingere, -tigī, -tactum, *to touch, reach;* impers. + dat., *to happen, be granted*
continuō, adv., *immediately*
contundō, -tundere, -tudī, -tūsum, *to pound to bits; to bruise, make sore*
conueniō, -uenīre, -uēnī, -uentūrum, *to assemble, meet;* + dat., *to be suited (to), befit, harmonize (with)*
conuīcium, -ī, n., *a reproach*
conuincō, -uincere, -uīcī, -uictum, *to overcome; to prove*
conuīua, -ae, m., *a table companion, guest*
cor, cordis, n., *the heart*
Corinna, -ae, f., *Corinna, the narrator's mistress*
corneus, -a, -um, *made of horn*
cornū, -ūs, n., *an animal's horn, an object made of horn*
corōna, -ae, f., *a crown*
corpus, -oris, n., *the body*
Corsicus, -a, -um, *Corsican, of the island of Corsica*

cortex, -icis, m., *the bark of a tree*
cothurnus, -ī, m., *a high boot worn by actors of tragedy; tragedy*
crās, adv., *tomorrow*
crēdibilis, -e, *believable, conceivable*
crēdō, -dere, -didī, -ditum, + dat., *to trust, believe*
crepusculum, -ī, n., *evening twilight, dusk*
crēscō, -ere, crēuī, crētūrum, *to be born, arise; to increase, change into (by growing); to grow, bud*
Cressus, -a, -um, *of Crete, Cretan*
crīmen, -inis, n., *charge, accusation; misdeed, crime; reproach, blame*
crīnis, -is, m., *a lock of hair;* pl. or collective sg., *hair*
crūdēlis, -e, *cruel, merciless*
crūs, -ūris, n., *the shin, leg*
crux, -ucis, f., *a cross*
cubō, -āre, cubuī, cubitum, *to lie, rest*
culpa, -ae, f., *fault, blame, guilt*
cultus, -a, -um, *elegant, polished, sophisticated; well-groomed, spruced up*
cultus, -ūs, m., *adornments, clothes, finery*
cum, prep. + abl., *with*
cum, conj., *whenever, since, when, although*
Cupīdō, -inis, m., *Cupid, Venus's son and god of physical love*
cupiō, -ere, cupīuī, cupītum, *to wish, want, desire*
cūr, interr., *why?*
cūra, -ae, f., *worry, care; love*
currō, -ere, cucurrī, cursum, *to run*
currus, -ūs, m., *a chariot*
cursus, -ūs, m., *a running, flow, motion*
cuspis, -idis, f., *a sharp point, tip (esp. of a spear)*
custōs, -ōdis, m./f., *a guard*

Cytherēa, -ae, f., *the Cytherean, i.e., Venus, named for Cytherea, an island in the Aegean sacred to her*

D

damnum, -ī, n., *financial loss; loss*
dē, prep. + abl., *down from, from; concerning, about*
dea, -ae, f., *a goddess*
dēbeō, -ēre, -dēbuī, dēbitum, *to owe, ought*
dēbitor, -ōris, m., *a debtor, one who is indebted (for a service)*
decens, -ntis, *having a pleasing appearance*
decet, -ēre, decuit, *to be proper or suitable; to befit; to be becoming, adorn*
dēcipiō, -cipere, -cēpī, -ceptum, *to deceive*
dēdecet, -decēre, -decuit, *to be unbecoming to*
dēdicō (1), *to declare; to dedicate*
dēdignor (1), *to scorn, despise; to refuse scornfully*
dēdūcō, -dūcere, -dūxī, -ductum, *to lead away, draw down, draw out, spin*
dēfendō, -fendere, -fendī, -fensum, *to defend, plead for (in court)*
dēficiō, -ficere, -fēcī, -fectum, *to run short, fail*
dēfungor, -fungī, -functus sum, *to have died*
dēicio, -icere, -iēcī, -iectum, *to cast down*
dēmens, -ntis, *out of one's mind, insane*
dēmō, -ere, dēmpsī, demptum, *to remove, take away; to cut off*
dēnique, adv., *finally, in the end; in point of fact*

dens, -ntis, m., *a tooth*
dēnsus, -a, -um, *thick, dense; frequent*
dēpereō, -perīre, -periī, *to perish, go to ruin*
dēpre(he)ndō, -pre(he)ndere, -pre(he)ndī, -pre(he)nsum, *to catch, seize*
dērigō, -rigere, -rexī, -rectum, *to guide*
dēripiō, -ripere, -ripuī, -reptum, *to tear off, snatch away*
dēserō, -serere, -seruī, -sertum, *to leave, abandon*
dēseruiō, -seruīre, + dat., *to serve, be a slave to*
dēsidia, -ae, f., *idleness, inactivity*
dēsidiōsus, -a, -um, *idle, lazy*
dēsinō, -sinere, -sīuī, -situm, *to cease (from)*
dēsistō, -sistere, -stitī, *to cease (from)*
dēspiciō, -spicere, -spexī, -spectum, *to look down (on); to be contemptuous of*
dēsultor, -ōris, m., *a leaper, a circus rider who leaps from horse to horse*
dēsum, -esse, -fuī, + dat., *to be lacking*
dētractō (1), *to refuse to undertake, decline; to recoil from*
dētrahō, -trahere, -traxī, -tractum, *to pull off, remove*
dēuoueō, -uouēre, -uōuī, -uōtum, *to curse*
deus, deī, m., *a god*
dextra, -ae, f. *the right hand*
dīcō, -ere, dīxī, dictum, *to say, tell*
dīdūcō, -dūcere, -dūxī, -ductum, *to split, tear apart*
diēs, diēī, f., *day*
difficilis, -e, *difficult; troublesome, hard to deal with*

dīgerō, -gerere, -gessī, -gestum, *to scatter, spread out; to organize, arrange*
digitus, -ī, m., *a finger; toe*
dīgnus, -a, -um, *worthy (of)*, + abl.
dīligō, -ligere, -lexī, -lectum, *to prize, love, esteem highly*
dīmittō, -mittere, -mīsī, -missum, *to send away; (mil.) to discharge*
Diōnē, -ēs, f., *Dione, the mother of Venus; Venus herself*
dīrus, -a, -um, *grim, terrifying, horrible*
discēdō, -cēdere, -cessī, -cessūrum, *to leave, go away*
discīnctus, -a, -um, *unbelted, in loose-fitting attire; easygoing, undisciplined*
discō, -ere, didicī, *to learn*
disertus, -a, -um, *skilled in speaking, eloquent*
dispendium, -ī, n., *loss, cost*
dispōnō, -pōnere, -posuī, -positum, *to arrange, put in place; (mil.) to post, station*
distrahō, -trahere, -traxī, -tractum, *to tear to pieces*
diū, adv., *for a long time*
dīues, -itis, *rich, wealthy*
dīuidō, -uidere, -uīsī, -uīsum, *to separate*
dīuiduus, -a, -um, *divided, parted*
dō, dare, dedī, datum, *to give, offer give over; to allow; to produce*
docilis, -e, *ready to be taught, responsive*
doctus, -a, -um, *learned; expert, skilled (at)*
doleō, -ēre, doluī, dolitūrum, *to grieve, be sad, hurt, feel pain*
dolor, -ōris, m., *pain, distress, grief*

Vocabulary 153

domina, -ae, f., *the female head of the household, mistress*
dominus, -ī, m., *the master of the household*
domō, -āre, domuī, domitum, *to subdue, tame, conquer*
domus, -ūs (abl., domō; acc. pl., domōs), f., *a house, home*
dōnec, conj., *as long as, while, until*
dōnō (1), *to give as a present*
dōs, dōtis, f., *a gift, talent*
dubitō (1), *to doubt; to hesitate*
dubius, -a, -um, *uncertain, doubtful, of uncertain outcome*
dūcō, -ere, dūxī, ductum, *to lead, take, bring*
dulcis, -e, *sweet; delightful; beloved*
dum, conj., *while, as long as, in or by (doing something)*
dummodo, conj., *provided that, if only, as long as*
duo, -ae, -o, *two*
duplex, -icis, *double, folded; two-faced, deceitful, duplicitous*
duplicō (1), *to fold over; to double in amount/size*
dūrō (1), *to last, endure*
dūrus, -a, -um, *hard, firm; harsh, unfeeling*
dux, -cis, m., *leader, commander*

E

ē/ex, prep. + abl., *out of, from; in accordance with*
ecce, adv., *behold! look!*
edax, -ācis, *gnawing, destructive*
ēdiscō, -discere, -didicī, *to learn by heart*
ēdō, -dere, -didī, -ditum, *to bring forth; to engage in; to narrate*
effectus, -ūs, m., *an effect, result; success*
effundō, -fundere, -fūdī, -fūsum, *to pour out, stream forth, let loose*
ego, *I*
ei (hei), interj., *oh! alas!*
ēloquium, -ī, n., *eloquence, manner of speaking*
emō, -ere, ēmī, emptum, *to buy, purchase*
ēmodulor (1), *to measure out; to put into meter*
ēn, interj., *behold, look!*
Ennius, -ī, m., *Ennius, a Roman poet of the late third/early second century* BCE
eō, īre, iī, ītūrum, irreg., *to go, pass (by)*
Eōus, -a, -um, *of/connected with the dawn, of the lands to the east*
ephēmeris, -idis, f., *a (daily) account book*
epula, -ae, f., *a banquet, dinner party*
equa, -ae, f., *a horse, mare*
eques, -itis, m., *a horse soldier; a knight*
equus, -ī, m., *a horse, stallion*
ergō, conj., *therefore*
errō (1), *to wander, roam; to act in error*
error, -ōris, m., *wandering; a mistake; delusion*
ērubescō, -rubescere, -rubuī, *to blush*
ērudiō, -rudīre, -rudiī, -ruditum, *to instruct, train*
et, conj., *and*; adv., *also, even*; et . . . et, *both . . . and*
etiam, adv., *also, even*
ēuentus, -ūs, m., *an outcome, result*
ēuocō (1), *to call out (from)*
Eurōtās, -ae, m., *the Eurotas River, on which Sparta stands*
Eurus, -ī, m., *the east wind*
exanimis, -e, *lifeless; faint with fear*

excipiō, -cipere, -cēpī, -ceptum, *to receive, welcome*
excitō (1), *to wake up, rouse*
exclūdō, -clūdere, -clūsī, -clūsum, *to shut out*
excubiae, -ārum, f. pl., *the keeping of a watch, a watch*
excutiō, -cutere, -cussī, -cussum, *to shake out, throw off*
exemplum, -ī, n., *a sample; example*
exeō, -īre, -iī, -itum, *to go or come out*
exerceō, -ercēre, -ercuī, -ercitum, *to keep busy, keep in practice, put to use*
exigō, -igere, -ēgī, -actum, *to drive out; to finish, complete; to exact, call for*
exiguus, -a, -um, *small, slight*
eximō, -imere, -ēmī, -ēmptum, *to remove*
exitium, -ī, n., *death, destruction*
experiens, -ntis, *active, enterprising*
externus, -a, -um, *external, outside; foreign*
exterō, -terere, -terīuī, -terītum, *to rub away, wear down; to crush*
exterritus, -a, -um, *badly frightened*
extrēmus, -a, -um, *outermost, at the edge*
exultō (1), *to leap for joy, rejoice mightily*

F

fabrilis, -e, *of a craftsman, of a blacksmith*
fābula, -ae, f., *talk, gossip; a story, tale*
faciēs, -ēī, f., *physical appearance, looks; beauty*
facinus, -oris, n., *a crime, outrage*
faciō, -ere, fēcī, factum, *to make, do;* + *ut* or subjn., *see to it (that)*
fallax, -ācis, *tricky, deceitful*
fallō, -ere, fefellī, falsum, *to deceive, mislead*
falsus, -a, -um, *false, untrue, mistaken*
falx, -cis, f., *a scythe, sickle*
fāma, -ae, f., *glory, renown; rumor, report*
fateor, -ērī, fassus sum, *to acknowledge, admit, confess*
fātum, -ī, n., *destiny, fate; death*
fax, -cis, f., *a torch*
fēlix, -īcis, *fruitful, rich; lucky, happy, fortunate*
fēmina, -ae, f., *a woman*
fēmineus, -a, -um, *of women, proper to women*
femur, -oris, n., *the thigh*
fenestra, -ae, f., *a window*
fera, -ae, f., *a beast, wild animal*
ferē, adv., *almost; generally, usually*
ferō, ferre, tulī, lātum, irreg., *to carry, bring, bear; to carry off or away; to suffer, endure; to deal (a blow); to get, derive; to report, allege*
ferox, -ōcis, *fierce, savage, ferocious, savage*
ferreus, -a, -um, *made of iron; hard-hearted, cruel*
ferrum, -ī, n., *iron, steel; sword*
ferus, -a, -um, *wild*
feruidus, -a, -um, *intensely hot, blazing*
fidēs, -eī, f., *faithfulness, fidelity, belief*
fīdus, -a, -um, *loyal, faithful*
figura, -ae, f., *outward appearance, looks*
fīlius, -ī, m., *a son*
fīlum, -ī, n., *a thread, string*
findō, -ere, fidī, fissum, *to split apart*
fingō, -ere, finxī, fictum, *to fabricate, make up*
fīniō, -īre, *to set within limits; to end, finish*

fīnis, -is, m., *a boundary, border, end, limit (of time or distance)*
fīō, fīerī, factus sum, irreg., *to become, come into being, be made; to be done, happen*
flāgitō (1), + double acc., *to demand or press for* (x) *from* (y)
flāmen, -inis, n., *a gust, blast (of wind)*
flamma, -ae, f., *a flame*
flāuens, -ntis, *golden, yellow*
flāuus, -a, -um, *golden; fair-haired, blonde*
fleō, -ēre, flēuī, flētum, *to weep, weep for*
flexus, -ūs, m., *a curve, curl; change*
flōs, -ōris, m., *a flower*
flūmen, -inis, n., *a stream, river*
flūmineus, -a, -um, *of a river*
fluō, -ere, fluxī, fluxum, *to flow, stream*
forās, adv., *outside, out*
foris, -is, f., *the door, entrance (of a building* or *room);* pl., *double doors*
forma, -ae, f., *shape, beauty*
formīdō (1), *to fear, dread*
formōsus, -a, -um, *shapely, beautiful*
fors, -tis, f., *chance, luck*
forsitan, adv., *perhaps*
forte, adv., *by chance*
fortis, -e, *brave, strong, forceful*
fortūna, -ae, f., *chance, fate, luck, fortune*
Forum, -ī, n., *the Forum, the center of political and legal business*
foueō, -ēre, fōuī, fōtum, *to warm; to caress*
frangō, -ere, frēgī, frāctum, *to break, crush*
fraudō (1), *to cheat, swindle (out of)*
frēnum, -ī, n., *a bridle, rein*
fretum, -ī, n., *strait, channel;* pl., *sea*
frīgidus, -a, -um, *cold*
frīgus, -oris, n., *the cold, cold spell*
frons, -tis, m., *the forehead, brow*
frux, -ūgis, f., *crops, fruits, grain*
fugiō, -ere, fūgī, fugitūrum, *to flee*
fulciō, -īre, fulsī, fultum, *to fortify*
fulgeō, -ēre, fulsī, *to shine brightly*
fulmen, -inis, n., *a lightning bolt; threat of destruction*
fulminō (1), *to flash like lightning*
fultus, -a, -um: pple. of fulciō
fūnebris, -e, *connected with a funeral*
furor, -ōris, m., *violent madness, frenzied passion*
furtim, adv., *stealthily, slyly*
furtīuus, -a, -um, *stolen; stealthy, secret*
futūrum, -ī, n., *the future;* pl., *future events*

G
galea, -ae, f., *a helmet*
Gallus, -ī, m., *C. Cornelius Gallus, a Roman poet of the first century* BCE
Gangētis, -idis, *of the Ganges River (in India)*
garrulus, -a, -um, *chatty, wordy*
gaudeō, -ēre, gauīsus sum, *to rejoice*
geminus, -a, -um, *twin, double*
gemma, -ae, f., *a gem, jewel*
gena, -ae, f., *the cheek*
genitor, -ōris, m., *the begetter, father*
gens, -ntis, f., *a race, people*
genū, -ūs, n., *the knee*
Germānia, -ae, f., *Germany*
gerō, -ere, gessī, gestum, *to wear; bear; wage*
glomerō (1), *to form into a ball; to mass together*
gracilis, -e, *slender, thin*
grāmen, -inis, n., *grass; herbs*

156 Vocabulary

grandis, -e, *full-grown, great, large; old*
graphium, -ī, n., *a stylus, a sharply pointed instrument for inscribing*
grātia, -ae, f., *gratitude, thanks; favor; prestige*
grātus, -a, -um, *grateful, thankful; pleasing, dear*; grātīs, abl. pl. as adv., *without payment, for nothing*
grauis, -e, *heavy, massive; weighty, serious, solemn; hard to capture*
gremium, -ī, n., *the lap*
grex, -egis, m., *a flock, herd*
guttur, -uris, n., *the windpipe, throat*
gypsātus, -a, -um, *whitened with gypsum (= chalk)*

H

habeō, -ēre, habuī, habitum, *to have, hold, keep, possess; to have on, wear*
habilis, -e, *easy to handle, available; suitable, fit*
Haemonius, -a, -um, *from Thessaly*
haereō, -ēre, haesī, haustum, *to stick, cling; to fasten one's gaze (on); to be hesitant, be uncertain*
harundō, -inis, f., *a reed*
Hector, -oris, m., *Hector, eldest son of King Priam, hero of Troy*
Helicōnius, -a, -um, *of Helicon, a mountain in Boeotia sacred to Apollo and the Muses*
herba, -ae, f., *an herb (used for magical purposes)*
Hesperius, -a, -um, *of the lands to the west*
heu, interj., *alas!*
hic, haec, hoc, *this; the latter*
hiems, -mis, f., *winter*
hinc, adv., *from here*
hodiē, adv., *today*

Homērus, -ī, m., *Homer, poet of the Iliad and Odyssey*
homō, -inis, m., *a man, human being*
honor (honōs), -ōris, m., *glory, high esteem*
hōra, -ae, f., *an hour*
hortor (1), *to encourage, exhort, urge*
hostis, -is, m./f., *an enemy*
hūc, adv., *to here, to this place*
humus, -ī, f., *the earth, ground*

I

iaceō, -ēre, iacuī, *to lie, to be lying down; to lie dead, die*
iaciō, -ere, iēcī, iactūrum, *to throw*
iactō (1), *to throw; to toss about, to wave, shake*
iactūra, -ae, f., *loss, deprivation*
iam, adv., *now, already, soon*
iānitor, -ōris, m., *a doorkeeper*
iānua, -ae, f., *the door of a house*
ibi, adv., *there*
īciō, -ere, īcī, ictum, *to strike*
Īda, -ae, f., *a mountain range in Phrygia*
Īdē, -ēs, f.: see Īda
īdem, eadem, idem, *the same*
ignāuus, -a, -um, *lazy, idle*
ignis, -is, m., *fire*
ille, illa, illud, *that, that famous; the former; he, she, it*
imber, -ris, m., *rain*
immemor, -oris, *not remembering, forgetful*
immitis, -e, *hard, harsh, cruel*
immundus, -a, -um, *unclean, foul; slovenly in appearance*
impellō, -pellere, -pulī, -pulsum, *to strike or beat against; to push; to urge on, stimulate*
imperium, -ī, n., *supreme power, authority*

impius, -a, -um, *lacking respect for gods, parents, country; wicked*
impōnō, -pōnere, -posuī, -positum, *to put, lay, place in or upon*
imprimō, -primere, -pressī, -pressum, *to apply with pressure, press onto, imprint*
improbus, -a, -um, *shameless*
īmus, -a, -um, *lowest, bottommost*
in, prep. + abl., *in, on, among; in dealing with;* + acc., *into, onto, to; against; for*
inānis, -e, *foolish, of little importance*
inaurātus, -a, -um, *overlaid with gold*
inbellis (imbellis), -e, *not suited for warfare*
incertus, -a, -um, *uncertain; confused; in disarray*
inclāmō (1), *to shout at*
inclūdō, -ere, -clūsī, -clūsum, *to shut in; confine*
incuruus, -a, -um, *curved, crooked, bent*
inde, adv., *from there, then*
indignus, -a, -um, *unworthy, beneath one's dignity*
inemptus, -a, -um, *unpurchased, obtained for free*
ineptus, -a, -um, *foolish, silly*
inermis, -e, *unarmed, defenseless*
iners, -tis, *crude, lacking skill; lazy, idle*
infāmis, -e, *notorius, ill-reputed*
infēlix, -īcis, *unlucky, unsuccessful, causing misfortune, announcing disaster*
inferior, -ius, comp., *lower; following, subsequent*
infestus, -a, -um, *hostile, savage*
infirmus, -a, -um, *weak*
ingeniōsus, -a, um, *clever, innately gifted, naturally talented*

ingenium, -ī, n., *inherent nature; innate talent*
ingenuus, -a, -um, *freeborn; tender, delicate*
ingrātus, -a, -um, *unpleasant; ungrateful*
iniciō, -icere, -iēcī, -iectum, *to throw on or over*
innumerus, -a, -um, *countless*
inoffensus, -a, -um, *not tripping, not stumbling*
inops, -pis, *poor, destitute*
insānus, -a, -um, *crazed, insane*
insignis, -e, *conspicuous, remarkable*
instar, n., *the equivalent (of), like,* + gen.
instruō, -struere, -strūxī, -strūctum, *to equip, furnish*
insum, -esse, -fuī, *to be present (in, on, or among)*
inter, prep. + acc., *between, among*
intonō, -tonāre, -tonuī, *to thunder forth*
inuādō, -uādere, -uāsī, -uāsum, *to attack*
inueniō, -uenīre, -uēnī, -uentūrum, *to come upon, find*
inuidiōsus, -a, -um, *causing ill will, odious*
inuidus, -a, -um, *jealous*
inuīsus, -a, -um, *hated*
inuītus, -a, -um, *unwilling*
inūtilis, -e, *serving no good purpose, useless*
iō, interj., *(part of a ritual shout with* triumphe*)*
Īō, f., *Io, daughter of Inachus loved by Jupiter*
ipse, ipsa, ipsum, *-self, the very*
īra, -ae, f., *anger*
īrascor, -ī, *to become angry, fly into a rage*

158 Vocabulary

īrātus, -a, -um, *angry, enraged*
is, ea, id, *he, she, it; this, that*
Īsis, -idis, f., *Isis, an Egyptian goddess*
iste, ista, istud, *that, that of yours; that nasty*
ita, adv., *so, thus, in this way*
iterum, adv., *again*
iubeō, -ēre, iussī, iussum, *to order, bid; to demand*
iūcundus, -a, -um, *pleasant, delightful to be with*
iūdex, -icis, m., *judge, juror*
iugōsus, -a, -um, *hilly, mountainous*
iugum, -ī, n., *a yoke; a ridge, cliff*
iunctus, -a, -um (pple. of iungō), *closely associated, connected*
iungō, -ere, iūnxī, iūnctum, *to join; to yoke*
iurgium, -ī, n., *a quarrel; scolding, reproach*
iūs, iūris, n., *the law, legal sanction; legal authority, right; control*
iustus, -a, -um, *fair, just*
iuuenālis, -e, *youthful*
iuuencus, -ī, m., *a young bull, bullock*
iuuenis, -is, m., *a young man*
iuuō, -āre, iūuī, iūtum, *to help, aid; to delight, please;* impers. + acc., *it delights, pleases*

L

lābellum, -ī, n., *a lip*
labor, -ōris, m., *work, toil, task*
lābor, -ī, lāpsus sum, *to slip, fall; to slip by*
labōrō (1), *to labor, toil; to have difficulty, be anxious*
lacertus, -ī, m., *the arm, esp. the upper arm*
lacrima (lacruma), -ae, f., *a tear*
lacrimō (1), *to cry, shed tears*

lacrimōsus, -a, -um, *teary, drippy*
laedō, -ere, laesī, laesum, *to injure, harm*
laesus, -a, -um: pple. of laedō
laetus, -a, -um, *happy*
Lāis, -idis, f., *Lais, a famous Greek courtesan*
lānificus, -a, -um, *wool-working, spinning*
laniō (1), *to tear to pieces*
lānūgō, -inis, f., *soft hair or down*
Lar, -ris, m., *the protective deity of the hearth and home; home*
lascīuia, -ae, f., *playfulness; licentious behavior*
lascīuus, -a, -um, *lewd, lustful, naughty*
lassō (1), *to make tired, weary*
lassus, -a, -um, *tired, weary*
lātē, adv., *widely, far and wide, over a large area*
latebra, -ae, f., *a hiding place, concealment*
lateō, -ere, *to be concealed, lie hidden*
latus, -a, -um, *wide*
latus, -eris, n., *side, flank, hip; the strength of the side of the upper body*
laudābilis, -e, *praiseworthy*
laudō (1), *to praise*
lauō, -ere, lāuī, lātum, *to wash*
laurus, -ī, f., *a laurel tree, crown of laurel; victory*
laus, -dis, f., *praise, cause of renown*
laxus, -a, -um, *loose, relaxed; wide open*
lectus, -ī, m., *a bed, couch*
Lēdē, -ēs, f., *Leda, mother by Jupiter of Helen, Clytemnestra, Castor, and Pollux*
legō, -ere, lēgī, lēctum, *to gather, collect, select; to read*

lēna, -ae, f., *a brothel-keeper, procurer*
lēnis, -e, *slow and quiet, slowly moving, gentle*
lēnō, -ōnis, m., *a pimp, procurer*
lentus, -a, -um, *resistant; slow*
leuis, -e, *light; trivial; gentle; insubstantial, thin*
leuō (1), *to raise; to relieve, ease*
lēx, -gis, f., *a law; rule, regulation, order*
līber, -era, -erum, *being a free man, free*
Līber, -erī, m., *Bacchus, god of wine; wine*
lībō (1), *to touch; to taste*
lībum, -ī, n., *a cake*
liceor, -ērī, licitus sum, *to bid for*
licet, -ēre, licuit, impers., + dat., *it is allowed*; with subjn., *although*
līcium, -ī, n., *a length of thread or cord*
lignum, -ī, n., *firewood; wood*
līmen, -inis, n., *a threshold, doorway*
lingua, -ae, f., *the tongue, language, eloquence*
liquidus, -a, -um, *gliding, flowing*
līs, lītis, f., *a dispute, lawsuit*
lītoreus, -a, -um, *of or situated by the seashore*
littera, -ae, f., *a letter, character*; pl., *writing; letter, missive*
līueō, -ēre, *to be black and blue*
līuidus, -a, -um, *black and blue, bruised*
līuor, -ōris, m., *envy, spite, malice*
locō (1), *to hire out*
locus, -ī, m. (pl., loca, -ōrum, n.) *a place*
longē, adv., *far, far off*
longus, -a, -um, *long, tall (= upwardly long)*

loquax, -ācis, *talkative; talking, expressive*
loquor, -ī, locūtus sum, *to speak*
lōrum, -ī, n., *a leather thong*; pl., *reins*
Lūcifer, -erī, m., *the morning star; morning, day*
Lucrētius, -ī, m., *T. Lucretius Carus, a first-century* BCE *Roman poet*
lucrōsus, -a, -um, *profitable*
lucrum, -ī, n., *a profit*
luctor (1), *to wrestle; to struggle*
lūdō, -ere, lūsī, lūsum, *to play; to amuse oneself with; to deceive*
lūmen, -inis, n., *light; eye*
lūna, -ae, f., *the moon*
Lūna, -ae, f., *Luna, goddess of the moon*
lūnō (1), *to make crescent-shaped, bend back*
lupāta, -ōrum, n. pl., *a bit with jagged teeth*
lūpus, -ī, m., *a wolf*
lūsus, -ūs, m., *a game; lovers' game*
lūx, -cis, f., *light*
Lycōris, -idis, f., *Lycoris, the mistress of the narrator in Gallus's elegies*
lyra, -ae, f., *a lyre*

M

madeō, -ēre, *to be wet; to be drunk*
madidus, -a, -um, *wet, well moistened; drunk*
Maenalius, -a, -um, *of Mt. Maenalus in Arcadia; Arcadian*
Maenas, -adis, f., *a female follower of Bacchus, Bacchante, Maenad*
Maeonidēs, -ae, m., *offspring of Maeonia, the eastern part of Lydia; the Lydian, i.e., Homer*
maestus, -a, -um, *sad, grieving*
magis, adv., *more*

magister, -trī, m., *the commander of a military force; a teacher, schoolmaster*
magnificus, -a, -um, *splendid, excellent*
magnus, -a, -um, *big, great*
magus, -a, -um, *magic*
maior, -ius, comp., *greater*
male, adv., *badly, basely; barely*
malignus, -a, -um, *ill-disposed, grudging*
malus, -a, -um, *bad, evil, base*
mandō (1), *to order, command, bid*
māne, adv., *in the morning*
maneō, -ēre, mānsī, mānsūrum, *to remain, stay*
manifestus, -a, -um, *clear, visible, evident*
manō (1), *to trickle*
manus, -ūs, f., *the hand; band (of men)*
marceō, -ēre, *to wither, droop, be feeble*
mare, -is, n., *the sea*
margō, -inis, m., *a rim; border, edge; margin*
marītus, -ī, m., *a husband*
Mars, -tis, m., *Mars, god of war; war*
māter, -tris, f., *mother*
māteria, -ae, f., *building material; material, subject matter*
māteriēs, -eī, f.: see māteria
māternus, -a, -um, *of a mother*
medicō (1), *to treat, medicate (with); dye (with)*
medius, -a, -um, *mid-, middle (of)*
mel, mellis, n., *honey*
melior, -ius, *better*
melius, adv., *better*
membrum, -ī, n., *a part of the body, limb, member*
meminī, -isse (defective), *to remember*
memor, -oris, *mindful, remembering*

Memnōn, -onis, m., *Memnon, king of Ethiopia*
Menandros, -ī, m., *Menander, a fourth-century BCE Greek comic poet*
menda, -ae, f., *a fault; defect, blemish*
mēns, -tis, f., *the mind; intention*
mēnsa, -ae, f., *a table*
mercābilis, -e, *able to be purchased, for sale*
mercēs, -ēdis, f., *a price, payment*
mereō, -ēre, meruī, meritum, *to earn, deserve*
meretrix, -icis, f., *a courtesan, kept woman*
meritō, adv., *deservedly, duly, rightfully*
meritum, -ī, n., *due reward; meritorius action, service*
meritus, -a, -um, *deserved; deserving*
merus, -a, -um, *pure, undiluted;* as a noun, merum, -ī, n., *wine unmixed with water*
merx, -cis, f., *merchandise, goods*
metuō, -ere, metuī, *to fear, be afraid of*
metus, -ūs, m., *fear*
meus, -a, -um, *my, mine*
mīles, -itis, m., *a soldier*
mīlia, -um, n. pl., *thousands*
mīlitia, -ae, f., *military service*
mīlitō (1), *to serve as a soldier*
mille, indecl., *thousand, one thousand*
minae, -ārum, f. pl., *threats*
Minerua, -ae, f., *Minerva, goddess of wisdom and warfare*
minimus, -a, -um, *smallest; youngest; lowest*
ministerium, -ī, n., *the activity of a servant, service; support; duty*
ministra, -ae, f., *a maidservant; an accomplice*
ministrō (1), *to serve*

minium, -ī, n., *cinnabar (used for red dye and medicine)*
minuō, -ere, minuī, minūtum, *to reduce, make thin; to lessen, diminish*
minus, adv., *less; not*
mīror (1), *to express wonder, marvel (at)*
misceō, -ēre, miscuī, mixtum, *to mix*
miser, -era, -erum, *unhappy, wretched*
mitis, -e, *mild, soft, ripe*
mittō, -ere, mīsī, missum, *to send (off), let go*
moderābilis, -e, *controlled, controllable*
modestus, -a, -um, *respectful, unassuming*
modicus, -a, -um, *moderate (in amount)*
modo, adv., *only; recently, just*
modo . . . modo, *at one time . . . at another*
modus, -ī, m., *a way, method; rhythm*
mōlior, -īrī, mōlītus sum, *to set in motion (with effort)*
molliō, -īre, mollīuī, mollītum, *to soften; to weaken*
mollis, -e, *soft, tender; gentle*
moneō, -ēre, monuī, monitum, *to warn, advise*
monīle, -is, n., *a necklace*
monimentum (monumentum), -ī, n., *an example*
mōns, -tis, m., *a mountain*
monstrō (1), *to show; to show how to (+ inf.)*
mora, -ae, f., *a delay*
morbus, -ī, m., *disease*
morior, -ī, mortuus sum, *to die*
moror (1), *to delay, keep waiting; to hold the attention of; to last, linger*
mors, -tis, f., *death*
mortālis, -e, *mortal, belonging to man*
mōs, -ris, m., *practice, custom, usage, habit;* pl., *character*
mōtus, -ūs, m., *a movement, motion*
moueō, -ēre, mōuī, mōtum, *to move, set in motion, shake; to disturb, disarrange; to affect; to direct*
mox, adv., *soon, after a short time*
mulier, -ris, f., *a woman*
multum, adv., *much, greatly*
multus, -a, -um, *much, great is size;* pl., *many*
mūnīmen, -inis, n., *defense, fortification*
mūnus, -eris, n., *a gift; a gift in payment*
Mūsa, -ae, f., *a Muse, goddess of music, literature and the arts; genius, inspiration*
mustum, -ī, n., *the juice of the grape*
mūtō (1), *to change*
myrtus, -ī, m./f., *myrtle, a flowering plant with fragrant white blossoms and blue-black berries containing several seeds*

N
nam, conj., *for*
Napē, -ēs, f., *Nape, Corinna's maidservant*
narrō (1), *to tell, talk*
nāscor, -ī, nātus sum, *to be born (for)*
Nāsō, -ōnis, m., *Naso (Ovid's cognomen: Publius Ouidius Naso)*
nātīuus, -a, -um, *natural, real*
nāuita, -ae, m., *a sailor, seaman*
nē, conj., (+ subjn.), *so that . . . not, lest;* (as the negative in prohibitions and wishes)
nec, conj., *and . . . not;*
nec . . . nec, *neither . . . nor*
nectō, -ere, nexī, nexum, *to weave, bind*

neglegō, -legere, -lexī, -lectum, *to disregard (one's dress, appearance, etc.)*
negō (1), *to say . . . not, refuse; to refuse to give, withhold*
nēmō, -inis, m., *no one, nobody*
nempe, adv., *of course, certainly*
neque, conj., *and . . . not;* neque . . . neque, *neither . . . nor*
nequīquam, adv., *in vain, for nothing*
neruus, -ī, m., *a muscle, nerve; a cord, string*
nesciō, -scīre, -scīvī, -scītum, *to not know, be ignorant of*
nescioquis, nescioquid, *some unknown, some unimportant*
nescius, -a-, -um, *not knowing, ignorant*
nēue, conj., = et nē, *and so that . . . not*
neuter, -tra, -trum, *neither (of two)*
nexilis, -e, *woven together*
niger, -gra, -grum, *dark in color, black*
nihil (nīl), n., indecl., *nothing;* adv., *not at all*
nimbus, -ī, m., *a rain cloud; shower, rain*
nimium, n., *too much;* adv., *too, excessively*
nisi, conj., *if not, unless; except*
niteō, -ēre, nituī, *to shine, sparkle*
nix, niuis, f., *snow*
nocens, -ntis, *injurious, harmful; guilty*
noceō, -ēre, nocuī, + dat., *to hurt, cause harm*
nocturnus, -a, -um, *at night, of the night*
nōlō, nōlle, nōluī, *to not wish, to be unwilling*
nōmen, -inis, n., *a name*
nōn, adv., *not*
nōndum, adv., *not yet*

nōnne (asks a question that expects a "yes" answer)
nōnnumquam, adv., *sometimes*
nōs, *we (I)*
nōscō, -ere, nōuī, nōtum, *to get to know;* in perf. tense, *to know;* + inf., *know how (to)*
noster, -tra, -trum, *our*
nota, -ae, f., *a mark; signal, sign*
notō (1), *to mark, brand, scar; to notice; to inscribe*
Notus, -ī, m., *the south wind*
nōtus, -a, -um (pple. of noscō), *known, well-known*
nouem, indecl., *nine*
nouus, -a, -um, *new*
nox, -ctis, f., *the night*
nūbes, -is, f., *a cloud*
nūbilum, -ī, n., *darkness; cloud*
nūbō, -ere, nupsī, nuptum, + dat., *to marry*
nūdus, -a, -um, *naked, exposed; unadorned*
nullus, -a, -um, *not any, no; no one*
num (asks a question that expects a "no" answer)
nūmen, -inis, n., *a divinity, deity*
numerō (1), *to count; to count out (money) as payment*
numerus, -ī, m., *a number; meter*
nunc, adv., *now*
nūper, adv., *not long ago, recently*
nūsquam, adv., *nowhere, not . . . anywhere*
nūtrix, -īcis, f., *a nurse*
nūtus, -ūs, m., *a nod; nod of agreement*

O

obiciō, -icere, -iēcī, -iectum, *to throw up (to), reproach; to charge, accuse*
oblīquus, -a, -um, *slanting*

oborior, -orīrī, -ortus sum, *to spring up, arise*
obsideō, -sidēre, -sēdī, -sessum, *to beseige*
obstipēscō, -stipēscere, -stipuī, *to be struck dumb, be stunned*
obstō, -stāre, -stitī, -stātūrum, *to block, hinder*
obsum, -esse, -fuī, + dat., *to be a hindrance (to), be a nuisance (to)*
obuius, -a, -um, *so as to meet or confront,* + dat.
occulō, -culere, -culuī, -cultum, *to hide, conceal*
occultē, adv., *secretly*
ōceanus, -ī, m., *the ocean*
ocellus, -ī, m., *a (little) eye*
oculus, -ī, m., *an eye*
ōdī, -isse, ōsum, defective, *to hate*
officium, -ī, n., *a service, duty; ceremony, rite*
Olympus, -ī, m., *Mount Olympus, a lofty mountain on the borders of Thessaly and Macedonia, home of the gods*
ōmen, -inis, n., *an omen, augury; ill omen*
omnis, omne, *all, every, each*
onerō (1), *to weigh down, overload*
onus, -eris, n., *a load, burden*
oppositus, -a, -um, *forming a barrier, hostile*
ops, opis, f., *might, ability; aid, help; resources; wealth*
optō (1), *to wish, desire*
opus, -eris, n., *work, task; purpose;*
opus est, + abl., idiom, *there is need of*
ōra, -ae, f., *the edge, border*
orbis, -is, m., *a disc, any disk-shaped object; wheel; ringlet; orb (of a planet); the world, earth*

ōrdō, -inis, m., *a row, series, succession; social status, class; order, assigned position*
Orestēs, -is, m., *Orestes, son of Agamemnon and Clytemnestra*
orior, -īrī, ortus sum, *to rise, arise, begin*
Ōrīthyīa, -ae, f., *Orithyia, daughter of Erectheus, king of Athens*
ornātrix, -icis, f., *a servant who arranges one's hair*
ornō (1), *to decorate, beautify; to arrange (hair); to equip*
ōrō (1), *to pray (for), beg, ask*
ortus, -ūs, m., *the coming into being, rising*
ōs, ōris, n., *the mouth, face, expression, speech* (pl. common for sg.)
os, ossis, n., *a bone*
osculum, -ī, n., *a kiss*
ōtium, -ī, n., *leisure*
ouis, -is, f., *a sheep, ewe*
ōuum, -ī, n., *an egg*

P

paciscor, -i, pactus sum, *to negotiate, seek through bargaining*
pactus, -a, -um: pple. of pangō
paelex, -icis, f., *a mistress, rival*
pāgina, -ae, f., *a page*
palla, -ae, f., *mantle, cloak*
pallium, -ī, n., *a coverlet; cloak*
pandō, -ere, passum, *to spread; to open*
pandus, -a, -um, *spreading round in a wide curve*
pangō, -ere, pepigī, pactum, *to make a pact (for)*
papilla, -ae, f., *a nipple, breast*
pār, paris, *equal*
parātus, -a, -um (pple. of parō), *ready, prepared*

parcō, -ere, pepercī, *to spare, be sparing (to)* + dat.; *to refrain from* + inf.
parcus, -a, -um, *sparing, thrifty*
parēns, -ntis, m./f., *a parent; ancestor*
parentō (1), *to make an offering to the dead, esp. relatives*
Parius, -a, -um, *of the island of Paros*
parō (1), *to prepare, plan, intend; to obtain*
pars, -tis, f., *a part; a party, side (in war or politics)*
parum, n., *too little, not enough*; adv. *too little*
parvus, -a, -um, *small*
pascor, -ī, *to feed, graze*
pateō, -ēre, patuī, *to be open; to spread out*
pater, -tris, m., *a father; ancestor*
paternus, -a, -um, *of a father, ancestral*
patiens, -ntis, *long-suffering, patient; hardy*
patior, -ī, passus sum, *to suffer, bear, endure; to allow, permit; to leave alone, let be*
paucī, -ae, -a, *few, a few*
pauidus, -a, -um, *terror-struck, frightened, anxious*
pauper, -eris, *poor*
pāx, -cis, f., *peace*
pecten, -inis, m., *a comb*
pectus, -oris, n., *the chest, breast; heart, soul*
pecus, -dis, f., *any lifestock animal (esp. sheep)*
pellō, -ere, pepulī, pulsum, *to beat, strike; to drive away, repel*
pendeō, -ere, pependī, *to be suspended, hang; to hang down*
Pēnelopē, -ēs, f., *Penelope, wife of Odysseus*

penitus, adv., *in the innermost part; deeply, thoroughly*
pensum, -ī, n., *an allotment of wool to be spun*
per, prep. + acc., *through, along, over; by*
peragō, -agere, -ēgī, -āctum, *to chase; to complete; to go through (space or time); to live out, complete*
perarō (1), *to plow through; to incise, inscribe*
percellō, -cellere, -culī, -culsum, *to strike, knock down, wound*
perdō, -ere, peperdī, perditum, *to destroy; to waste*
perennis, -e, *lasting through the year; lasting, durable*
pereō, -īre, -iī, -itum, *to perish, die*
perferō, -ferre, -tulī, -lātum, *to carry straight to; to endure*
perfidus, -a, -um, *treacherous, deceitful*
periūrium (pēiūrium), -ī, n., *a false oath, lie*
periūrō (pēierō) (1), *to swear a false oath*
periūrus (pēiūrus), -a, -um, *oath-breaking*
perlegō, -legere, -lēgī, -lectum, *to read all the way through*
perpetior, -petī, -pessus sum, *to bear to the end, endure*
perpetuus, -a, -um, *continuous, unremitting*
peruigil, -ilis, *keeping watch all night, awake*
peruigilō (1), *to stay awake all night*
pēs, pedis, m., *the foot*
pessimus, -a, -um, *worst*
petō, -ere, petīuī, petītum, *to seek, look for; to attack*

pharetra, -ae, f., *a quiver*
pharetrātus, -a, -um, *wearing a quiver*
Phoebus, -ī, m., *Phoebus (Apollo, god of the sun and the arts); the sun*
Phrygius, -a, -um, *of Phrygia, Phrygian; Trojan*
Pīeris, -idos, f., *a daughter of Pierus, i.e., a Muse*
pingō, -ere, pinxī, pictum, *to paint, color, depict*
pinguis, -e, *fat, rich, luxuriant, fertile*
pinna, -ae, f. *a feather, wing*
placeō, -ēre, placuī placitum, + dat., *to please, be pleasing (to); to find favor (with)*
plānus, -a, -um, *flat*
plaudō, -ere, plausī, plausum, *to clap, applaud (for)*
plebs, plēbis, f., *the common people*
plectō, -ere, *to beat; to punish*
plēnus, -a, -um, *full, filled (with)*
plūma, -ae, f., *a feather; mass of feathers*
plūs, plūris, n., *more*
plūrēs, -a, *more in number, several*
poculum, -ī, n., *a cup*
poena, -ae, f., *a penalty, punishment*
pollex, -icis, m., *a thumb*
pompa, -ae, f., *a procession, parade*
pōmum, -ī, n., *a fruit*
pōnō, -ere, posuī, positum, *to put, place; to put down or aside*
pontus, -ī, n., *the sea*
pōpuleus, -a, -um, *of the poplar tree*
populus, -ī, m., *people, the people*
porrigō, -rigere, -rēxī, -rēctum, *to stretch forth, extend*
porta, -ae, f., *a gate*
portō (1), *to carry, bear*
poscō, -ere, poposcī, *to ask for, demand*
possideō, -sidēre, -sēdī, -sessum, *to have in one's control, hold, occupy*
possum, posse, potuī, irreg., *to be able; to have power*
post, prep. + acc., *after, behind*
postis, -is, m., *a doorjamb; door*
postmodo, adv., *later, presently*
potēns, -ntis, *powerful*
potentia, -ae. f., *the power, potency*
praebeō, -bēre, -buī, -bitum, *to display, show; to give, offer, supply*
praeceps, -ipitis, *rushing headlong*
praecipuē, adv., *especially*
praeda, -ae, f., *booty, plunder; prey*
praedor (1), *to rob, plunder, take as prey*
praegustō (1), *to taste before*
praemium, -ī, n., *a reward*
praeripiō, -ripere, -ripuī, -reptum, *to seize first, snatch away*
praestō, -stāre, -stitī, -stātum, *to bring to bear, apply*
praeter, prep. + acc., *except, in addition to*
praetereō, -īre, -iī, -itum, *to go past*
precor (1), *to pray for, beg*
pre(he)ndō, -ere, pre(he)ndī, pre(he)nsum, *to catch, round up*
premō, -ere, pressī, pressum, *to press, press upon; to oppress, crush; to be on top of, ride; to cover*
pretium, -ī, n., *a price, recompense, fee*
prex, -cis, f., *an entreaty, prayer*
Priamēis, -idos, f., *a daughter of Priam, i.e., Cassandra*
prīmum, adv., *first*
prīmus, -a, -um, *first*
prior, -us, *earlier, the first*
prō, prep. + abl., *for, on behalf of; in accordance with; in place of*
proauus, -ī, m., *a great-grandfather*

probō (1), *to approve (of), esteem; to regard as right and proper*
procul, adv., *far, far away*
prōcumbō, -cumbere, -cubuī, -cubitum, *to lie outstretched (in worship)*
prōditiō, -ōnis, f., *a betrayal, abandonment (of a cause)*
prōdō, -dere, -didī, -ditum, *to thrust forward, betray*
proelium, -ī, n., *a battle, conflict*
profiteor, -fitērī, -fessus sum, *to declare, claim*
prōiciō, -icere, -iēcī, -iectum, *to cast forth, throw out, fling to the ground*
prōmissum, -ī, n., *a promise*
properō (1), *to act with haste, be quick; to hurry, rush*
prōpōnō, -pōnere, -posuī, -positum, *to put forth; to set up as an intention*
prosequor, -sequī, -secūtus sum, *to follow, accompany*
prostituō, -stituere, -stituī, -stitūtum, *to prostitute, put to an unworthy use; to dishonor*
prostō, -stāre, -stitī, -stitum, *to offer oneself for sale*
prōsum, prōdesse, prōfuī, + dat., irreg., *to be of use (to), benefit, help; to be beneficial (to do something)* + inf.
prōtegō, -tegere, -texī, -tectum, *to cover, conceal; to protect*
proteruus, -a, -um, *bold, shameless*
prōtinus, adv., *immediately*
prōueniō, -uenīre, -uēnī, -uentūrum, *to come forth; to come about, turn out*
proximus, -a, -um, *nearest, next, immediately following*
pruinōsus, -a, -um, *full of frost, frosty*

pudīcus, -a, -um, *pure, chaste*
pudor, -ōris, m., *a sense of shame; decency, chastity*
puella, -ae, f., *a girl*
puer, -ī, m., *a child, boy; young male slave*
pugnō (1), *to fight*
pulsō (1), *to strike repeatedly*
puluerulentus, -a, -um, *covered with dust*
pūpula, -ae, f., *a little girl; the pupil of the eye*
purpureus, -a, -um, *crimson, rosy-red; glowing*
pūrus, -a, -um, *spotless, clean; faultless, innocent; clear*
putō (1), *to think, consider*

Q

quā, adv., *by what road, by which route*
quaerō, -rere, quaesīuī, quaesītus, *to seek, demand, require, ask*
quālis, -e, interr. adj., *what kind of?* rel. adj., *such a; such as*
quāliscumque, quālecumque, *such as (one) is*
quāliter, adv., *as, just as*
quam, adv., *how!*
quamlibet, adv., *however, in whatever degree*
quamuis, conj., *although*
quandō, interr., *at what time? when?* indefinite adv., *at any time, sometimes, ever*
quantus, -a, -um, interr. *how much? how great?*
quasi, conj., *as if, as though*
-que, enclitic, *and;* -que . . . -que, *both . . . and*
queror, -ī, questus sum, *to complain (about), protest*

quī, quae, quod, relative pron., *who, which, that*; interr. adj., *which? what?*
quia, conj., *because*
quīcumque, quaecumque, quodcumque, indefinite pron./adj., *whoever, whatever*
quid, interr., *what?* (see quis, quid); *why?; well?*
quīdam, quaedam, quiddam, *a certain*
quidem, adv., *indeed*
quiēscō, -ere, quiēuī, quiētum, *to sleep, rest, do nothing*
quīn, adv., *indeed, in fact;* + subjn., *but that, from*
quīnque, indecl., *five*
Quirīs, -ītis, m., *a citizen of Rome*
quis, quid, interr. pron., *who? what?*
quis, qua/quae, quid, indefinite pron., *someone, anyone, something, anything;* indefinite adj., *any, some*
quisque, quaeque, quidque, *each one*
quisquis, quicquid, indefinite rel. pron., *any who, whoever, whatever*
quīuīs, quaeuīs, quiduīs, pron., *anyone or anything at all*
quō, interr., *(to) where?*
quod, conj., *because; the fact that*
quondam, adv., *formerly, once, in the past*
quoque, adv., *also*
quot, interr., *how many?*
quotiēns, interr., *how often? how many times?*

R

rādō, -ere, rāsī, rāsum, *to scratch; to inscribe*
rāmus, -ī, m., *a branch*
rapidus, -a, -um, *swift*
rapīna, -ae, f., *forcible removal of property, plunder*
rapiō, -ere, rapuī, raptus, *to seize, seize and carry off; to ravish*
rārus, -a, -um, *thin, flimsy; rare*
ratiō, -ōnis, f., *a reckoning, calculation; reason, sense*
ratis, -is, f., *a ship, craft*
raucus, -a, -um, *hoarse, screechy, noisy*
recēns, -ntis, *recent, newly arrived; newly shed; recently caught; fresh*
recingō, -cingere, -cinxī, -cinctum, *to unbelt, ungird, loosen*
recipiō, -cipere, -cēpī, -ceptum, *to receive, make welcome*
recompōnō, -pōnere, -posuī, -positum, *to put back together; to arrange harmoniously*
recuruō (1), *to bend back; to turn back*
reddō, -dere, -didī, -ditum, *to give back, return, deliver, render; to discharge (a vow)*
redeō, -īre, -iī, -itūrum, irreg., *to come or go back, return*
redimiō, -imīre, -imiī, -imītum, *to encircle with a garland, wreathe around*
redimō, -imere, -ēmī, -emptum, *to buy back*
reditus, -ūs, m., *a return, revenue;* reditū esse, *to yield a monetary return*
referciō, -fercīre, -fersī, -fertum, *to cram or stuff full*
referō, -ferre, rettulī, relātum, irreg., *to bring back, give in return; to recall; to relate, report*
refertus, -a, -um: pple. of referciō
refugiō, -fugere, -fūgī, *to flee from*
rēgnō (1), *to rule, reign; to be in control*
rēgnum, -ī, n., *a kingdom*

168 Vocabulary

reiciō, -icere, -iēcī, -iectum, *to throw back or away; to reject with scorn, spurn*
relaxō (1), *to loosen, open*
relentescō, -ere, *to become less ardent, slacken off*
releuō (1), *to lighten, relieve*
religō (1), *to tie up, bind fast*
relinquō, -linquere, -līquī, -lictum, *to leave, leave behind, abandon*
remoueō, -mouēre, -mōuī, -mōtum, *to move away, remove*
renouō (1), *to restore, refresh, renew (with planting)*
reparābilis, -e, *able to be recovered or restored*
repellō, -pellere, reppulī, repulsum, *to push or drive away, repel*
rependō, -pendere, -pendī, -pensum, *to balance out, compensate*
reperiō, -perīre, -perrī, -pertum, *to find, discover*
repertor, -ōris, m., *a discoverer*
requiescō, -quiescere, -quiēuī, -quiētum, *to rest, take a rest; to rest in the grave*
rēs, -eī, f., *thing, matter, situation; fact reality*
resānescō, -sānescere, -sānuī, *to be healed*
rescrībō, -scrībere, -scrīpsī, -scrīptum, *to write back*
resecō, -secāre, -secuī, -sectum, *to cut, cut back*
resīdō, -sīdere, -sēdī, *to sit down, sink down, shrink*
respiciō, -spicere, -spexī, -spectum, *to look again, look back up*
restō, -stāre, -stitī, *to stop*
resurgō, -gere, -rēxī, -rēctum, *to rise again*
rēte, -tis, n., *a net, trap*

retineō, -tinēre, -tinuī, -tentum, *to hold back, check, restrain*
retorqueō, -torquēre, -torsī, -tortum, *to twist around or back, pull backward*
reuocō (1), *to summon back; to recall (to active duty)*
reus, -ī, m., *a defendant, the accused; the guilty party*
rēx, -gis, m., *a king*
Rhēsus, -ī, m., *Rhesus, an ally of Troy from Thrace*
rhombus, -ī, m., *an instrument whirled on a string*
rīdeō, -ēre, rīsī, rīsūrum, *to laugh, smile*
rigeō, -ēre, *to be unbending, be unmoved*
rigidus, -a, -um, *stiff, hard, unbending; rough*
rīpa, -ae, f., *bank of a river*
rītū, + gen., *in the manner of, like*
rīuālis, -is, m., *a rival (esp. in love)*
rōbur, -oris, n., *an oak tree; a hard wood; strength*
rōdō, -ere, rōsī, rōsum, *to gnaw, eat away; to erode*
rogō (1), *to ask (for);* + double acc., *to ask (x) for (y)*
Rōma, -ae, f., *Rome*
rōs, -ōris, m., *the dew*
rosa, -ae, f., *a rose*
roscidus, -a, -um, *dewy, moist with dew*
roseus, -a, -um, *rose-colored*
rota, -ae, f., *a wheel*
rubeō, -ēre, *to become red; to blush*
rubor, -ōris, m., *redness, shame*
rūga, -ae, f., *a wrinkle*
rūgōsus, -a, -um, *wrinkled*
rusticitās, -ātis, f., *a provincial nature, lack of sophistication*

S

Sabīnus, -a, -um, *Sabine, of the Sabines, an ancient people living northeast of Rome*
sacer, -cra, -crum, *holy, religious*
sacrilegus, -a, -um, *guilty of impiety or sacrilege*
saepe, adv., *often*
saeuus, -a, -um, *fierce, savage*
sagitta, -ae, f., *an arrow*
Samēramis, -idis, f., *Sameramis, a legendary queen of Assyria and daughter of a Syrian goddess*
sanctus, -a, -um, *holy*
sanguinulentus, -a, -um, *accompanied by bloodshed; blood-red*
sanguis, -inis, m., *blood*
sapiō, -ere, sapīuī, *to taste; to think, be wise, be sensible*
satis, n., indecl., *enough;* adv., *enough*
saucius, -a, -um, *wounded*
saxum, -ī, n., *a stone*
scelus, -eris, n., *a crime*
Schoenēis, -idos, f., *daughter of Schoeneus, i.e., Atalanta*
scindō, -ere, scicidī, scissum, *to tear apart*
sciō, -īre, scīuī, scītum, *to know*
scrībō, -ere, scrīpsī, scrīptum, *to write*
scrīptum, -ī, n., *an inscription; writing*
secundus, -a, -um, *following; second (to), second-rate*
secūrus, -a, -um, *free from fear, confident*
sed, conj., *but*
sedeō, -ēre, sēdī, sessūrum, *to sit, stay fixed*
sēdulus, -a, -um, *attentive, careful*
sēgnis, -e, *disinclined to exert oneself, inactive, slow-moving*
sēligō, -ligere, -lēgī, -lectum, *to pick out, choose*
sēmiadapertus, -a, -um, *half-open*
sēmisupīnus, -a, -um, *half-reclining on one's back*
semper, adv., *always*
senecta, -ae, f., *old age*
senectūs, -ūtis, f., *old age*
senescō, -ere, senuī, *to grow old, deteriorate*
senex, -is, m., *an old man;* adj. *old*
senīlis, -e, *of an old man, in old age, aged*
senior, -ius, comparative adj. of *senex*
sentiō, -īre, sensī, sensum, *to feel, experience; to perceive by one of the senses*
sēparō (1), *to sever, separate*
septemplex, -icis, *sevenfold*
sepulcrum, -ī, n., *a tomb, grave*
sequor, -ī, secūtus sum, *to follow, pursue; to side with; to go with, accompany*
sera, -ae, f., *a bar, bolt*
Sēres, -um, m. pl., *the Chinese or their neighbors*
sermō, -ōnis, m., *one's words, speech*
seruitium, –i, n., *slavery, service*
seruō (1), *to guard, keep under observation, watch*
seruus, -ī, m., *a slave*
seruus, -a, -um, *subject to servitude*
sex, indecl., *six*
sī, conj., *if*
sīc, adv., *thus, in this way*
siccus, -a, -um, *dry, desiccated*
sīdus, -eris, n., *a heavenly body, star*
signum, -ī, n., *a sign, mark, indication; sign of the zodiac; military standard*
sileō, -ēre, siluī, *to make no sound, be silent*

silex, -icis, n., *flint; any hard rock*
silua, -ae, f., *the woods, forest*
similis, -e, *like, similar (to)*
Simoīs, -entis, m., *the Simois, a tributary of the River Scamander at Troy*
simplex, icis, *simple, free from complication*
simplicitās, -ātis, f., *simplicity; lack of sophistication, ignorance*
simulācrum, -ī, n., *an image, likeness*
simulō (1), *to pretend; to produce, simulate, feign*
simultās, -ātis, f., *hostility, a quarrel*
sine, prep. + abl., *without*
singulus, -a, -um, *single, separate, one at a time*
sinō, -ere, sīuī, situm, *to let, allow, permit*
sinuōsus, -a, -um, *bent, curved*
sinus, -ūs, m., *a curve, curl; fold (of toga); lap, bosom*
sitis, -is, f., *thirst, lack of drink*
situs, -ūs, m., *neglect, disuse; rot, mold*
sōbrius, -a, -um, *not intoxicated, sober, sensible*
socius, -a, -um, *keeping company with; shared, in common;* (mil.) *allied*
sōl, sōlis, m., *the sun*
soleō, -ēre, solitus sum, *to be accustomed*
solidus, -a, -um, *solid, tight-packed, firm*
sollemnis, -e, *yearly; solemn, religious*
sollers, -rtis, *skilled, clever*
sollicitō (1), *to harass, attack*
sollicitus, -a, -um, *anxious, troubled, in turmoil*
soluō, -luere, -luī, -lūtum, *to loosen, undo; to settle* or *discharge (a debt)*

sōlus, -a, -um, *alone*
somnus, -ī, m., *sleep*
sonō, -āre, sonuī, sonitum, *to make a noise*
Sophoclēus, -a, -um, *of Sophocles*
sōpiō, -īre, sōpīuī, sōpītum, *to cause or lull to sleep; to render senseless*
sopōrātus, -a, -um, *lulled to sleep, asleep*
sordēs, -is, f., *dirt, stain, baseness*
sordidus, -a, -um, *filthy, foul, tarnished by greed*
soror, -ōris, f., *a sister*
sors, -tis, f., *lot, fortune, fate*
spargō, -ere, sparsī, sparsum, *to scatter*
spatiōsus, -a, -um, *ample, long*
spectābilis, -e, *outstanding in appearance, noteworthy*
spectō (1), *to watch, look at*
speculātor, -ōris, m., *a scout, spy*
speculum, -ī, n., *a mirror*
spērō (1), *to hope*
spēs, -eī, f., *hope*
spīculum, -ī, n., *a sharply pointed weapon like a spear or arrow*
spissus, -a, -um, *thick, dense*
splendidus, -a, -um, *bright, shiny; spotless*
spolium, -ī, n., *spoils (of war), booty*
spondeō, -ēre, spopondī, sponsum, *to pledge to pay a bond/surety (in court)*
sponte, abl. sg. as adv., *naturally, by nature; voluntarily*
statiō, -ōnis, f., *the usual position; military position of alert*
stella, -ae, f., *a star*
sternō, -ere, strāuī, strātum, *to spread out; to strike down with a blow, lay low*
stillō (1), *to drip*

stipula, -ae, f., *stalks left as stubble after the reaping*
stō, -āre, stetī, statūrum, *to stand*
strātum, -ī, n., *bedding, coverlet; (often in pl.) bed*
strēnuus, -a, -um, *prompt, vigorous*
stringō, -ere, strinxī, strictum, *to bare, unsheathe; to skim, brush*
strix, -gis, f., *a screech owl*
studium, -ī, n., *zeal, ardor, devotion*
suādeō, -ēre, suāsī, suāsum, *to recommend, urge*
sub, prep. + abl., *under, beneath;* + acc., *up under, beneath, at the foot of*
subdūcō, -dūcere, -dūxī, -ductum, *to take away, remove; to reduce*
subeō, -īre, -iī, -itum, irreg., *to come up, approach; to steal in, sneak up; to undergo, endure*
subiciō, -icere, -iēcī, -iectum, *to throw or place or set under or near*
subiectus, -a, -um (pple. of subiciō), *lying close (to)*
subitus, -a, -um, *sudden, unexpected*
sublīmis, -e, *lofty, elevated*
sublūceō, -lūcēre, *to shine faintly, glimmer*
subscrībō, -scrībere, -scrīpsī, -scrīptum, *to write at the bottom*
succurrō, -currere, -currī, -cursūrum, *to run/go under; to undergo; to come to mind*
sum, esse, fuī, futūrum, irreg., *to be*
summus, -a, -um, *very great, the greatest; the highest, the top of*
sūmō, -ere, sūmpsī, sūmptum, *to take*
sumptus, -ūs, m., *cost, expense*
super, prep. + acc., *over, above, on top of*
superbus, -a, -um, *proud, haughty, arrogant*

supercilium, -ī, n., *the eyebrow*
superō (1), *to conquer, overcome*
superstes, -itis, *surviving, remaining alive after death*
supersum, -esse, -fuī, *to remain*
supplex, -icis, *making humble entreaty*
supprimō, -primere, -pressī, -pressum, *to press down; to hold back, check*
suprēmus, -a, -um, *final*
surdus, -a, -um, *deaf*
surgō, -gere, -rēxī, -rēctum, *to get up, rise up, rise*
surripiō, -ripere, -ripuī, -reptum, *to steal; to snatch on the sly*
suspendium, -ī, n., *a hanging (of oneself, esp. suicide)*
suspendō, -pendere, -pendī, -pensum, *to hold up, check,*
suspicor (1), *to suspect, imagine*
sustineō, -tinēre, -tinuī, *to hold up, support, bear; to sustain;* + inf., *to allow (oneself)*
suus, -a, -um, *his, her, its, their (own)*
Sygamber, -bra, -brum, *of the Sugambri (a German tribe)*

T
tabella, -ae, f., *a flat board, tablet;* pl., *writing tablet*
tabula, -ae, f., *a tablet; legal document, will;* pl., *account books*
taceō, -ēre, tacuī, tacitum, *to be silent*
tacitus, -a, -um, *silent*
Tagus, -ī, m., *the Tagus River in Spain*
tālis, -e, *such (a), like this, of this kind*
tam, adv., *so, to such a degree;* tam ... quam, correlatives, *as ... as*
tamen, conj., *however, nevertheless, yet*
tamquam, adv., *just as, as if, as though*

tangō, -ere, tetigī, tāctum, *to touch*
tantum, adv., *only*
tantus, -a, -um, *so great, such a big*
tardus, -a, -um, *slow*
Tatius, -ī, m., *Tatius, king of the Sabines*
taurus, -ī, m., *a bull*
tectum, -ī, n., *a roof; a roofed building, house*
tectus, -a, -um (pple. of tegō), *covered, hidden, secret*
tegō, -ere, tēxī, tēctum, *to cover; to hide, conceal*
tēlum, -ī, n., *a weapon*
temerō (1), *to violate, desecrate*
temerārius, -a, -um, *reckless, impetuous*
temere, adv., *recklessly, without thought or reason; by chance*
Tempē, n.pl., *Tempe, the valley of the Peneus River between Mts. Ossa and Olympus in Thessaly*
temperō (1), *to control, regulate*
templum, -ī, n., *a sacred space; temple*
temptō (1), *to test; to attack*
tempus, -oris, n., *moment, hour, time; the side of the forehead, temple*
tendō, -ere, tetendī, tentum, *to extend, stretch forth, spread; to proceed*
tenebrae, -ārum, f. pl., *darkness*
Tenedos, -ī, f., *Tenedos, an island in the Aegean Sea*
teneō, -ēre, tenuī, tentum, *to hold, keep*
tener, -era, -erum, *tender, delicate, soft*
tenuis, -e, *slender, thin*
tenuō (1), *to make slender or thin*
tepidus, -a, -um, *warm*
ter, adv., *three times*
tergum, -ī, n., *the back, rear; hide*
terra, -ae, f., *earth, ground*

testificor (1), *to testify solemnly to*
testis, -is, m., *a witness*
thalamus, -ī, m., *the marriage bed; bedchamber*
Thēsēus, -ī, m., *Theseus, slayer of the Minotaur*
Thrācius (Thrēicius), -a, -um, *Thracian, of Thrace*
Tibullus, -ī, m., *Albius Tibullus, an elegiac poet of first-century BCE Rome*
tigris, -is, f., *a tiger*
timeō, -ēre, timuī, *to fear*
timidus, -a, -um, *fearful, timid, shy*
timor, -ōris, m., *fear*
tingō, -ere, tinxī, tinctum, *to color, tint*
Tithōnus, -ī, m., *Tithonus, husband of Aurora, given immortality without eternal youth*
Tītyrus, -ī, m., *Tityrus, a herdsman in pastoral poetry*
tollō, -ere, sustulī, sublātum, *to remove, take away*
torqueō, -ēre, torsī, tortum, *to twist, wrench; to torment, torture*
torrens, -ntis, m., *a rushing stream*
tortus, -a, -um, *twisted, coiled; rotating, whirling*
torus, -ī, m., *a couch, bed*
tot, indecl. adj., *so many*
totiens, adv., *so many times*
tōtus, -a, -um, *all, the whole*
trabs, -is, f., *a wooden beam*
tractō (1), *to handle, manipulate; to pluck*
trādō, -dere, -didī, -ditum, *to hand over, surrender*
trahō, -ere, trāxī, trāctum, *to drag, pull, draw*
trāiciō, -icere, -iēcī, -iectum, *to throw across; to pierce*

trānseō, -īre, -iī, -itūrum, irreg., *to cross, go across, cross over or through*
tremō, -ere, tremuī, *to tremble*
tribūnal, -ālis, n., *a platform fom which a Roman magistrate pronounced official judgments; a court of law*
tribuō, -ere, tribuī, tribūtum, *to grant, bestow, award*
tristis, -e, *sad, unhappy*
triumphō (1), *to triumph over; to celebrate a triumph, exhibit in a triumphal parade*
triuium, -ī, n. (often pl.), *a crossroads*
triumphus, -ī, m., *a triumph, the procession of a victorious Roman general*
Trōs, Trōis, m., *a Trojan*
tū, *you* (sg.)
tueor, -ērī, tuitus sum, *to look at, observe; to watch over, protect*
tumeō, -ēre, tumuī, *to swell, bulge*
tumidus, -a, -um, *swollen; enraged, violent*
tunc, adv., *then, at that time*
tundō, -ere, tutudī, tunsum, *to pound*
tunica, -ae, f., *a tunic, the standard gament of clothing*
turba, -ae, f., *a mob, crowd, throng*
turpis, -e, *foul; disgusting; shameful*
tūtus, -a, -um, *safe, secure*
tuus, -a, -um, *your* (sg.)
Tȳdīdēs, ae, m., *son of Tydeus, Diomedes*

V

uacca, -ae, f., *a cow*
uacō (1), *to be empty, be free (from)*
uacuus, -a, -um, *empty, hollow; carefree, available; devoid (of), free (from)* + abl.
uadimōnium, -ī, n., *a guarantee of appearance in court*
ualeō, -ēre, ualuī, *to be strong, be well; to have power, be effective;* ualē/ualēte, *Goodbye!*
uallēs, -is, f., *a valley*
uallum, -ī, n., *a palisade of stakes for fortification*
uānescō, -ere, *to melt away, vanish*
uānus, -a, -um, *empty, insubstantial*
uapor, -ōris, m., *steam; heat*
uariō (1), *to adorn with various colors*
Varrō, -ōnis, m., *Varro, a first-century Roman poet and translator*
uārus, -a, -um, *crooked, bent*
uātēs, -is, m., *prophet; bard, poet*
ubi, conj. *when;* interr., *where?*
ubīque, adv., *anywhere, everywhere*
ūdus, -a, -um, *wet*
-ue, enclitic, *or*
uehō, -ere, uexī, uectum, *to convey, carry, bring*
uel, conj., *or;* adv., *at least, actually;* uel . . . uel, *either . . . or*
uēlāmen, -inis, n., *a covering, garment*
uēlō (1), *to cover, veil, envelop*
uēlum, -ī, n., *a sail; fabric*
uēna, -ae, f., *a blood vessel; a supply, store*
uendō, -dere, -didī, -ditum, *to seek or offer to sell*
uenēnum, -ī, n., *poison*
uenia, -ae, f., *pardon, forgiveness*
ueniō, -īre, uēnī, uentūrum, *to come*
uenter, -ris, m., *stomach, belly*
uentilō (1), *to wave in the air, brandish*
uentus, -ī, m., *wind*
Venus, -eris, f., *Venus, goddess of sexual love and Cupid's mother; lovemaking*

uerber, -eris, n., *a whip; a beating or blow with a whip*
uerbōsus, -a, -um, *wordy, long-winded*
uerbum, -ī, n., *word*
uērē, adv., *really, truly*
uerēcundus, -a, -um, *bashful, modest, shy*
uerrō, -ere, uerrī, *to sweep, sweep over, skim*
uersō (1), *to turn, spin; to turn back and forth, twist; to torment*
uersus, -ūs, m., *a line of writing, line of verse*
uertex, -icis, m., *the topmost part; the top of the head*
uertō, -ere, uertī, uersum, *to cause to turn, spin; to change, change form*
uērum, conj., *but*
uērus, -a, -um, *true, real*
uēsānus, -a, -um, *wild, frenzied*
uester, -tra, -trum, *your* (pl.)
uestigium, -ī, n., *a footprint; any mark or print*
uestis, -is, f., *clothing, piece of clothing, garment*
uetō (1), *to forbid, prevent*
uetus, -eris, *ancient, old*
uexō (1), *to attack constantly*
uia, -ae, f., *a road, street; journey;* (mil.) *march*
uiātor, -ōris, m., *a traveler*
uibrō (1), *to move to and fro*
uīcīnus, -a, -um, *neighboring, close at hand*
uicis (gen.), f., *repayment, recompense*
uictor, -ōris, m., *the victor, conqueror, winner*
uictrīx, -cis, adj., *victorious, triumphant*
uideō, -ēre, uīdī, uīsum, *to see*

uideor, -ērī, uīsus sum, *to seem*
uigil, -ilis, m., *a sentry, guard*
uīlis, -e, *cheap, worthless; contemptible; of inferior rank*
uincō, -ere, uīcī, uictum, *to win, conquer, overcome*
uinculum (uinclum), -ī, n., *a chain, shackle*
uindex, -icis, m., *a champion, defender; avenger*
uindicta, -ae, f., *vengeance*
uīnum, -ī, n., *wine*
uiolentus, -a, -um, *violent, savage*
uiolō (1), *to profane, dishonor, do violence to*
uir, -ī, m., *a man, husband*
uirgineus, -a, -um, *maidenly, of a virgin*
uirgō, -inis, f., *a maiden*
uiridis, -e, *green, abounding in green vegetation*
uīrus, -ī, m., *a secretion*
uīs, uis, f., *violence, violent attack;* pl., *physical strength*
uiscus, -eris, n., *the internal organs; womb*
uītis, -is, f., *a vine*
uitium, -ī, n., *a flaw, defect*
uitreus, -a, -um, *glassy*
uītricus, -ī, m., *a stepfather*
uittātus, -a, -um, *wearing a ritual headband*
uīuō, -ere, uīxī, uīctūrum, *to live*
uīuus, -a, -um, *living, alive*
uix, adv., *scarcely, with difficulty*
ullus, -a, -um, *any*
ultimus, -a, -um, *last*
ultor, -ōris, m., *an avenger*
umbra, -ae, f., *shade, darkness, shadow, ghost; retirement*
ūmeō, -ēre, *to be wet*
umerus, -ī, m., *the shoulder*

umquam, adv., *ever, at some time*
unda, -ae, f., *a wave, water*
ūndēnī, -ae, -a, *eleven each, eleven at a time*
unguis, -is, m., *a fingernail; claw, talon*
ūnus, -a, -um, *one, a single, alone*
uocō (1), *to summon, call*
uolātilis, -e, *able to fly, fleeting*
uolitō (1), *to fly, fly about*
uolō (1), *to fly*
uolō, uelle, uoluī, irreg., *to wish, want, be willing*
uoluō, -ere, uoluī, uolūtum, *to roll*
uoluptās, -ātis, f., *delight, pleasure*
uōs, *you* (pl.)
uōtum, -ī, n., *a vow, prayer, wish*
uōx, -cis, f., *the voice; words*
urbs, -is, f., *city*
urgeō, -ēre, ursī, *to press, spur on; to insist*
urna, -ae, f., *a vessel for holding water, pitcher, urn*
ūrō, -ere, ussī, ustum, *to destroy by fire, set on fire, burn; to cause to burn with grief*

ūsque, adv., *all the way (to); continuously, constantly*
ūsus, -ūs, m., *use, employment; something useful; the right to use or enjoy; habit*
ut (utī), conj., + indicative, *as, just as, when;* + subjn., *so that, in order that, that; how*
uterque, utraque, utrumque, *each (of two), both*
ūtilis, ūtile, *useful*
ūtor, -ī, ūsus sum, + abl., *to use, enjoy, take advantage of*
ūua, -ae, f., *grape*
uulgus, -ī, n. (m.), *the common people; the multitude*
uulnus, -eris, n., *a wound*
uultur, uulturis, m., *vulture*
uxor, -ōris, f., *a wife*

Z
Zephyrus, -ī, m., *the west wind*
zōna, -ae, f., *a girdle, belt*

Bibliography

Adams. J. N. 1990. *The Latin Sexual Vocabulary*. Baltimore, Md.: Johns Hopkins University Press.
Armstrong, R. 2005. *Ovid and His Love Poetry*. London: Duckworth.
Barsby, J. A., ed. and trans. 1973. *Ovid's* Amores: *Book One*. Oxford: Clarendon Press.
Bartman, E. 2001. "Hair and the Artifice of Roman Female Adornment." *American Journal of Archeology* 105: 1–25.
Boyd, B. W. 1997. *Ovid's Literary Loves*: 117–22. Ann Arbor: University of Michigan Press.
Buchan, M. 1995. "*Ovidius Imperamator*: Beginnings and Ends of the Love Poems and Empire in the *Amores*." *Arethusa* 28.1: 53–85.
Cahoon, L. 1988. "The Bed as Battlefield: Erotic Conquest and Military Metaphor in Ovid's *Amores*." *Transactions of the American Philological Association* 118: 293–307.
———. 1985. "A Program for Betrayal: Ovidian *Nequitia* in *Amores* 1.1, 2.1, 3.1." *Helios* 12: 29–39.
Cairns, F. 1993. "Imitation and Originality in Ovid, *Amores* 1.3." In *Roman Poetry and Prose, Greek Rhetoric and Poetry*, ed. F. Cairns and M. Heath: 101–22. Leeds: Francis Cairns.
Carcopino, J. 2003. *Daily Life in Ancient Rome: The People and the City at the Height of the Empire*. New Haven, Conn.: Yale University Press.
Clausen, W. V. 1964. "Callimachus and Latin Poetry." *Greek, Roman, and Byzantine Studies* 5: 181–96.
Copley, F. O. 1956. *Exclusus Amator: A Study in Latin Love Elegy*. Madison, Wis.: American Philological Association.
Curran, L. C. 1966. "*Desultores Amoris*: Ovid *Amores* 1.3." *Classical Philology* 61: 47–49.
———. 1964. "Ovid, *Amores* 10." *Phoenix* 18: 70–87.
Davis, J. T. 1977. *Dramatic Pairings in the Elegies of Propertius and Ovid*. Noctes Romanae 15. Bern: Paul Haupt.
———. 1988. "*Desultores Amoris*, Publicity-Seeking and Ovid, *Amores* 1.3." *Augustan Age* 8: 22–26.
———. 1992. "Thou Shalt Not Cuddle: *Amores* 1.4 and the Law." *Syllecta Classica* 4: 65–70.

Bibliography

Davis, P. J. 1999. "Ovid's *Amores*: A Political Reading." *Classical Philology* 94: 431–49.
DuQuesnay, I. M. Le M. 1973. "The *Amores*." In *Ovid*, ed. J. W. Binns, 1–48. London: Routledge and Kegan Paul.
Elliot, A. G. 1973. "*Amores* 1.13. Ovid's Art." *Classical Journal* 69: 127–32.
Ferguson, J. 1978. "Notes on Some Uses of Ambiguity and Similar Effects in Ovid's *Amores*, Book 1." *Liverpool Classical Monthly* 3: 121–32.
Ford, G. B. 1966. "An Analysis of *Amores* 1.4." *Helikon* 6: 645–52.
Galinsky, K. 1969. "The Triumph Theme in Augustan Elegy." *Weiner Studien* 82: 75–107.
Giangrande, G. 1981. "Hellenistic *topoi* in Ovid's *Amores*." *Museum Philologum Londoniense* 4: 25–51.
Green, P., ed. and trans. 1982. *Ovid: The Erotic Poems*. New York: Penguin Books.
Greene, E. 1999. 1998. *The Erotics of Dominaton: Male Desire and the Mistress in Latin Love Poetry*. Baltimore, Md.: Johns Hopkins University Press.
———. "Travesties of Love: Violence and Voyeurism in Ovid, *Amores* 1.7." *Classical World* 92: 409–18.
Gross, N. 1995–96. "Ovid *Amores* 1.8: Whose Amatory Rhetoric?" *Classical World* 89: 197–206.
Hallett, J. P. 1973. "The Role of Women in Roman Elegy: Counter-Cultural Feminism." *Arethusa* 6: 103–24.
Hardie, P. R. 2002. *Ovid's Poetics of Illusion*. Cambridge: Cambridge University Press.
Hinds, S. 1987. "Generalising about Ovid." *Ramus* 16: 4–31.
Holzberg, N. 2002. *Ovid, The Poet and His Work*. Translated by G. M. Goshgarian. Ithaca, N.Y.: Cornell University Press.
Huntingford, N. P. C. 1981. "Ovid, *Amores* 1.5." *Acta Classica* 24: 107–15.
Hutchinson, G. O. 1988. "Roman Poetry." Chapter 6 of *Hellenistic Poetry*. Oxford: Clarendon Press.
James, S. L. 2001. "The Economics of Roman Elegy: Voluntary Poverty, the *Recusatio*, and the Greedy Girl." *American Journal of Philology* 122: 223–53.
———. 2003. "Her Turn to Cry: The Politics of Weeping in Roman Love Elegy." *Transactions of the American Philological Association* 133: 99–122.
———. 2005. "A Courtesan's Choreography." In *Defining Gender and Genre in Roman Elegy: Essays Presented to William S. Anderson on his Seventy-fifth Birthday*, ed. W. Batstone and G. Tissol, 269–99. New York: Peter Lang.
Keith, A. M. 1992. "*Amores* 1.1 and the Propertian Programme." *Studies in Latin Literature* (Collection Latomus) 6: 327–44.
———. 1994. "*Corpus Eroticum*: Elegiac Poets and Elegiac *Puellae* in Ovid's *Amores*." *Classical World* 88: 27–40.

Kennedy, D. F. 1993. "Love's Figures and Tropes." In *The Arts of Love: Five Studies in the Discourse of Roman Love Elegy*: 46–63. Cambridge: Cambridge University Press.

Khan, H. Akbar. 1966. "*Ovidius Furens*: A Revaluation of *Amores* 1,7." *Latomus* 25: 880–94.

LaFleur, R. A. 1995. *Love and Transformation: An Ovid Reader*. Reading, Mass.: Addison-Wesley Publishing Company.

Lyne, R. O. A. M. 1980. *The Latin Love Poets from Catullus to Horace*. Oxford: Clarendon Press.

Mack, S. 1988. *Ovid*. New Haven, Conn.: Yale University Press.

McCarthy, K. 1998. "*Seruitium Amoris: Amor Seruitii*." In *Women and Slaves in the Greco-Roman Culture*, ed. S. R. Joshel and S. Murnagham, 174–92. London: Routledge.

McKeown, J. C. 1995. "*Militat omnis amans*." *Classical Journal* 90: 295–304.

———. 1987. *Ovid*: Amores, *Text, Prolegomena, and Commentary in Four Volumes*. Vol. 1: *Text and Prolegomena*; Vol. 2: *A Commentary on Book One*. Leeds: Francis Cairns.

Meyer, E. 2001. "Wooden Wit: *Tabellae* in Latin Poetry." In *Essays in Honor of Gordon Williams: Twenty-five Years at Yale*, ed. E. Tylawski and C. Weiss, 201–12. New Haven, Conn.: Henry R. Schwab Publishers.

Miller, J. F. 1995. "Reading Cupid's Triumph." *Classical Journal* 90: 287–94.

Miller, P. A., ed. 2002. *Latin Erotic Elegy: An Anthology and Reader*. London: Routledge.

———. 2004. *Subjecting Verses: Latin Erotic Elegy and the Emergence of the Real*. Princeton, N.J.: Princeton University Press.

Moles, J. 1991. "The Dramatic Coherence of Ovid, *Amores* 1.1 and 1.2." *Classical Quarterly* 41: 551–54.

Morrison, J. V. 1992. "Literary Reference and Generic Transgression in Ovid, *Amores* 1.7: Lover, Poet, Furor." *Latomus* 51: 571–89.

Murgatroyd, P. 1999. "The Argumentation in Ovid, *Amores* 1.9." *Mnemosyne* 52: 569–72.

Myers, K. S. 1996. "The Poet and the Procuress: The *Lena* in Latin Love Elegy." *Journal of Roman Studies* 86: 1–21.

Nicoll, W. S. M. 1977. "Ovid, *Amores* 1.5." *Mnemosyne* 30: 40–48.

Olstein, K. 1975. "*Amores* 1.3 and Duplicity as a Way of Love." *Transactions of the American Philological Association* 105: 241–57.

———. 1980. "*Amores* 1.9 and the Structure of Book 1." *Studies in Latin Literature and Roman History* (Collection Latomus) 2: 286–300.

Parker, D. 1969. "The Ovidian Coda." *Arion* 8: 80–97.

Poliakoff, M. 1985. "Clumsy and Clever Spiders on Hermann's Bridge." *Glotta* 63: 248–50.

Ramsby, T. R. 2007. *Textual Permanence: Roman Elegists and the Epigraphic Tradition*. London: Duckworth.
Rayor, D. J., and W. W. Batstone, eds. 1995. *Latin Lyric and Elegiac Poetry: An Anthology of New Translations*. New York: Garland Publishing.
Sebesta, J. L., and L. Bonfante. 2001. *The World of Roman Costume*. Madison: University of Wisconsin Press.
Vessey, D. W. T. 1981. "Elegy Eternal: Ovid, *Amores* 1.15." *Latomus* 40: 607–17.
Watson, L. C. 1982. "*Amores* 1.6: A Parody of a Hymn?" *Mnemosyne* 35: 92–102.
Wyke, M. 1989. "Mistress and Metaphor in Augustan Elegy." *Helios* 16: 25–47.
———. 1994. "Women in the Mirror: The Rhetoric of Adornment in the Roman World." In *Women in Ancient Societies: "An Illusion of the Night,"* ed. L. J. Archer, S. Fischler, and M. Wyke, 134–51. New York: Routledge.
Yardley, J. C. 1978. "The Elegiac Paraclausithyron." *Eranos* 76: 19–34.

Index

Accius, 136, 141
Achilles, 77, 95, 99, 124
Actium, 4
Aeneas, 42, 79, 81
Aeschylus, 77
Agamemnon, 77, 95, 99, 100, 105
Ajax, 74, 77
Alcinous, 109
Alcmaeon, 109
Alcmena, 127
Alliteration, 19, 37, 39, 45, 53, 57, 61, 72, 80, 81, 88, 91, 92, 97, 106, 108, 119, 124, 135
Amica, 71–72. See also *Domina*; Mistress; *Puella*
Amor, 38, 47, 69, 92, 98; personified, 9, 38–39, 42, 46, 71, 95, 106, 131. See also Cupid
Amymone, 102, 105
Anaphora, 16, 19, 29, 40, 47, 55, 62, 69, 88, 107, 108, 114, 125, 132
Anastrophe, 19, 113
Anceps, 13
Anchises, 81
Ancilla, 87, 93, 113
Andromache, 100
Andromeda, 105
Anthithesis, 16, 19, 53, 58, 80, 142
Antony, Mark, 4
Anus, 87
Aphrodite, 79, 134
Apodosis, 30, 71, 80, 89, 132
Apollo, 30, 46, 78, 91, 133, 137, 142
Apollonius, 141

Apostrophe, 19, 99, 109, 141
Apelles, 134
Aratus, 140–41
Archaic diction, 30, 53, 55, 56, 58, 79, 81, 92, 108, 126, 134
Archaic Greek poetry, 6, 15, 32
Ariadne, 78, 105
Aristophanes, 68
Arma, 27, 29, 31, 33, 39, 54, 71, 99, 109, 125, 141
Assonance, 19, 30, 61, 81, 119, 139
Asyndeton, 19, 33, 41, 42, 55, 69
Atalanta, 78
Athena, 78, 122
Atreus, 22, 100
Augustus, 4–6, 8, 35, 42, 134, 135
Aulus Gellius, 6
Aurora, 122, 124–28

Bacchante, 100, 133. See also Maenad
Bacchus, 22, 41, 42, 46, 72, 100, 133. See also Dionysus
Balanced structure, 15, 16, 39, 46, 60, 90–91, 95, 98, 140
Boreas, 72
Bracketing, 20, 47, 48, 53, 62, 77, 98, 121, 139
Briseis, 95, 99

Caesar, Julius, 4, 22, 42, 134
Caesura, 13, 15, 20
Callimachus, 6, 32, 56, 136, 138, 140, 141
Capitoline Hill, 40, 115

Index

Captatio Beneuolentiae, 68, 70
Carmen et error, 5
Cassandra, 22, 78, 100
Castor, 105
Catullus, 7–8, 9, 11, 32, 37, 61, 62, 113, 132; poems cited: (*c*.5) 9; (*c*.50) 37; (*c*.64) 78; (*c*.68) 11, 62; (*c*.85) 7. *See also* Iuuentius; Lesbia
Centaurs, 53–54
Cephalus, 127
Ceres, 140
Cerinthus, 10
Chiasmus, 16, 20, 33, 41, 42, 53, 56, 69, 80, 89, 99, 106, 107, 125, 132, 139, 142
Cicero, 47, 108
Circe, 87
Clytemnestra, 105
Comedy, influence of, 6, 33, 68, 83, 87, 89, 93, 113, 127, 136, 140
Corinna, 59, 61–63, 111, 113–15, 117, 119
Courtesans, 61–62
Cupid, 27, 29–33, 35, 38–42, 43, 45, 46, 69, 71, 91, 97, 101, 106, 137. *See also Amor*
Cynthia, 9, 27, 33, 105, 106, 131

Damnatio Memoriae, 8
Danaids, 105
Delia, 9, 27, 47
Diaeresis, 13, 14, 20, 29, 93
Diana, 31
Diastole, 20, 56
Diminutive, 20, 80, 90
Dinner parties, 10, 50, 53, 54
Diomedes, 79, 99
Dionysus, 133. *See also* Bacchus
Dipsas, 87–93, 119, 121
Disyllabic ending, 15
Diues Amator, 89, 91. *See also* Rival
Docta puella, 113

Domina, 9, 77, 79. *See also Amica*; Mistress; *Puella*; *Seruitium Amoris*
Double entendre, 53, 63, 68, 99. *See also* Sexual innuendo

Ellipsis, 20, 31, 37, 38, 39, 47, 48, 55, 57, 58, 63, 69, 72, 89, 91, 108, 110, 114, 121, 125, 127, 132, 133
End-stopping, 14, 16, 20
Endymion, 127
Enjambment, 14, 20, 46, 53, 109, 113
Ennius, 136, 141
Epic poetry, 6, 7, 12, 21, 27, 29, 30, 81, 99, 100, 136, 137, 139, 140, 141; gods and goddesses, 100, 122, 125, 126; heroes, 100; meter, 5, 12, 14, 29, 32, 136; style and diction, 12, 14, 20, 32, 38, 41, 56, 99, 100, 133, 141. *See also* Love elegy, versus epic; Tragedy
Epigram, Hellenistic, 68
Equestrian class, 3, 46
Eriphyle, 102, 109
Europa, 43, 48, 106
Exclusus Amator, 11, 57, 65, 93. *See also Paraclausithyron*
Exempla, 125, 140; mythological 30, 43, 54, 78, 95, 102, 105

Fides, 40, 47
Furies, 77, 78
Furor, 37, 40, 41, 74

Gallus, Cornelius, 8, 136, 141–42. *See also* Lycoris
Ganymede, 106
Genre, 5, 6, 7, 8, 12, 21, 56, 100, 132, 133, 142
Germans, 4, 132, 134, 135
Golden line, 16, 21, 46, 91, 125, 140
Gnomic perfect, 21, 92, 98, 99
Greek anthology, 6

Greek words, 6, 29, 32, 61, 77, 87, 124, 138; forms and usage, 30, 31, 32, 54, 61, 63, 72, 78, 99, 100, 105, 113, 119, 120, 133, 134, 139, 140

Hair, 32, 61, 74, 77–78, 100, 111–13, 124, 129–30, 131–34
Hector, 95, 100
Helen, 102, 105
Helicon, Mount, 31
Hellenistic poetry, 6, 32, 68, 136, 140, 141
Hemistich, 12–15, 39
Hendiadys, 21, 57, 71, 100, 134
Hercules, 127
Herodas, 6
Hesiod, 32, 136, 140
Hiatus, 21
Hippodamia, 54
Homer, 3, 77, 81, 90, 99, 100, 122, 136, 139, 140, 141; *Iliad*, 79, 99, 100; *Odyssey*, 81, 87, 90, 100, 109, 122
Horace, 4, 30, 114, 115, 120, 139, 142; poems cited: (*c*.1.5) 115; (*c*.2.3) 120; (*c*.3.30) 139
Humor, 11, 27, 35, 66, 69, 70, 106, 107, 117, 125
Hyperbaton, 21, 39, 63, 70, 115
Hyperbole, 21, 74, 79

Ianitor, 11, 68–74, 127
Imagines, 92
Immortality, Poetic, 8, 11, 43, 48, 102, 103, 110, 133, 136, 138, 139, 140. See also *Nomen*
Inspiration, poetic, 27, 30, 32–33, 38, 48, 137, 142
Interlocked word order, 21, 46, 61, 68, 72, 98
Invective, 22, 102
Io, 43, 48

Irony, 38, 50, 69, 73, 78, 80, 92, 116
Isis, 93
Iuuentius, 32

Jason, 141
Juno, 48
Jupiter, 40, 43, 48, 69, 102, 105, 106, 115, 127

Lena, 83, 87, 89, 91, 92, 94, 139, 140
Leda, 43, 48, 102, 105
Legal language. *See* Archaic diction
Lesbia, 7, 9
Litotes, 22, 41, 63, 108
Livy, 80
Love elegy: development of, 6–12; elegiac couplet, 4, 5, 7, 11, 12–14, 15, 16, 20, 27, 29, 32, 46, 48, 53, 115, 132; features of, 8–9, 29, 45, 46, 50, 57, 58, 65, 89, 140; versus epic and tragedy, 6, 12, 20, 27, 29–33, 38, 56, 99, 100, 125–26, 133, 137, 142. *See also* Ovid; Poetic catchwords
Lucretius, 30, 136, 141
Luna, 127
Lycoris, 8, 142
Lygdamus, 10; poem cited: (Tib. 3.13) 10. *See also* Neaera

Maecenas, 4
Maenad, 100. See also *Bacchante*
Magic, 8, 65, 70, 83, 87–88, 126, 134. *See also* Witch; Witchcraft
Marathus, 9, 32
Marriage, 5, 45, 90, 124
Mars, 40, 89, 90, 95, 99, 100
Materialism, 83, 90, 92, 102–103, 106
Matrona, 90, 125
Medea, 141
Medea, tragedy by Ovid, 5
Memnon, 87, 124, 127

Menander, 136, 140
Menelaus, 105
Messalla, 4, 10
Metaphor, 31, 33, 35, 44, 46, 59, 65, 72, 92, 93, 99, 101, 117, 142. See also *Militia Amoris*; *Seruitium Amoris*
Meter. *See* Epic poetry; Love elegy; Ovid
Metonymy, 22, 55, 97, 140
Militia Amoris, 8, 59, 62, 69, 72, 95, 114, 115
Mime, 6, 70, 83, 87, 136
Minerva, 31, 78
Minos, 78
Mistress: of Catullus, 7, 61; a convention of love elegy, 8, 35, 44, 47, 68, 83, 131; of Gallus, 142; of Ovid, 10–11, 43, 50, 54, 57, 59, 61, 62, 65, 66, 68, 74, 77, 81, 92, 102, 109, 117, 124, 129; of Propertius, 9, 63, 77; of Tibullus, 9, 77. See also *Amica*; *Domina*; *Puella*
Muses, 10, 30, 31, 33, 46, 111, 142. *See also* Pierides

Nape, 111, 113–17, 119, 121, 127
Neaera, 10
Nemesis, 9
Neptune, 102, 105
Nero, 4
Noctes Atticae, 6
Nomen, 46, 48, 87

Octavian, 4. *See also* Augustus
Odysseus, 81, 90, 109
Omens, 9, 117, 119, 120
Orestes, 74, 77
Orithyia, 72
Ovid: approach to love elegy, 10–12; life and works, 1–6; metrical practices, 14–15, 38, 39, 40, 61, 88, 90, 106, 142; style, 15–17, 19–24. *See also* Poetic catchwords

Paraclausithyron, 11, 65, 68. See also *Exclusus Amator*
Parcae, 47
Paris, 102, 105
Parthians, 4
Patronymic, 22, 30, 79, 100, 139, 140, 141
Paupertas, 46, 89, 91, 92, 102
Penelope, 90
Pentameter, 8, 12, 14, 15, 20, 29, 39, 98, 142
Periphrasis, 22, 31, 46, 78, 87, 126, 141
Persona, 6, 7, 29
Personification, 22, 38, 40, 41, 119, 129, 136, 138, 142
Phoebus, 31, 46. *See also* Apollo
Pierides, 30, 33. *See also* Muses
Plautus, 68, 87, 127. *See also* Comedy
Poetic catchwords: *aranea*, 132; *durus*, 11, 56; *fortis*, 11, 69; *grauis*, 32, 41–2, 46; *leuis*, 32, 41, 42, 56, 69; *mollis*, 56, 100, 120; *rara*, 62; *tener*, 9, 56, 125; *tenuis*, 11, 32, 38, 56, 69, 125, 132
Pollux, 105
Polysyndeton, 22, 32, 41, 46, 94
Praeceptor Amoris, 5, 83
Praeda, 35, 43, 44–45
Praetor, 56, 108, 126
Prayer: address to deity, 40, 45, 47, 69, 114; characteristics of, 122, 125, 126, 134; kletic hymn, 125
Priam, 78, 100
Prolepsis, 22
Propertius, 4, 8–9, 11, 27, 30, 33, 40, 45, 55, 63, 68, 77, 87, 105, 131, 133; poems cited: (1.1) 9, 21, 27,

33, 106; (1.2) 131; (1.3) 105, 133; (1.6) 45; (1.16) 68; (2.1) 44; (2.5) 77; (2.10) 40; (2.15) 63; (2.18b) 131; (2.34) 8; (3.2) 46, 48; (3.3) 30; (3.8) 55; (4.5) 87. *See also* Cynthia

Protasis, 45, 80, 90

Puella, a convention of love elegy, 8, 10, 32, 43, 45, 47, 83, 98, 113, 117, 131; of Catullus, 7; of Gallus, 8; of Ovid, 10–11, 35, 43–48, 50, 53–57, 61, 65, 73, 74, 78–81, 83, 87, 89, 102, 106–107, 122, 129, 133–34, 140; of Propertius, 9, 27, 46, 133; of Tibullus, 9. See also *Amica*; *Domina*; Mistress

Quintilian, 8

Recusatio, 11, 30

Refrain, 15, 65, 70, 127

Repetition: of clauses, 70, 127; of consonant sounds, 19, 37, 45, 80, 88, 124; of syllables, 29; of vowel sounds, 30; of words, 19, 29, 40, 41, 45, 54, 57, 69, 88, 90, 93, 140, 141. *See also* Alliteration; Anaphora; Assonance

Rhetorical question, 23, 30, 78

Rhetorical training, 15–17, 47, 63, 68, 141

Rhyme, 98; internal, 15, 16, 39, 115, 133

Ring composition, 23, 63, 101, 128, 135

Rival, 8, 50, 53, 56, 83, 87, 89. See also *Diues Amator*

Roman comedy. *See* Plautus

Romulus, 90

Sacra Via, 94

Saga, 87. *See also* Witch

Sappho of Lesbos, 7

Semiramis, 61

Sententia, 16, 23, 38

Seruitium Amoris, 9, 11, 35, 39, 43, 45, 72, 74, 77, 79, 92. See also *Domina*

Sexual innuendo, 31–32, 33, 39, 57, 60, 90, 99, 106, 125–26, 132, 133. *See also* Double entendre

Simile, 81, 133

Sophocles, 31, 77, 136, 140

Sphragis, 139

Suasoria, 16, 45, 70

Sulmo, 3

Sulpicia, 10; poem cited, (Tib. 3.5) 10. *See also* Cerinthus

Synchesis, 21, 46, 72. *See also* Interlocked word order

Syncope, 23, 45, 72, 93, 98, 127

Synecdoche, 23, 41, 124, 127

Synizesis, 23, 78, 91, 135

Systole, 23, 90, 116

Tarpeia, 102, 109

Tatius, 90

Theocritus, 6, 70

Theogony, 32

Theseus, 78, 105

Tiberius, 6

Tibullus, 4, 8–10, 27, 32, 55, 68, 77, 87, 89, 136, 141; poems cited: (1.1) 9, 45, 47; (1.2) 55, 68, 87; (1.5) 87, 89; (1.8) 87; (1.10) 77; (2.3) 9. *See also* Delia; Marathus; Nemesis

Tithonus, 124

Tmesis, 23, 54

Tomis, 5–6

Tragedy, 5, 12, 21, 74, 133, 137, 140

Transferred epithet, 23, 100, 113

Tricolon, 16, 24, 62; *crescens*, 24, 62, 107, 114, 125

Triumph, 35, 40, 80, 115, 137

Trojan War, 77, 79, 90, 99, 105, 124, 140
Tunic, 59, 61, 62, 132

Variatio, 16
Variant readings, 56, 91, 93, 98, 115
Varro, Terentius, 30
Varro Atacinus, 136, 141
Vates, 30, 33, 91
Venus, 10, 31, 39–40, 42, 45, 55, 58, 79, 90, 99, 100, 107, 108, 111, 115, 134; and myrtle, 34, 39, 137, 142; as a planet, 89
Vergil, 4, 8, 30, 81, 136, 141; *Aeneid*, 27, 40, 41, 78, 81, 14; *Eclogues*, 8, 30, 141; *Georgics*, 141
Vesta, 40, 126

Vestal, 109
Vibius Sequester, 8
Vir, 50, 53, 56, 57
Vulcan, 40, 100

Witch, 70, 83, 87, 88. See also *Saga*
Witchcraft, 9, 87, 134. *See also* Magic
Word picture, 24, 33, 56, 57, 61, 114
Word placement, 29, 31, 40, 47, 61, 97, 98, 113, 115, 119, 127, 133, 134; juxtaposition, 53, 58, 71, 89, 93, 105, 120. *See also* Word picture
Wordplay, 38, 41, 54, 56, 61, 69, 77, 98, 100, 101, 108, 132

Zeugma, 24, 135

CPSIA information can be obtained at www.ICGtesting.com
Printed in the USA
BVOW07s2233201113

336797BV00001B/1/P